NAPOLEON'S DOWNFALL

MADAME RÉCAMIER AND HER BATTLE WITH THE EMPEROR

TO MY SISTERS
all five of them

NAPOLEON'S DOWNFALL

MADAME RÉCAMIER AND HER BATTLE WITH THE EMPEROR

GERI WALTON

PEN & SWORD
HISTORY

AN IMPRINT OF PEN & SWORD BOOKS LTD.
YORKSHIRE – PHILADELPHIA

First published in Great Britain in 2020 by
PEN AND SWORD HISTORY
an imprint of
Pen and Sword Books Ltd
Yorkshire – Philadelphia

ISBN 978 1 52673 459 4

A CIP record for this book is available from the British Library

Typeset in Times New Roman 11/13.5 by
Aura Technology and Software Services, India.
Printed and bound in the UK by TJ International

Pen & Sword Books Ltd incorporates the imprints of Pen & Sword
Archaeology, Atlas, Aviation, Battleground, Discovery,
Family History, History, Maritime, Military, Naval, Politics, Railways,
Select, Social History, Transport, True Crime, Claymore Press,
Frontline Books, Leo Cooper, Praetorian Press, Remember When,
Seaforth Publishing and Wharncliffe.

For a complete list of Pen & Sword titles please contact
PEN & SWORD BOOKS LIMITED
47 Church Street, Barnsley, South Yorkshire, S70 2AS, England
E-mail: enquiries@pen-and-sword.co.uk
Website: www.pen-and-sword.co.uk

Or
PEN AND SWORD BOOKS
1950 Lawrence Rd, Havertown, PA 19083, USA
E-mail: Uspen-and-sword@casematepublishers.com
Website: www.penandswordbooks.com

MIX
Paper from
responsible sources
FSC
www.fsc.org
FSC® C013056

Contents

Author's Notes ... vi

Chapter 1 Napoleon ... 1
Chapter 2 Juliette ... 9
Chapter 3 Life's Changes ... 16
Chapter 4 The Directory ... 24
Chapter 5 Houses and Salons ... 34
Chapter 6 Lucien ... 42
Chapter 7 Friendships ... 48
Chapter 8 Intrigues and Assassination Attempts ... 56
Chapter 9 It's Business ... 68
Chapter 10 Losses ... 78
Chapter 11 Love is in the Air ... 86
Chapter 12 War, Marriage, and Exile ... 95
Chapter 13 Juliette's Exile ... 104
Chapter 14 The Russian Campaign ... 111
Chapter 15 Rome, Naples, and Paris ... 119
Chapter 16 Elba and One Hundred Days ... 128
Chapter 17 Waterloo ... 139
Chapter 18 Buonaparte ... 148
Chapter 19 Death ... 155
Chapter 20 Continued Fascination ... 164

Notes ... 173
Bibliography ... 183
Index ... 189

Author's Notes

Napoleon has long been a fascinating figure and many people are familiar with his military genius and his strategic skills on the battlefield. Yet, his life is more fascinating than his military prowess. It is his personal and social life that reveal a different Napoleon than the one his enemies faced in battle.

His rich social life introduced him to another well-known and enigmatic personality named Juliette Récamier. She was a wealthy socialite busy leading a life of glittering sophistication and, because of her stunning beauty, men such as Napoleon where highly intrigued. In addition, she attracted both those who supported and opposed Napoleon to her salon.

Juliette came to oppose Napoleon, and it is their story of opposition that brings to life what it was like to live in the late 1700s and early 1800s. It also demonstrates how a different kind of battlefield occurs when the powerful and the rich are pitted against one another. Here is that story.

Chapter 1

Napoleon

Little Meddler.
(Napoleon's childhood nickname)

On Tuesday, 15 August 1769, a small but bright nebulosity was seen in the darkened sky. It slowly traversed the horizon of the constellation Aries and was no ordinary occurrence. Those on the island of Corsica and elsewhere who saw it believed it foreshadowed some divine omen or momentous celestial event. Exactly what that was, no one knew for sure, but the strange occurrence accompanied the birth of a baby boy on the island.

The first person to notice the nebulosity was the French astronomer Charles Messier. He saw it when he looked through his telescope about 11pm on 8 August at the Naval Observatory in Paris. The next night, Messier confirmed it was a long-period comet, and he was able to observe it with his naked eye. By the day of the baby boy's birth on 15 August, Messier noted that the comet had grown quite bright and had a startling long tail.

By the end of August, sailors at sea could easily see the comet as it had increased even more in brightness. Speculators thought it was as large as the Moon with a tail that had a 'lucid vapour' of nearly 30 million miles. Newspapers throughout Europe reported on it, and reports indicated that it appeared to have a bright reddish head. During this time, Messier continued to observe what would become known as a Great Comet because of its outstanding brightness.

The comet was not the only thing heralding the baby boy's birth. A celebration for a major feast known as the Feast of the Assumption of Our Lady the Virgin Mary was being held the same day. The baby's parents, 23-year-old Carlo and 19-year-old Letizia (Ramolino) Buonaparte, were in attendance when Letizia suddenly felt the excruciated pains of labour. Fortunately for her, the Ajaccio Cathedral was near her house and Letizia's sister-in-law, Gertrude Paravicini, helped her home.

Letizia had no time to reach the bedroom because the baby was coming fast. Instead, she threw herself onto an uncomfortable couch in a narrow, ill-lit salon and gave birth with the aid of Paravicini and a maid-servant named Mammucia Caterina. A baby was born 'with a big head and a very intelligent face, who screamed loudly, and soon began sucking his thumb, which was considered a good augury among the peasants of Corsica'.[1] He was Letizia's fourth child and third son. One of his brothers and a sister had died in infancy and so the new baby had just one older brother, Joseph, and later a slew of younger siblings – Lucien, Elisa, Louis, Pauline, Caroline and Jérôme – would follow.

The boy's name was Napoleone di Buonaparte.

Napoleone spent his early years using the Italian spelling of his name, but at the age of 27, he changed it to the French-sounding Napoleon Bonaparte. The new Napoleon was by then a military man serving in the French army. Thus, some historians claim the name change demonstrated his final break with his Corsican roots.

In April 1795, he was assigned to command an infantry unit in the armée de l'Ouest (Army of the West) that was struggling against royalist counter-revolutionaries in the west central region of France known as the Vendée. Commanding such an infantry unit was essentially a demotion and, to avoid it, Napoleon claimed poor health. Because he refused to serve in the Vendée, his name was stricken from the list of generals, and he was sidelined. His future seemed bleak. However, soon after, in October, royalist sympathizers declared a rebellion against the National Convention. The Convention had been created after the insurrection of 10 August 1792. It also had no connection to the monarchy and was organized as a republic, so its members were worried. They formed three battalions for their defence, but they were severely outnumbered by the approaching royalist rebels. They called on Napoleon to protect them and he was told to use whatever was necessary to crush the revolt.

He agreed to do so if he was allowed complete freedom of movement. He was also already familiar with the September Massacres where hundreds of prisoners and priests were killed, and he knew what had happened on 10 August 1792 when insurgents stormed the Tuileries Palace and massacred Louis XVI's Swiss guard. Thus, Napoleon knew artillery would be key to protecting the National Convention and he ordered large cannons be retrieved from the sandy plains of Sablons so that he could place them in strategic spots to create a perimeter.

An intense two-hour engagement ensued. Napoleon's horse was shot out from under him and the cannons he strategically placed around Paris produced an effect like a giant shotgun because they were filled with small musket balls tightly packed into muslin or canvas bags. When the cannons fired, they scattered balls everywhere and devastated the charging enemy. The result of the encounter was that he repelled the royalist rebels and cleared the streets with what the famous nineteenth-century historian Thomas Carlyle called a 'whiff of grapeshot'.

Besides receiving the patronage and wealth of the Directory, which was France's new government set up in November of 1795, Napoleon also earned unexpected fame. It was a remarkable success that probably would have surprised many who knew him from birth.

Despite his early upbringing being the subject of many stories and myths, no one, not even Napoleon's mother, had written down details about his birth. The story of Letizia having no time to reach the bedroom and delivering him in the salon is the accepted version. It comes from a biography written about her in the 1800s by Félix Hippolyte Larrey. However, Larrey's version is disputed by Napoleon's brother, and, moreover, Joseph supposedly told his good American friend, Charles Ingersoll, that the story of Napoleon being born in the salon was untrue.

Even if that was untrue, it was true that when Carlo married Letizia, he was on a slightly lower social rung to that of his wife. Yet when it came to wealth, the couple stood on nearly equal footing. Letizia was her father's only child. So, when he died in 1755, it was she who inherited his home and vineyards.

Carlo became an attorney shortly after Napoleon's birth. In September 1771, Carlo's nobility was confirmed with help from the governor of Corsica. Carlo then became an assessor and deputy. He also became a member of the Twelve Nobles of Dila in May 1772, Deputy of the Nobility of Corsica in July 1777 and a Corsican representative at Louis XVI's court at Versailles in 1778. Besides these titles and honours, Carlo obtained a substantial inheritance. He also owned land, but his land was heavily mortgaged because of risky investments and because he liked to gamble. Thus, he and his children relied primarily upon Letizia for support.

Letizia's stately beauty, majestic figure, and imperial dignity were praised regularly by her peers. Yet, despite her grace and beauty, 17-year-old Carlo could not stop thinking of another girl whom he loved. When he married the 13-year-old Letizia, he was forced to give up this love because his and Letizia's marriage was arranged by their families to achieve a proper alliance.

Letizia's beauty endured as she aged. In fact, later in her life, one person wrote that '[she] was the best-looking woman of her age I ever beheld, [she was nearly seventy], and must formerly have been very handsome; but her countenance was at once sweet and dignified.'[2]

Like many of his ancestors, Carlo died young. He succumbed to stomach cancer on 24 February 1785 at just thirty-nine years old. This left his 34-year-old wife to pay the family's debts and raise the children alone. However, she did have her half-brother, Joseph Fesch, who would rise to prominence after Napoleon's 1799 coup d'état to become Archbishop, Cardinal and eventually Ambassador to Rome. She could rely on Fesch to serve as a protector to the Bonaparte family.

Many reports characterize Letizia as a harsh, austere and domineering mother. She was also said to be thrifty, practical and affectionate. Further, she thought nothing of sending her children to bed hungry because she viewed it as a good way to toughen them for life's challenges.

Letizia's qualities affected her children. Napoleon was certainly affected by her mothering skills and demonstrated a toughness from an early age. His nursemaid reported that when he was reprimanded, he seldom cried. The nursemaid also said that when he was beaten for having committed some offence, 'he would sometimes shed a few tears, but they were soon over; and he would never utter a word in the way of begging pardon'.[3] When he was older, he said of his mother:

> 'She had … the head of a man on the shoulders of a woman. Left without a guide and protector, she was compelled to take upon herself the direction of affairs; and the burden was not too much for her strength. She administered every thing with a degree of sagacity not to be expected from her age and sex.'[4]

While others may have seen Letizia as a harsh and domineering mother, she thought of herself as a good mother and once wrote:

> 'I consecrated myself wholly to my duties as a mother, and rarely went out except to mass. My presence at home was always necessary to control my little children. My mother-in-law and husband were so indulgent that at the least cry or reprimand they ran to them and gave them a thousand caresses. As for me I was severe or indulgent as needed. Thus, I was loved and obeyed by my children who have always shown me love and respect.'[5]

Corsica, known as the 'ile de beauté' because of its beautiful mountains, spectacular coastline, and tropical flair, is located off France's southeast mainland in the Mediterranean Sea. The Republic of Genoa ruled it until officially ceding it to Louis XV in 1768. Nevertheless, Corsicans were unhappy with Genoese rule and a struggle for Corsican independence began in 1729.

One Corsican who fought against the Genoa rule was Pasquale Paoli's father, which resulted in Paoli and his father being exiled to Naples. While living in Naples, Paoli's father spared no expense in educating his 14-year-old son and Paoli grew into a magnetic man who served as an idol to many Corsicans seeking liberty. He certainly inspired Carlo as he was extremely loyal to him and even Napoleon would later find Paoli a pivotal figure in his life.

Eventually, Paoli devised a plan to establish a native Corsican government and a republic with a representative democracy was proclaimed under his leadership in 1755. Once the Republic of Genoa realized they had lost control of Corsica, they sold it to France, who was willing to buy the island because they wanted to reinforce their position in the Mediterranean.

Unaware that France was furtively replacing Genoese soldiers with French ones, Corsicans remained unhappy and continued fighting for independence. During this struggle, Paoli suddenly found himself fighting a guerrilla war against France instead of Genoa. France was determined to win, but it still took a large army led by the Count of Vaux to crush Corsican resistance at the Battle of Ponte Novu in May 1769.

During the guerrilla war, Paoli won some engagements, but it was not enough to stop French forces. When the Battle at Ponte Novu occurred, despite stories stating otherwise, he and Carlo were both absent: Paoli had disappeared into the hills and Carlo was probably with Paoli's staff. With France having essentially gained control of Corsica, annexation by France occurred the following year.

After the loss at Ponte Novu, Carlo remained loyal to Paoli and wrote in his memoirs that he would have left his pregnant wife and followed him into exile if Paoli had not reminded him that his first duty was to his family. Thus, a dutiful Carlo returned to the small-populated harbour town of Ajaccio with his wife. That trip home resulted in many tales. However, the tales lauded Carlo's wife and her bravery rather than his, and those tales became part of the Bonaparte folklore after Napoleon became famous.

The story was that a pregnant but heroic Letizia willingly traversed forbidden snowy passes, forded swift-moving rivers and suffered hunger, thirst and fatigue. Then, in Corsica's highest mountains, in what was said to be 'Fugitives' Grotto,' freezing and hungry, she courageously faced death.

She also rallied Carlo and her countrymen to make one last stand against the invading French forces, crying, 'Let us fight to the last man, and conquer or die!'[6]

It was true that Letizia was pregnant and that the trip to Ajaccio would have been difficult even if she had not been. It was also true that a sudden snowstorm occurred and that she displayed great fortitude in making the arduous trip. Nonetheless, the claims about Letizia's heroic bravery were wholly untrue. The Bonapartes returned home practically alone, which means there were no countrymen for Letizia to rally or inspire in any grotto. That was the stuff of legends and it was such legends that made Napoleon bigger than life.

As a boy, Napoleon grew up in Ajaccio in the family's ancestral home of 'Maison Bonaparte.' Although the Corsican island had an abundance of wine, chestnuts and oil, most goods had to be shipped to the island. Demonstrative of the lack of goods available on the island is what happened to Letizia in 1797. At the time she had begun to restore Maison Bonaparte and noted that 'rolls of paper of a red ground with roses'[7] had to come from the Continent.

Maison Bonaparte was a plain four-storey building located on rue St. Charles. It was the home where all of Napoleon's siblings, except for Joseph, were born. At the time of Napoleon's birth, Carlo owned the first three floors, and the fourth floor was owned by another family, although the Bonaparte family would eventually own the whole building. In 1774, Carlo added a terrace and, in 1780, he made repairs and redecorated several rooms.

During Napoleon's early years, Carlo characterized his son as having a 'penetrating disposition', wishing to know everything and being extremely observant. The boy was also considered feisty and hot-tempered and though smaller than Joseph, Napoleon usually defeated his older brother in fights. In addition, Napoleon was described as an instigator and mischievous, so much so that he acquired a nickname meaning 'little meddler.'

Napoleon also embraced a Spartan and military lifestyle from an early age. Perhaps, his mother's arduous trip over the mountains affected him somehow in the womb. He liked to play soldier and one modern-day historian maintained that 'he befriended the French garrison, and appalled Letizia by preferring their coarse rations of black bread to family meals'.[8]

Napoleon's upbringing was also modest. Nonetheless, his family was of minor nobility and rich enough to allow him to enjoy certain opportunities unavailable to other children. When Napoleon was nine years old, he was sent to the French mainland at Autun and enrolled at a religious school with the help of educational scholarships granted by the king. Five months later, in May 1779, the 10-year-old Napoleon was transferred to the Military School at Brienne where he began learning French. At the time he spoke and read only Corsican and Italian and although he would become fluent in French, he always spoke with a strong Corsican accent and struggled to spell French words properly.

School was not necessarily a happy experience for Napoleon. A sympathetic schoolmate, named Louis Antoine Fauvelet de Bourrienne (who later became his secretary), reported on Napoleon's time at school. Bourrienne noted that Napoleon had a stern character and was naturally reserved. In addition, fellow students teased him for his accent, bullied him because of his birthplace and ridiculed him for his mannerisms. The teasing, bullying and ridiculing caused Napoleon to find solace in books, particularly history books.

It also did not help that he was naturally unsocial. The following story demonstrates his unsociability and shows why Napoleon was disliked and unpopular with his school peers:

> 'Gloomy and even savage, almost always self-absorbed, one would have supposed that he had just come from some forest … he detested games and all manner of boyish amusements. One part of the garden was allotted to him and there he studied and brooded, and woe to him who ventured to disturb him! One evening the boys were setting off fireworks and a small powder-chest exploded. In their fright the troop scattered in all directions and some of them took refuge in Napoleon's domain, whereat he rushed upon the fugitives in a passion and attacked them with a spade.'[9]

Despite Napoleon's unpopularity and troubles at school, his mathematics teacher, Father Patrauld, genuinely liked him and became attached to him. Napoleon was said to excel in maths and even won a prize. Yet, in his other subjects, his abilities did not foreshadow any extraordinary success. An evaluation of him noted that he was an excellent sailor, functioned 'very passably' in history and geography and barely knew Latin. However, his success was enough for him to be transferred to the Paris École Militaire two months after he turned fifteen.

Unfortunately, at École Militaire, he fared no better socially than he had at Brienne. Part of the problem was his vocal criticisms that the school was not up to par for a military school. He wrote a letter to the vice-principal expressing his disappointment and noting that the education was 'pernicious and far from being calculated to fulfil the object … [of inspiring] pupils'.[10] He reasoned that the school was too easy and suggested students eat coarse bread instead of devouring two-course meals. He also requested that students brush their own clothes and clean their own boots rather than a have groom or attendant do it for them.

He had other contrary opinions about his education and freely expressed them. Of course, such criticisms did not sit well with his superiors. His situation was made worse when his father died. He found that his brother Joseph was unfit to fill his father's shoes and so Napoleon assumed the role taking care of his family. His father's death also reduced his income and with a reduced income and unhappy supervisors, his time at school was accelerated so that he completed his education in about half the time usually required for graduation and became the first Corsican to graduate from the school.

In September 1785, he obtained the post of second lieutenant in La Fère artillery regiment and departed for his garrison in October. He served in Valence and Auxonne, where he found garrison life not as expected and reported it was tedious. He read novels and often found himself dreaming of an ideal world that he compared against his everyday reality. Moreover, just as he had behaved at school, Napoleon was unsocial with his garrison comrades.

Chapter 2

Juliette

Perfect harmony was the characteristic of this harmonious woman.
Alphonse of Lamartine on Juliette

About a year before Napoleon was sent to Autun, on 4 December 1777, a girl of unspeakable beauty was born in Lyon who would come to play a role in his life. She was christened Jeanne-Françoise-Julie-Adélaïde Bernard, and her father was the handsome Jean Bernard. Yet, handsome as Monsieur Bernard was, he was also said to be dull, uninteresting and of mediocre intelligence, although he did serve as a notary and was Louis XVI's counsellor.

Monsieur Bernard's wife was the former Marie-Julie Matton. Like her husband, Madame Bernard was remarkably attractive, being described as strikingly beautiful with blonde hair, fair skin, brilliant black eyes, rosy cheeks and a white lovely neck. However, unlike her husband, she was vivacious, capable and exceedingly intelligent. She even amassed a great fortune through speculation using her business acumen.

Apart from her intelligence and talents, Madame Bernard was extremely conscientious of her looks and she focused on the external charms of others over their inner character. In fact, it has been noted that she strove throughout her life to maintain a youthful appearance until her last dying breath.

Monsieur and Madame Bernard's daughter, Juliette, as she was called, reputedly had all the features that marked a beauty: a bewitching face, luxuriously thick chestnut hair, rosy red lips, brilliant white teeth and sparkling, passionate eyes. Yet, of all the gifts that the beautiful Juliette possessed, the one gift people often thought most pronounced was her dazzling complexion, which was said to be of a colour so rare the gods envied it. Because she had inherited her mother's exquisite beauty, people almost always described Juliette in glowing physical terms, as did the French writer and poet Alphonse of Lamartine who wrote:

> 'A woman I did not know was standing with her arms on the mantel-shelf, warming her little cold feet at the half-burnt-out embers in the fireplace. I scarcely had time to see, as one

> sees the groups of stars in a dark sky, a white forehead, bay-coloured hair, a Grecian nose, eyes that had been dipped in the bluish dew of the soul, a mouth the flexible corners of which contracted slightly when she smiled, or expanded gravely with feeling: cheeks that were neither tinted nor pale, but like velvet, stirred by a constant shiver of autumn air. Perfect harmony was the characteristic of this harmonious woman.'[1]

Juliette's extraordinary beauty even captured Queen Marie Antoinette's attention. It all began with the Grand Couvert, a ceremony that consisted of the royal family dining in public and spectators filing past as the royal family devoured meats, sipped soup and feasted on dessert. One day, Juliette, who was just a child at the time, was among the spectators and the Queen was so enamoured of her beauty that she invited her to her private apartments. There, she met the Queen's daughter, Marie-Thérèse Charlotte, known as Madame Royale, who was her age.

Prior to Juliette meeting Marie Antoinette, around 1784, Juliette's father obtained work in Paris, and she was sent to live temporarily with one of her mother's sisters named Madame Blachette. There, Juliette had a playmate the same age, a little boy named Renard Humblot, who some say became her first admirer.

Soon after, she was enrolled at Couvent des Benédictines de la Déserte, a convent at Lyon where one of her mother's sisters was a nun. Juliette supposedly enjoyed her time there and was in fact reluctant to leave. So, in 1787, when she was told she had to move to Paris to live with her parents, she lamented:

> 'The night before my aunt was to come for me, I was sent for by the Lady Abbess to receive her blessing. The next day, bathed in tears, I passed over the threshold of that door, the opening of which to admit I could scarcely remember. I was put into a carriage with my aunt, and we set off for Paris.'[2]

The Paris Juliette found in the late 1780s was very different from the Paris that Monsieur Bernard entered in 1784. One change originated from problems that had occurred in 1774, when Parisian cemeteries were overflowing with dead bodies and, in some cases, decomposing improperly and presenting a health risk. The resulting putrid odours and ongoing sanitary problems, resulted in the closure of some cemeteries, which created more problems.

To permanently deal with the dead, a law was passed in 1785 to move bodies from the overflowing cemeteries to an underground sepulchre, known as the Catacombs of Paris. Beginning in April 1786, dead bodies were exhumed every night and fat was collected from them and turned into candles or soap. The bones were transferred in black cloth-draped wagons to the underground ossuaries of the catacombs in jumbled piles.

Another interesting change for Parisians was when the first luxury restaurant opened in 1786. It was located at the Palais-Royal where it was owned and operated by Antoine B. Beauvilliers, who was probably among the first to term his eating establishment a restaurant. Beauvilliers had started his culinary career as a boy in the kitchens of Louis XVI's brother, the Count of Provence, who later became Louis XVIII. The Beauvilliers' elegant restaurant was called La Grande Taverne de Londres and was known for its high-priced menu, luxurious accommodations, superior cooking, excellent wines and finely trained waiters.

Besides Beauvilliers' restaurant, Parisians were soon able to patronize a new exhibition known as the Caverne des Grands Voleurs (Cavern of the Grand Thieves). It opened in 1787 and offered a gory and bloody display like what we know today as 'The House of Horrors.' Philippe Guillaume Mathé Curtius was its owner. He had originally been a physician but became a wax modeler. He was also the uncle and mentor to the famous wax sculptress Madame Tussaud.

Despite all the changes associated with the Catacombs, Beauvilliers' restaurant, and Curtius' wax exhibition, other more momentous changes were in store for France. It all began in the year 1789 on a Tuesday in July when revolutionaries stormed the seemingly impassable, wide and deep ditches of the Paris prison called the Bastille. To the revolutionaries, the Bastille represented everything wrong with the monarchy. Storming the Bastille and gaining control of this monarchical symbol was as inspiring to the revolutionaries as when they afterwards gathered at the Hôtel de Ville with their new provisional government.

There were other changes resulting from the storming of the Bastille. First, the Marquis who gained hero status for his participation in America's Revolutionary War, Marie-Joseph Paul Yves Roch Gilbert du Motier, known simply as Lafayette, was appointed as commander of the newly established National Guard. Parisians appointed a new mayor too. He was a French astronomer, politician, and mathematician named Jean Sylvain Bailly. Revolutionaries also adopted the tricolour (blue and red for the colours of Paris and white an ancient colour for France), and these three colours, often worn in the form of a cockade, became a symbol of the revolution and the new republican nation.

The storming of the Bastille threatened the security of France's nobility. Terror and fear drove many nobles to flee France and among those who fled was Louis XVI's youngest brother, the Count of Artois, who later became Charles X. As for the royal family, they were forced to leave Versailles on 5 October after a hungry mob, composed primarily of women, marched on the Palace of Versailles and demanded food to feed their hungry families. Ultimately, Lafayette rescued the king and queen, but because Versailles was far away from Paris, they felt that they had no choice but to satisfy the mob by moving to the Tuileries Palace located in Paris.

Amid all these changes, Juliette arrived in Paris. She lived with her parents at No. 13, rue des Saint-Pères. Upon her arrival, Madame Bernard immediately had her daughter focus on improving her feminine charms. This meant learning how to dress, spending hours in front of the mirror and devoting herself to an excruciating long toilette that sometimes took hours. Years later, Juliette would remember her toilette routine with distaste.

Madame Bernard also did not neglect her daughter's education. Despite Louis XIV's second wife, Madame de Maintenon, founding a famous school for girls in the 1600s, most French girls were still educated at home, as was Juliette. Moreover, whether a girl attended a school or was taught at home, her education still focused on the skills and talents necessary to create a good wife and mother. This was because women were still considered 'weak' and serious subjects such as philosophy, science, or politics considered inappropriate for the female mind.

Juliette was proficient in her studies. Her education included the arts and she displayed a special gift for them. She studied music, attended dance lessons and practiced the harp and piano. Although she later gave up the harp, her love of the piano lasted a lifetime and she memorized many pieces by heart. She was also fortunate to take singing lessons from the famous composer of operas, François-Adrien Boieldieu. However, her voice lacked power despite having good tone and expression.

As the Bernards maintained a box at Théatre Française (also called the Comédie Française), the theatre supplemented Juliette's education. Performers whom she might have seen in the early 1790s included the comic actor Dazincourt, the Belgian actress Mademoiselle Fleury, the talented Louise-Fançoise Contant, Abraham-Joseph Bénard (considered one of the greatest comedians at the time) and the actor Grandmesnil, who debuted at the theatre on 31 August 1790. There was also the famous tragedienne Mademoiselle Raucourt, who was extremely popular until news of her offstage romances with both men and women ended her career.

Juliette's home life educated her in another unusual way. Living with the Bernards was the childhood companion of Monsieur Bernard, a man named Simonard, who was the opposite of Monsieur Bernard in many ways. He was a short, squat widower with an extra-large nose, but he was quick-witted and lively, whereas Monsieur Bernard was rather slow-witted and listless.

Simonard was also a Voltairean, a staunch Catholic and a devoted royalist enchanted by Marie Antoinette. In fact, after he moved to Paris, he did everything to meet the queen. He did ultimately encounter her, but his first meeting proved unsatisfying. So, he decided to meet her again.

The second meeting took place when the queen attended a grand hunt at St. Germain. He hired a nag, travelled there and positioned himself near her at the start of the hunt. Once the hunt began, he made a comical sight as he and his nag could not keep up with the queen. Still, he faithfully pursued her with his hair flowing and his coat flapping in the wind.

The Queen could not help but notice him and, amused by his antics, she finally stopped. She asked him how long he intended to stay with the chase. He replied, 'As long, madame, as the legs of my horse will carry me.'[3] Supposedly, at that precise moment his poor horse expired; the queen chuckled, gave him a nod, and cantered away. While the story might not have been true, he told it to anyone who complained the queen was haughty.

He also had a son about Juliette's age who was, if not wayward, at least very mischievous. The son regularly raided the neighbour's grape vines and used his charisma to encourage Juliette to assist him. Unfortunately, one of their raids went bad. It happened because the owner of the vines suffered so many losses that he was on guard to catch the culprits in the act. Simonard's son escaped, while Juliette was caught red-handed atop the wall mid-flight.

What happened next explains the appeal of Juliette's beauty. It so disarmed the neighbour that, rather than scold the tearful and trembling girl, he begged her to stop crying. He also promised not to tell her parents about the thefts and even sent her home with her pinafore full of grapes.

When not raiding grape vines, the young Juliette often socialized with the numerous guests that frequented the Bernards' home when Madame Bernard hosted dinners twice a week. Literary people were the family's favourite guests and the slightly coquettish Madame Bernard was extremely skilled at 'attracting, retaining, and grouping … men whose sentiments were often in conflict'.[4] The dinners proved to be a great education for the young inquisitive girl and the skill of handling conflict would become one of Juliette's greatest talents.

The Bernards' entertaining also allowed Juliette to rub elbows with some of France's most elite people. For instance, one friend of the Bernard family was Pierre-Édouard Lémontey, from Lyon. He was a politician, scholar, historian and editor of a royalist newspaper. He was also extremely intelligent and twice selected as laureate of the learned society Académie de Marseille, first in 1785 and then in 1788. One person remarked of him that he was so educated he always talked as if his was a professor at a lectern.

Another frequent visitor was Bertrand Barère de Vieuzac, a French politician and journalist who became one of the most prominent members of the National Convention. He also served on the Committee of Public Safety and later presided over the trial of Louis XVI when he was charged with committing crimes against the state and high treason. Barère proved to be a valuable friend to the Bernards, as it is likely that because of their relationship with him they escaped the guillotine.

A third regular visitor was Jacques-Rose Récamier. He was to become one of the most important people in Juliette's life. In fact, he would affect her life in profound ways. His family originated from an area located between Lyon and Geneva, known as the Bugey region, but it was Lyon where he was born in 1751. His father was François Récamier, a respectable hat shop owner and his mother was Emmeraude Delaroche. Jacques-Rose grew into a tall, handsome, well-built man with a light complexion, thick fair hair and large blue eyes.

As a young man, Jacques-Rose travelled frequently with his father to Spain on business and learned to speak Spanish fluently. He also read and spoke Latin and enjoyed interspersing his conversations with quotes from Horace or Virgil, to the amazement of his listeners. Additionally, he became interested in finance and banking after he began working and travelling with his father.

From these early experiences, Jacques-Rose developed relationships with several Parisian banking houses. With a knack for finance and frugality, he soon become head of one of the first banking houses in Paris, which he further developed into a prosperous business. His business was further enhanced because of his tact with clients and because he wore the latest fashions, thereby presenting a fine, distinguished appearance.

As far as character went, he was generous to a fault and willing to give away money, advice, or time to any friend who asked. He was also polite, kind and light-hearted. Friends noted he was optimistic to excess, loved pleasure and frivolousness and could weave a tale with the best story tellers. Yet, there was one quality most people claimed was missing: Jacques-Rose was incapable of deep feelings. One writer said of him, '[Let a] friend be taken away by death, he would scarcely give two days to regret. "Another drawer closed," he would say, and there ended his sensibility.'[5]

When he came to visit the Bernards, he was always kind and considerate to Juliette. He told her wonderful stories and frequently brought gifts. Among these gifts were sweets, puppets, and dolls, called *poupees* in French. The *poupees* were always expensive and attired in luxurious fashions. On occasion, he may have even brought paper dolls, but if he did, they were probably intended for Juliette's parents as they were considered a form of adult entertainment with their painted and jointed bodies that resembled famous people.

Chapter 3

Life's Changes

I had nevertheless already found my conqueror.
Jacque-Rose on Juliette

As Jacques-Rose was visiting the Bernard family and bringing gifts to 11-year-old Juliette, Napoleon was taking leave in the late summer of 1789 to visit Corsica. The French Revolution created an upheaval that made life uncertain, created disorder and encouraged unrest. It also resulted in Paoli returning to Corsica from Britain where he had been exiled.

At the time, Napoleon was an ardent Corsican nationalist. He was also supportive of the republican Jacobin movement and involved in the complex three-way struggle involving revolutionaries, royalists and Corsican nationalists. In addition, he practically worshipped Paoli and supposedly once wrote of his patriotic feeling towards Corsica:

> 'As the nation was perishing I was born. Thirty thousand Frenchmen were vomited on to our shores, drowning the throne of liberty in waves of blood. Such was the odious sight which was the first to strike me. From my birth, my cradle was surrounded by the cries of the dying, the groans of the oppressed and tears of despair. You left our island and with you went all hope of happiness. Slavery was the price of our submission. Crushed by the triple yoke of the soldier, the law-maker and the tax inspector, our compatriots live despised.'[1]

Between 1786 and 1793, Napoleon took several military leaves that allowed him to come and go from Corsica. He had good reason to return to the island. Besides being ambitious in furthering his career, he also wanted to protect and improve his family's interests on the island. To do so, he thought it important to support the French Revolution and was among the first in Ajaccio to buy up church property after it was nationalized and became available for sale by the new government.

Although Paoli could see advantages if France controlled the island, he advocated for an independent Corsica. He also worried that France might try to rid itself of Corsica and wondered what would happen if that occurred. In addition, he was unhappy with the failed attempts by Frenchmen to materially ingratiate themselves with Corsicans.

Because of Paoli's attitude, his loyalty to the French Revolution was eventually questioned. Napoleon tried to clear Paoli's name and bolster his reputation by declaring him supportive of the Revolution. In early 1793, an opportunity presented itself that would have helped both men improve their reputations with the French government: Paoli had a chance to prove his patriotism and Napoleon had an opportunity to distinguish himself in the army.

It began after France ordered Corsican soldiers to invade Sardinia. Instead of sending a large, well-trained troop, Paoli sent a handful of poorly trained fighters. During the invasion, Napoleon distinguished himself, but most of Paoli's Corsican fighters withdrew at an inopportune time. The withdrawal turned into a fiasco and resulted in Paoli being branded a traitor in Paris.

In the meantime, problems continued to erupt between Napoleon and Paoli. Napoleon's young brother Lucien then openly declared Paoli a traitor at a Jacobin meeting. Lucien's accusation offended many Corsicans and they vociferously defended Paoli. Napoleon was with Paoli at Corte when Paoli learned of Lucien's accusation. According to tradition, the accusation meant that Napoleon was against Paoli, and thus, on 30 April, Napoleon fled from Corte to Ajaccio because he knew Lucien's accusations put his entire family at risk.

The risk became more perilous on 31 May 1793 when Paoli sealed the fate of the Bonaparte family be declaring of them that they were 'born in the mud of despotism, nourished and raised high under the eye … to their perpetual infamy'.[2] This declaration was a death warrant for the family. To save their lives, they were forced to flee. Napoleon had already escaped to a town on the northwest coast of Corsica called Calvi. There he finalized arrangements for a French ship to take his family to safety:

> 'Elisa took Pauline and Caroline by the hand, Letizia carried Jérome in her arms, and they fled to the beaches, where they waited in the open until the rescue ship arrived on 2 June and took them to Napoleon. … Nine days later the Buonaparte sailed for Toulon. Corsica was over for them.'[3]

Although life on Corsica may have ended for the Bonaparte family, for Juliette life was just beginning. For some time, 41-year-old Jacques-Rose had been thinking about marriage. He was a rich aristocrat and he had decided in early 1793 to offer his hand to 15-year-old Juliette. When she accepted his offer, he wrote a letter to a friend dated 22 February 1793 discussing his feelings:

> 'Last year, my dear friend, I hinted to you that the thought of marriage was beginning to have more charm for me. The idea was still a vague one, uncertain as to choice, and devoid of any fixed determination. I had nevertheless already found my conqueror, though I was as yet unaware of the power of her weapons, and never reckoned on my own defeat. … Unfortunately, she is too young, she is not more than sixteen. Others may possess greater beauty, but I have never seen any which answered better to my heart's desire. … I have always treated her with affectionate tenderness, she has always shown me a special regard, which has been developed by her childish caresses and her own innocent ardour, though veiled by the timid reserve of a tender heart just beginning to be stirred. … I am not in love with her, but I feel for her a genuine and tender attachment which convinces me that this interesting creature will be a partner who will ensure the happiness of my whole life and, judging by my own desire to ensure her happiness, of which I can see she is absolutely convinced, I have no doubt that the benefit will be reciprocal.'[4]

Avoiding death was another good reason for Jacques-Rose to marry Juliette. Aristocrats were regularly viewed as being disloyal to the revolutionary cause and many ended up with their heads severed by the guillotine. His marriage to Juliette would have diverted suspicion regarding his political beliefs because her parents were viewed in good political stead.

Whatever Jacques-Rose's reasoning for offering his hand to Juliette, there was apparently no reluctance or apprehension on her part. She willingly accepted his proposal. Thus, the wedding took place on 24 April 1793. It was a civil ceremony conducted at the Hôtel de Ville without any religious service. Some people may have thought that odd since she had been raised in a convent and always embraced her religion, but there were two good reasons to forgo religious services at the time.

First, Jacques-Roses' occupation as a banker was extremely unpopular with revolutionaries, and second, it would have been dangerous to have any priestly participation after many priests had been murdered by revolutionaries. These murders happened during the September Massacres of 1792 and among the first priests killed were twenty-four attacked while being transported to the prison of the Abbey of Saint-Germain-des-Prés. In a letter dated 3 September, the English Ambassador of Paris, the Earl of Gower, reported that the priest's deaths stating they were 'shocking' and full of 'barbarity.' Priests of the Carmelite Convent were also murdered after their removal to the rue Vaugerard. Their throats were slit and then their 'bodies were fixed on pikes and exhibited to the wretched victims who were next to suffer'.[5]

Because the French Revolution was volatile and because revolutionaries tended to react, it was prudent to keep any wedding celebration low-key. So, after the ceremony, Juliette and Jacques-Rose returned to the Bernards' home for a small, unassuming reception. That night, the bride slept at her new home located at No. 12 rue du Mail, but she did not consummate her marriage with Jacques-Rose. Apparently, their marriage took place in name only and, in fact, Juliette remained a virgin until she was at least forty years old.

Exactly why no consummation happened has been debated for years. One version is that Jacques-Rose had an affair with Juliette's mother and was her natural father. Supposedly, this rumour was known during Juliette's lifetime and was first made public in *Les Mémories d'une Inconnue, publiés sur le Manuscript original, 1780-1816,* by Madame Cavaignac, who was the mother of General Louis-Eugène Cavaignac and politician Éléonore Louis Godefroi Cavaignac.

Supporting this allegation was Mary Elizabeth (Clarke) Mohl, nicknamed 'Clarkey'. She was a salon hostess in Paris and an ardent Francophile. Later in life, her landlady was Juliette, from whom she sublet accommodations at Abbaye-aux-Bois. Mohl supported the story that Jacques-Rose was Juliette's biological father. Furthermore, some people contend that Cavaignac and Mohl's allegations are supported by the following passage written by Jacques-Rose:

> 'It may be said that my feelings for the daughter arise out of those I have had for her mother; but all those who frequent the house are well aware that what took me there was pure friendship – a friendship which had grown out of the possibly

> somewhat warmer feeling I may have had in the earlier days of our acquaintance. At present, having reached an age when all other pretensions are past, she only wishes to educate her child, and make her a virtuous and good woman.'[6]

Despite all the support for Jacques-Rose being Juliette's father, that claim seems to have been eventually debunked. A more logical explanation for no consummation between the couple originated with a French archaeologist and historian of the nineteenth century named Prosper Mérimée. He states Jacques-Rose never consummated the marriage because Juliette suffered from a physical condition that caused sex to be painful. A French doctor, historian, and author of numerous works of both fiction and history, Augustin Cabanès, also remarked on her physical condition in the late 1800s, likening her condition to that of Queen Elizabeth I. He indicated that Juliette likely had some impenetrable membrane or vaginal band that prohibited or greatly deterred sex.

As Juliette was embracing a life of virginal domesticity, the French military commander and former minister of war, General Charles François Dumouriez, defected to Austria. From Austria, he then threatened to march on France. People in France were nervous just like they had been a year earlier when the September Massacres occurred. Thus, to protect the newly established republic against foreign attacks and internal rebellion, the Committee of Public Safety was created.

Around this same time, Napoleon and his family washed up on the shores of Toulon in southern France off the coast of the Mediterranean. They had no land, no money and few prospects. Napoleon's military pay was the family's only hope for survival at the time. However, there was also one other promising thing in the family's favour. The strife created by the French Revolution allowed for rapid military and political advancement for those willing to seize it.

Napoleon was willing to grab any opportunity given for advancement and focused all his energies on improving his career. He had previously been promoted to captain in the regular army and, in July 1793, he was ordered to pick up gunpowder in Avignon. When he reached that city, he found it had fallen to anti-Convention forces, the Federalists. He claims that Federalists arrested him, but no records support his claim. However, records do indicate he was arrested by National Convention forces because of suspicions that he was a nobleman. A fellow Corsican, Antoine Christophe Saliceti, fortunately vouched for Napoleon and he was released.

After his release, Napoleon published a pamphlet called *Le souper de Beaucaire* (Supper at Beaucaire). He probably wrote the pamphlet to clear his name and show that he was not disloyal. The pro-republican pamphlet garnered the attention of Maximilien Robespierre's younger brother, Augustin. It also resulted in Augustin and Saliceti, helping the penniless Napoleon be appointed the republican force's artillery commander at the Siege of Toulon that began on 29 August of 1793.

The siege was one of the Federalist revolts that broke out during the French Revolution in various parts of France in the summer of 1793. The Federalists as a group were upset about what was happening in the Convention and included disgruntled Girondins. First, power had centralized in Paris and this made some provinces unhappy and, second, the more radical Jacobins had gained authority in the Convention and then excluded the Girondins from power. When they did that, Federalists saw it as the last straw and revolted.

Toulon was a major French naval base that had been taken by Federalists. It was being defended by them and a powerful British fleet that was sitting in the harbour. The Convention had sent their forces to take it, but they could not have been more unprepared or ill-suited for the task. The only advantage the Convention forces had was that Napoleon was given carte blanche to organize the rag-tag, ill-trained soldiers.

Convention strategists soon realized that there was no way to retake the city without first taking the harbour's entrance. Unfortunately, this was controlled by Fort Eguilette, which was protected by the British fleet. To oust the Federalists and the British fleet, Napoleon worked jointly with a French general, Jacques François Coquille – more usually called Dugommier – who was the overall commander.

Napoleon contributed all his resourcefulness, creativity and initiative to establish an indomitable galvanized force that would menace the enemy. This was his chance and he grabbed it with both hands. Historian and author Michael Broers wrote:

> 'Starting with a couple of mortars, four cannon and a few light field guns manned by untrained volunteers, Napoleon forged a force to be reckoned with. Somehow, he collected more and more large guns – 24 pounds – and long-range mortars fit for siege warfare, he searched out retired army artillery officers in the area and set them to work. He filled the ranks by retaining regular infantry intensively, under his direct

> supervision … [so that] by early November, he had a hundred cannon and siege mortars, regular supplies of ammunition, and good gunners. They were well placed and sited, all thanks to Napoleon, in positions to cause the city and the British fleet maximum damage. … He pounded Toulon and its harbour for twenty hours a day, day in, day out. It was superhuman effort, if on a small scale.'[7]

Although the plan for taking Toulon had been devised jointly by Dugommier and Napoleon, Napoleon reworked the plan substantially by the time it was submitted to the Convention in Paris. Broers provides this account:

> 'Napoleon … proved himself again an able and very brave field commander, not just a skilled gunner. He soon had ten cannon trained on the inner harbour. When he opened a murderous fire on the British ships in the harbour, Admiral Lord Hood, the commander-in-chief at Toulon, ordered a general evacuation. It was over.'[8]

Also involved in the siege, besides Augustin and Salicetti, was Paul François Jean Nicolas, Vicomte de Barras, commonly known as Paul Barras. He was born to a noble family in Provence and became a well-known French politician during the French Revolution. He also sought to overthrow Robespierre's faction and went on to become the main executive leader of the Directory regime.

On 19 December 1793, Convention forces entered Toulon victorious and fearful citizens scrambled to get aboard one of the many British ships fleeing the harbour. Thousands made it, but thousands did not. As the refugees sailed away, they reported the panic they witnessed back on shore. Citizens rushed to the waterfront hoping to be saved as the Convention's advancing soldiers pursued them and fired upon them indiscriminately. Those making haste to escape were either shot, crushed, or drowned in the harbour.

Napoleon suffered a bayonet wound to his leg after his horse was shot out from under him, and as he was being treated for his wound, the aftermath of the siege played out in a blood bath of suppression. Savage revenge was enacted by Barras and another French politician, Stanislas Fréron, on the Toulon citizens who had turned against the Convention. Convention troops created havoc murdering the citizenry and executing hundreds of prisoners at Toulon's Champ de Mars.

Unrest had been building in France, and during the Siege of Toulon a period of intense violence broke out between the two opposing political factions, the Girondins and the Jacobins. Moreover, the civil unrest and counter-revolutions caused French politicians in Paris to worry another September Massacre might occur. To guard against such an occurrence, politicians decided it was better the government direct the violence and one politician declared, 'Let us make terror the order of the day'.[9]

Beginning in September 1793 and continuing for the next year and a half, the Reign of Terror became like a snowball rolling downhill. Once it began rolling, the momentum kept it going and it grew larger as it went. Anyone who opposed the Terror was suspect themselves and so rather than become a victim of the Terror, people often complied and went along. Those people who did not comply were considered an enemy of the Revolution and were sent to trial. To make it worse, trials didn't have to be completed for decisions to be rendered or for a person to be released or executed.

Amid the Reign of Terror, the Siege of Toulon proved beneficial to Napoleon's career. Although Dugommier was hailed as the hero, Napoleon was not overlooked. The 24-year-old had proven himself more than capable in his first major action, and his talent and skills were rewarded when he received a promotion to brigadier general. Still, despite his heroics, the Siege of Toulon did not launch his career. That would take another two years.

Chapter 4

The Directory

Whiff of grapeshot.
Thomas Carlyle

While Juliette and Jacques-Rose were leading an uneventful and low-profile life, Napoleon's career had been launched with the 'whiff of grapeshot' in 1795. He gained recognition and wealth from the Directory, which consisted of a five-member committee of directors who had been chosen by the Council of Ancients (upper house of the legislature of France) and the lower house, called the Council of Five Hundred. The five directors thanked Napoleon by appointing him commander of the Army of Italy on 2 March 1796.

That was not the only change for Napoleon. Earlier, he had met Marie Josèphe Rose Tascher de La Pagerie, whom he called Josephine probably based on her middle name Josèphe. She had been born in Les Trois-Îlets, Martinique, to a white Creole family that owned a sugarcane plantation. The family had been struggling financially since 1766 because hurricanes had destroyed their estate.

During these years of struggle, Josephine's paternal aunt became mistress to a wealthy French aristocrat, François, Vicomte de Beauharnais. When he fell ill, he wanted to ensure that his money and estates stayed in the Beauharnais hands, and so Josephine's aunt helped him arrange a marriage for his 19-year-old son Alexandre that also happened to benefit Josephine's family.

Alexandre had heard about 15-year-old Josephine, but he thought she was too old and was instead interested in her 12-year-old sister Catherine-Désirée. Unfortunately, before he could marry her, Catherine-Désirée died of yellow fever. To replace her, Josephine's youngest sister, 11-year-old Manette, was suggested. However, she became ill with a fever and could not travel. That left Josephine. So, on 13 December 1779, Josephine and Alexandre married.

Alexandre was a good-looking, well-built, young man 'with wide-set intense blue eyes, a long curved nose and full lips. His hair, meticulously coiffed and powered, was pulled back into a neat bow at the nape'.[1] He was also an army man, well-educated, and somewhat of lady's man, whereas Josephine was poorly educated, practically illiterate, and anything but worldly. Their marriage was not a happy one and in fact, Alexandre took a mistress. She was eleven years older and supposedly gave birth to his child the same year he married Josephine.

In 1781, two years after her marriage, Josephine gave birth to a son named Eugène and then two years later to a daughter, Hortense. Alexandre's career continued to improve during this time. He served in the American Revolutionary War, became a politician, and then in 1792 was promoted to a general. However, in 1793, during the Siege of Mainz, he was so ineffective in defending the town that the new republic questioned his loyalty. He was arrested, convicted and guillotined during the Reign of Terror.

Josephine herself was also imprisoned during that same time. When the Terror ended, she, like many others, was released. Husbandless, Josephine needed to survive and reportedly had several love affairs with various powerful political figures. Among those she has been alleged to have had an affair with was Barras, the same man who had suppressed Toulon. At the time of their relationship, Barras was one of the main executive leaders of the Directory. He had obtained a position of importance because he had earlier voted for Louis XVI's death and sided with those who wanted to overthrow Robespierre. In addition, he rose to prominence during the interim period between the National Convention and the establishment of the Directory, known as the Thermidorian Reaction, which ended the most radical phase of the French Revolution.

Although there were allegations that Josephine and the cultured, intelligent, and worldly Barras were lovers, it is highly doubtful that their relationship was anything more than friendship, even though she frequently served as his hostess. He was probably homosexual (or at the least, bisexual). Moreover, their relationship seems to have operated on a level where he helped her financially and she aided him by improving his business connections.

There are several stories about how Napoleon and Josephine met. One legendary story claims they met in October 1795 after Parisians were ordered to give up their swords in a general disarming of Paris. Supposedly, Josephine's 14-year-old son Eugène went to Napoleon and appealed to keep his father's sword because his father had been guillotined. His appeal so touched Napoleon that he asked to meet the boy's mother, who turned out to be Josephine, who likewise charmed Napoleon.

Napoleon provided two different versions of how he met Josephine and several other slightly different versions also exist. However, despite Napoleon's support for the sword story, Barras claims that the couple met long before the sword incident. He maintains he introduced Napoleon to Josephine. According to Barras, they were at a mutual friend's house when he provided the introductions.

Whether Barras made the introductions or not, a romantic relationship existed between Napoleon and Josephine by the end of 1795. Napoleon was infatuated with her great political connections, high social status and extreme grace. The femme fatale saw him as her protector and provider. They soon decided to marry, and Barras is often credited as the person who facilitated their marriage. Their banns of marriage were published on 7 February 1796 and the wedding was set for 9 March 1796 at 8pm.

Josephine arrived on time, but Napoleon was nowhere in sight. Among those at the civil ceremony were four witnesses and a public officer in the municipality named Charles-Theodore-François Leclerc. He arrived at 6pm but got tired waiting for Napoleon and went home to bed. Napoleon did not arrive until 10pm as he had become side-tracked pouring over maps.

Among the witnesses to Josephine and Napoleon's marriage were Barras and three others. Leclerc had left an acting registrar in his place, a man named Antoine Collin-Lacombe. The marriage took less than 30 minutes to complete. Unfortunately, the wooden-legged Collin-Lacombe had no authority to marry anyone, but that did not stop Leclerc from signing and attesting to the fact that the marriage occurred. Afterwards, Leclerc noted:

> 'After Napolione Buonaparte and Marie-Joseph-Rose Detascher had declared, with a loud voice, that they took each other, by mutual consent, for husband and wife, I promised, with a loud voice, Napolione Buonaparte, and Marie-Joseph-Rose Detascher, to be united in marriage, and that in the presence of witnesses, of the age of majority … all of whom, the parties, and myself had signed after reading.'[2]

The wedding certificate purposely contained all sorts of false information. Josephine's birth date was changed from 23 June 1763 to 23 June 1767, which made her four years younger and, perhaps out of gallantry, Napoleon's birth date was also changed to make him 18 months older. Napoleon's impassioned love for Josephine reputedly resulted in him later destroying the certificates of their baptism, so that he could spare her any humiliation she might feel that she was six years older than him.

Like the Récamier's marriage, there was no religious ceremony and afterwards no celebration. Everyone just went home. Napoleon went with Josephine to the house she was leasing at No. 6 rue Chantereine, located in a fashionable part of Paris called the Chaussée d'Antin.

The wedding night appears to have had problems just like the wedding. Josephine owned a pug named Fortuné and, apparently, he was greatly disinclined to share the bed with Napoleon, even on his wedding night. When the new husband attempted to get into bed, Fortuné bit him on the shin.

The newlyweds also hardly enjoyed a honeymoon. Napoleon was feeling great pressure to leave and two days after his marriage, he rode out of Paris to join his army in Italy. Before he left, he told Josephine:

> 'I must hasten to my post … for an army without a chief is like a widow who can commit foolish deeds and endanger her reputation. I am responsible for the army's conduct from the moment of my appointment.'[3]

During the Directory, which lasted until 1799, the new government attempted to restore order and many émigrés began returning to France. As these changes occurred, French society bloomed. The bloom was accompanied by the fashion of male *incroyables* (incredible) and their female counterparts *les merveilleuses* (marvellous), who were often members of France's ruling class and among the leading figures at the time. During this time, the incroyables and merveilleuses not only affected fashion but also politics and art as well.

Incroyables were seen on streets decked in flamboyant, beribboned and eccentric attire. Because of their outlandish clothing, they were sometimes described as fops or dandies. They wore tight breeches, leather boots, redingotes, thick glasses, and huge neckties while carrying canes or hats that were topped by 'dog ears' because their foppish powdered long hairstyles fell over their ears. Some of them even sported monocles, affected a lisp, or assumed a stooped posture.

Les merveilleuses were as noticeable as the incroyables on the streets. The female versions embraced the *à la grecque* fashions that rejected the Ancien Régime. They also shed their stays and corsets for scandalous flowing gossamer muslin dresses that sported revealing décolleté and raised waists. Shawls were also in style, as were delicate slippers and sandals reminiscent of Greek or Roman footwear. Hair was often worn short or cropped, the style called *à la victime*, in honour of those who became victims of the guillotine during the Terror.

Many historians believed that these flamboyant and excess fashions were a manifestation of the renewed freedom the French people suddenly enjoyed when the Terror ended. In fact, the day after Robespierre's execution, it was reported that ornate carriages appeared on Parisian streets and, shortly thereafter, heady pleasure seekers invaded Paris. Moreover, women began to take on more visible roles, sociality resumed and promenades in parks and along the boulevards became fashionable once again.

Among those frequently mentioned as les merveilleuses were Juliette, Josephine and Thérésa Cabarrus, called Madame Tallien. She was a Spanish-born French noble. Her father was an ethnic Basque French-born Spanish financier and her mother the daughter of a French industrialist based in Spain. Her father founded and governed the bank of San Carlos, which became the Royal Bank of Spain and, in 1789, Charles IV of Spain ennobled him with the title of count.

At twelve years old, her father sent her to France to complete her education and get married. Wanting to strengthen his position in France, he then arranged for the by now 14-year-old to marry a rich powerful Frenchman Jean Jacques Devin Fontenay, the last Marquis de Fontenay. When her husband fled France at the outbreak of the Revolution in 1789, she obtained a divorce and resumed her maiden name. She then met and married Jean Lambert Tallien, a commissioner of the National Convention.

The three beauties – Juliette, Josephine and Thérésa – were dubbed the 'Three Graces' because of their trend-setting fashion sense. Twentieth century historian Édouard Herriot wrote of them:

> 'These three ladies … drove Paris wild, and saw the most illustrious personages at their feet, – those lovely feet which they wore bare, except for sandals, and with emeralds on their toes. They were seen everywhere, at the concerts, … – at the balls … – They were the soul of all gaiety.'

Paris was also wild in another way. For example, when public worship was re-established, parishioners who had been restrained from attending church began to attend in vast numbers. This resulted in chapels overflowing with nowhere for worshippers to sit or stand. Moreover, the packed chapels made it difficult for the plate passers to manoeuvre through the thick crowds. But it was well worth it to pass the plate, as churches received donations that amounted to thousands of francs.

Juliette and Jacques-Rose were some of the parishioners caught up in the excitement of returning to church. On one church visit, Juliette was requested to hold the plate for the collection of the poor and her beauty so intrigued everyone that her friend wrote:

> 'The crowd climbed on chairs, on columns; and it was as much as the two gentlemen appointed to attend her, according to the custom, could do to prevent her from being crushed to death by public admiration.'[4]

Like other wealthy French citizens, the couple enjoyed the happiness that was flourishing in France. As France was blooming with gaiety, Juliette was also blossoming. She changed from a young girl into a youthful woman:

> 'Her beauty had fully developed; … A figure, flexible and elegant; a well-poised head; throat and shoulders of admirable form and proportions; beautiful arms, though somewhat small; a little rosy mouth, pearly teeth, black hair that curled naturally; a delicate and regular nose, but *bien-français*; an incomparable brilliancy of complexion; a frank, arch face, rendered irresistibly lovely from its expression of goodness; a carriage slightly indicative of both indolence and pride … Wherever she went, her beauty called forth a murmur of admiration, curiosity, and enthusiasm.'[5]

Others also noted Juliette's beauty. The Frenchman Lamartine, a writer and poet who awoke one day to find himself famous because of his masterpiece *Les Méditations Poétiques*, wrote of Juliette, 'Her angelic face can bear no other name; one look suffices to bind your heart to her for ever'.[6] Even England's famous Field Marshal Arthur Wellesley, better known as the Duke of Wellington or the 'Iron Duke', was smitten by Juliette's beauty and never failed to call on her when he visited Paris.

Napoleon also noticed Juliette but not in the way she might have desired. It happened after his stunning success in Italy and his return to Paris on 5 December 1797. Everyone wanted to pay homage to the conquering hero and celebrate his genius, so the Directory decided to host some brilliant festivities to honour him. Five days after his return, a fete was held at Luxembourg Palace in an immense outdoor court.

A lofty platform was erected with an altar to France that contained three gigantic statues representing Freedom, Equality, and Peace. A second platform was also constructed around the first platform. It was covered with a canopy and was constructed to hold the five directors, the Council of Five-Hundred, and other important dignitaries.

On the day of the fete, Josephine was not seated on the platform; rather, she was watching from a window inside the Luxembourg palace. Juliette and her mother, however, were in attendance and seated close to the action. Juliette was particularly enthusiastic about seeing Napoleon as his name was on everyone lips, and, she, like Parisians in general, was curious to see him and hear what he had to say.

Although the directors made a theatrical appearance decked out in classical antique robes, their arrival caused no sensation among the crowd. What did cause a sensation was the entrance of Napoleon. The general was dressed in a simple green uniform and accompanied by a few officers also outfitted in their ordinary uniforms worn on the battlefield. In addition, two generals carried the standards that had been presented to the Army of Italy in 1796, further adorned by the names of the 67 battles that had been won.

Although Juliette and her mother were seated somewhat close in reserved seating, they were still far away enough that it was difficult to see Napoleon. Having never seen him, and wanting to get a good look, Juliette stood and peered over the throng. Due to her beauty, a spontaneous murmur of admiration arose from the crowd and attention suddenly diverted to her. Napoleon heard the murmur and saw the heads of the crowd swivel elsewhere. He looked to see who had diverted their attention from himself and saw a beautiful woman draped all in white. One historian gave the following description of what happened next:

> 'Napoleon's vanity was hurt; he showed his impatience, and bent upon her one of his chilling condemnatory looks. She sat down at once. Thus in the outset of her life she had the satisfaction of rivalling Napoleon himself in popular admiration.'[7]

When the fete began, the laicized French bishop and well-known diplomat Charles Maurice de Talleyrand-Périgord, simply called Talleyrand, opened the festivities with a long speech. Talleyrand, who walked with a congenital limp since childhood, came from a well-regarded and ancient family. His family was not prosperous and that is probably why he chose the clergy, as it provided a pathway to wealth. He had been ordained a priest at the age of 25 and named Bishop of Autun in 1789. Shortly after, he attended the

Estates-General and represented the clergy. He also strongly supported anti-clericalism during the French Revolution and assisted in the appropriation of Church properties. However, despite his support for the revolution, the National Convention issued a warrant for his arrest and he left Paris for England in September of 1792. After the fall of Robespierre, Talleyrand successfully lobbied the Directory for his return and arrived back in France on 25 September 1796.

Talleyrand recognized the possibility of a successful political career for Napoleon during the Italian Campaign. Talleyrand then began to correspond with him and the two men became close allies. Now he was saluting Napoleon in the name of France at a festival honouring him. Josephine noted that an emotional Barras also welcomed Napoleon to the podium and after praising his outstanding accomplishments, Barras heartily embraced him, as did the four other directors.

The same year in which Juliette first saw Napoleon, she experienced another fateful meeting. She met Anne Louise Germaine de Staël-Holstein, commonly called Germaine or Madame de Staël. Germaine was 32 at the time and not particularly attractive. She had a full pouting mouth, swarthy complexion and masculine features; if any of her physical assets might be praised, it was her large eyes and buxom figure. Juliette's meeting with her came about because Jacques-Rose decided his house at rue du Mail was too small and he wanted something larger.

That was exactly what Germaine's father, Jacques Necker, was selling. Necker had served under Louis XVI as his Finance Minister, and Germaine was negotiating the sale of his home in the rue du Mont Blanc because he was living in Switzerland. During the negotiations, Jacques-Rose appeared one day in his drawing room accompanied by a woman whom he did not introduce and whom Juliette did not know. He left the strange woman alone with Juliette, who later wrote:

> 'Her costume was peculiar: she wore a morning-gown, and a small dress-hat trimmed with flowers. I took her for a foreigner. I was struck with the beauty of her eyes and her expression. I was not able to analyze my feelings; but it is certain that I thought more of finding out, or rather guessing, who she was, than of addressing to her the usual commonplaces, when she said to me with an impressive, graceful manner, that 'she was truly charmed to know me; that her father M. Necker,' — At these words I recognized

> Mme. de Staël. I did not hear the rest of her sentence. I blushed, and felt extremely embarrassed. I had just been reading her letters on Rousseau, which I exceedingly admired. My looks were more expressive than my words, as she both attracted and intimidated me. I felt at once her superiority and her genuineness. As for her, she fixed her large eyes upon me, but with a friendly scrutiny, and paid me some personal compliments, that would have been too exaggerated and direct, had they not seemed to escape her unconsciously, thus giving to them an irresistible fascination. My embarrassment did me no harm. She understood it, and expressed the hope that she might see a great deal of me when she returned to Paris; for she was on the point of leaving for Coppet. This interview was but a passing one; but it made a deep impression upon me. I only thought of Mme. de Staël, so much did I feel the influence of that strong and ardent nature.'[8]

Germaine had been married for nine years to Baron Erik Magnus Staël von Holstein, but Juliette learned there was no love between husband and wife. The Baron was described by contemporaries as being handsome, having polished manners and possessing great talent as a diplomat. He was also witty and charming and enjoyed fine wines, politics, and history. Yet, all those traits must not have won Germaine over as she and he were at odds with one another over politics.

Their marriage was also not based on love. What it offered was certain advantages: he acquired financial benefits and in exchange Germaine obtained a high position at court. Although loveless, their marriage was not acrimonious, but it did nevertheless prove not to be strong enough to keep them together. They separated in 1797, but never divorced. The Baron liked to gamble, incurring enormous debts, and thereafter, he relied upon the Necker fortune for his finances.

At the time of their marriage in 1786, Germaine's husband was serving as Ambassador to France, having been appointed a year earlier. His position granted Germaine certain privileges that other French citizens did not enjoy during the Revolution. One advantage was a salon frequented by powerful men, such as Talleyrand and Barras. However, the advantages and privileges afforded Germaine and her husband did not reduce her fears during the September Massacres and she fled from France (although it is unclear if she faced any real danger).

When she fled, Germaine went to live in a small village in Switzerland called Coppet. She also travelled to England, wrote a pamphlet about Marie Antoinette's execution, and created another popular salon that was patronized by a host of friends and émigrés. When Robespierre fell, and the Reign of Terror ended, Germaine returned to Paris but alternated her time between Paris and Coppet. It was also around this same time that she first began to oppose Napoleon for both political and personal reasons.

Chapter 5

Houses and Salons

O Juliette! life without love is only one long slumber.
Lucien Bonaparte to Juliette

Jacques-Rose liked Necker's Mont Blanc house, and a deal was struck. The deed of sale was signed on 16 October 1798 and immediately afterwards work began to enlarge, refurbish and transform the Mont Blanc house into a 'fairlyland'. To accomplish it, Jacques-Rose hired architect Louis Martin Berthault and gave him carte blanche so that no expense was spared on what was now christened the Hôtel Jacques-Rose. It did not take long before the house became the talk of the town. People who saw it noted that it was as elegant outside as luxurious inside and rumours swirled about the custom-made furnishings.

Everyone who heard about the house wanted a peek inside. In fact, one Parisian visitor, a Miss Berry, said she could not leave Paris without seeing it and fortune shone on her as she was lucky enough to get a look inside. She reported that there were no large rooms nor an abundance of rooms but rather the house was 'fitted up with all the recherché and expense possible in what is now called *le goût antique*'.[1] She also noted:

> 'All the chairs are mahogany, enriched with ormolu, and covered either with cloth or silk; those in the salon, trimmed with flat gold lace, in good taste. Her [Juliette's] bed is reckoned with the most beautiful in Paris; it too, is of mahogany, enriched with ormolus and bronze, and raised upon two steps of the same wood. Over the whole bed was thrown a great coverlid or veil of fine plain muslin, with rows of narrow gold lace at each end, and the muslin embroidered as a border. … At the foot of the bed stood a fine Grecian lamp of ormolu, with a little figure of the same metal bending over it; and at the head of the bed, another and upon which was placed a large ornamented flower-pot, containing a large artificial rose-tree, the branches

> of which must nod very near her nose, in bed. Out of this bedroom is a beautiful little *salle de bain*. The walls, inlaid with satin-wood. The bath presents itself as a sofa in a recess, covered with a cushion of scarlet cloth, embroidered and laced with black. Beyond this, again, is a very little boudoir, lined with quilted pea-green lustring, drawn together in a bunch in the middle of the ceiling.'[2]

Another visitor to Paris also saw the interior and wrote a description of Juliette's apartment declaring:

> 'The apartment consisted of a vestibule, two rooms on the right, Mme. Récamier's bedroom, the bathroom, and the boudoir. Whenever a lady entered, [Juliette] … said to her, "Would you like to see my bedroom?" … and whilst she was leading her to the most elegant room in the house, the men, "young and old," rushed forward to take their part in the show. … The bedroom is very large: the walls are almost completely covered with wide and tall mirrors in one sole piece. Between the windows and the great doors of marquetry very artistically worked, there is white wood with brown moudlings relieved by bronze ornaments. Opposite the windows the partition is almost entirely formed of one glass. The couch of the goddess is all white, covered with the finest Indian stuffs. The woodwork of the bed is of the fine antique form, and is also ornamented with bronze. Elegant vases are placed on the two steps of the platform that supports it. Behind are two tall candelabra each with six or eight branches. The curtains of the bed are white. The back is composed of a heavy curtain of violet damask well drawn up at the sides to reveal the mirror on the walls, so that Mme. Récamier being in bed can be seen reflected from head to foot.'[3]

The Mont Blanc house was not the only residence the Récamiers enjoyed. They had an elegant summer residence close to Paris in Clichy that Jacques-Rose had purchased three years earlier. The Clichy house had a fine lush green park with banks that sloped to the shores of the Seine. It was at Clichy that Juliette entertained her most intimate friends.

The Clichy house was decorated in floral patterns and because of the abundance of flowers in the gardens, Juliette filled its rooms with fragrant flower blossoms. She and her mother always went to Clichy in the springtime and remained there throughout the summer. During their time at Clichy, Jacques-Rose remained in Paris but drove out every night for supper and every Sunday he and his wife held some sort of dinner party for close friends.

In the spring of 1799, after Juliette and her mother had already nestled in at Clichy for the summer, a dinner invitation for the Récamiers arrived from Bagatelle. The invitation was from Dr Sapey, a military surgeon. He also invited Napoleon's younger brother, Lucien, who, at the time, was 24 years old.

Although Lucien had his brother's chin and resembled Napoleon facially, he was slightly taller, awkward, and gangly, with long legs, long arms, and big hands. Fifteen-year-old Napoleon wrote a description of Lucien when was he was a boy to his uncle:

> 'He is 9 years old, and 3 feet, 4 inches, and 6 lines tall. He is in the sixth class for Latin, and is going to learn all the subjects in the curriculum. He shows plenty of good disposition and has good intentions. It is to be hoped he will turn out well. He is a big upstanding boy, quick and impulsive, and he is making a good start.'[4]

By the time Lucien reached adulthood, the French writer Laure Junot described him a little differently:

> 'Lucien was very near-sighted, which made him half-shut his eyes and stoop his head. This defect would therefore have given him an unpleasing air, if his smile, always in harmony with his look, had not imparted something agreeable to his countenance. Thus, though he was rather plain than otherwise, he pleased generally.'[5]

Lucien was a mixture of traits and characteristics. He has been described as conceited, politically ambitious, articulate, bombastic and filled with bravado. He would pepper his speech with quotes, high-sounding phrases and aphorisms accompanied by continual gesturing. Furthermore, despite a pleasant attitude and a lively disposition, his near-sightedness and nervous eye twitch often gave him a hard appearance.

Like his brother, Lucien immediately noticed Juliette. He was a romantic who thought himself irresistible to women. He also fell in love easily and was almost instantaneously smitten with Juliette. It did not matter that years earlier, Lucien had married a pleasing woman, who though pitted with smallpox had an angelic disposition. Her name was Christine Boyer, and everyone who met her remarked on her kindness, affection and love for her husband. Yet, despite Christine's wonderful qualities, it was Juliette who captivated Lucien and garnered his attention.

Juliette so intrigued Lucien that he practically fell in love instantaneously. On the same evening that he met her, he requested permission to walk with her in the Bagatelle gardens. Then, before she left, he begged to be allowed to visit her at Clichy the following day. Juliette was unsure but allowed it.

A few days later, Lucien sent a passionate declaration of love to Juliette. The pronouncement was in the form of a literary composition and was signed 'Romeo' as he was now calling her his 'Juliette'. As she had never been the object of such a passionate love before, she was stunned. She was unsure what to do but politely read what he wrote and calmly returned it to him. Then, in the presence of others, she praised him but advised 'him to reserve himself for higher objects, and not waste in works of imagination'.[6]

Juliette's words did not deter Lucien from pursuing her. Indeed, it only made him bolder. The fact that he had to pursue her made him more determined, so he began a letter writing campaign where he openly declared his undying love and devotion. There were many passionate love letters with one of them containing the following lines:

> 'O Juliette! life without love is only one long slumber; the most beautiful of women ought to be impressible: happy the man who will become the friend of your heart!'[7]

Lucien's letters were far from literary masterpieces, and his corny words did not endear Juliette to him. With each letter, he grew bolder and with each letter, he pronounced with greater firmness his love for Juliette. She hardly knew what to do, although in private she laughed at his bombastic ways and perhaps pitied him knowing that she would never return his love.

Eventually, however, she reached her limit and showed his letters to her husband. She wanted him to forbid Lucien from visiting, but Jacques-Rose refused. He told her that to shut the door to Napoleon's brother was unthinkable because it might jeopardize his business and their finances. Instead, he counselled her to continue to demonstrate prudence and wisdom. In other words, she had to walk a fine line; offer Lucien nothing but at the same time not drive him to despair.

In the meantime, Juliette focused on an activity that originated around the time of Louis XIV's reign; the salon. The French court served as a powerful status symbol for the elite and a movement developed in the 1600s whereby royal academies were established for science and the arts. Although the academies solidified absolutist ideologies, salons tended to act as an extension of the royal court. However, unlike the court, a salon had no social hierarchy as nobles and the bourgeois mixed freely and men and women also socialized without restriction.

Besides being created for social reasons, salons were also created for intellectual reasons because they increased a participant's knowledge about the world through meaningful conversations. Salons were often composed of the most influential and famous of men, the *philosophes*, and the most influential and famous of women, the *salonnières*. Salons could also give or withhold their stamp of approval. For instance, approval might be granted for a brilliant play or a great poem; thus, the approval or lack of it determined the fate of the poem or play's author.

Women were key to the success of salons and did more than just facilitate conversation. In France, the first renowned salon was held by Catherine de Vivonne, marquise de Rambouillet, at the Hôtel de Rambouillet near the Palais du Louvre in Paris. To ensure a long-lasting and successful salon, the marquise established rules of etiquette that resembled the old ideas of chivalry. However, by the eighteenth century these rules were no longer in force.

Manners and established traditions replaced them. Salons also began to operate on the idea of good breeding and good taste rather than for ethical or moral reasons. One Victorian writer noted of these times:

> 'Honour was a religion; politeness and courtesy were the current, though by no means always genuine, coin of unselfishness and amiability; the amenities stood in the place of an ethical code. Egotism, ill temper, disloyalty, ingratitude, and scandal were sins against taste, and spoiled the general harmony. Evil passions might exist, but it was agreeable to hide them, and enmities slept under a gracious smile. … Vice in many veiled forms might be tolerated, but that which called itself good society barred its doors against those who violated the canons of good taste, which recognize at least the outward semblance of many amiable virtues. Sincerity certainly was not one of these virtues; but no one was deceived, as it was perfectly well understood

> that courteous forms meant little more than the dress which may or may not conceal a physical defect, but is fit and becoming.'[8]

By the end of the eighteenth century, leading salonists transformed the salon 'from a noble, leisure institution into an institution of Enlightenment … [where] nobles and non-nobles were brought together on a footing of equality'.[9] The late eighteenth century also saw gentlemen making daily rounds to certain salons where they discussed the hottest topics related to the arts, politics, literature, or philosophy. Because Jacques-Rose was one of the most respected and richest bankers of the time and because he had standing within the community, he encouraged Juliette to entertain and suggested she open a salon.

When she did, it did not take long for it to be filled with people of influence. Her salon was held on Mondays from 1799 to 1803, and it was at that time that Juliette established a presence as a political and social hostess. Visitors to her salon ranged from returning émigrés and prominent writers to influential financiers and persuasive intellectuals. It included such people as Germaine, Lucien, Mathieu of Montmorency-Laval who Juliette viewed as something of a father figure, the French general Jean-Victor-Marie Moreau, and Louis Marie Jacques Amalric (Comte de Narbonne-Lara). Politicians were also an important part of this cultural hub.

With all the differing opinions, it might seem as if Juliette's salon would be rife for arguments and conflict. However, from her mother, she had learned to be tactful and control difficult situations. One historian wrote, 'It was said that great men who often clashed outside because of their different political views brushed these differences aside in Juliette's salon and were very friendly toward each other.'[10]

Juliette's salons were also different from other salons because her aim was for salon guests to discuss and stick to one subject. She had learned composure from her mother and was artful in applying it. The famous French literary critic Charles Augustin Sainte-Beuve once said of her:

> 'Never a talent, a virtue was lost, she recognized every distinction; she was willing to recognize every merit, and bring it to light. She desired to place everyone in his right relation therefore creating a perfect harmony about her, and thus subordinated them to her.'[11]

Juliette also proved to be an attentive and graceful hostess. One contemporary declared she was meant to electrify the world. Yet, more than that, Juliette was said to possess the unique quality of 'beauty and brains', which perhaps prompted one contemporary to praise her thus:

> 'The fact, however, is that never was a woman as likable and as beautiful at the same time as Mme Récamier. Yet, never susceptible to the usual calculations of the mediocre people, she was never afraid to surround herself with women more witty than herself, and moreover, no woman has ever sacrificed more of her own charms to let the others shine, so thus she is adored by anyone who has genius, talent, or wit.'[12]

Madame Tallien also held a popular salon. She and Josephine had been in prison together at Carmes in 1794 and when Madame Tallien was freed, she quickly became a leader of Parisian social life. As a fashion trend setter and well-known merveilleuse, she once appeared at the Paris Opera wearing a white diaphanous gown with no underwear. Talleyrand was so shocked by the sheerness of her dress, he proclaimed, 'One could not be more richly unclothed!'[13]

Unlike Madame Tallien, when Juliette held her salons, she usually reclined on a chaise longue. In 1800, the great French Neoclassical painter Jacques-Louis David was commissioned to paint Juliette and he did so by painting her lounging on a Directory style sofa in a white 'negligée toga' with bare feet. Because he never finished the painting (either because he was too slow or because he abandoned the project), Juliette offered a commission to his student, François Gérard.

When David learned that Juliette had commissioned Gérard, he said, 'Madame, ladies have their caprices, and so have artists; allow me to satisfy mine, which is to keep your portrait in its present state.'[14] Juliette agreed, and David kept the unfinished painting in his possession. It remained unseen by the public until it entered the Louvre in 1826. Interestingly, around that time, a new type of chaise that had one end slightly higher than the other became known as the récamier, based on David's portrait of Juliette.

Meanwhile, Gérard, who was known for his nervous, irritable temper, was attempting to complete his painting of Juliette. It was difficult as he was constantly annoyed by her friends who wanted to view his progress or remain while she sat for him. For a time, he remained silent and patiently bore the daily interruptions, until one of Juliette's most ardent admirers,

Christian de Lemoignon, knocked and requested admittance. Gérard's face darkened and his fury resulted in an unexpected reaction.

> 'Going to the door, his pallet in one hand and his garde-main in the other, he flung it open, and in a voice hoarse with passion exclaimed, "Come in monsieur, come in, but afterwards I shall destroy my picture!" He almost pushed the intruder into the room … Lemoignon had the tact to apologise for his intrusion and withdraw, with the remark that he should be in despair if he were unfortunate enough to deprive posterity of one of M. Gérard's masterpieces.'[15]

In 1802, Gérard finally completed his painting of Juliette. Like David's, it depicts Juliette dressed in white and barefooted, but Gérard's portrait depicts a seductive air as she is facing forward, wearing a low-cut bodice, and gently smiling. Furthermore, his portrait, which can today be found in the Carnavalet Museum in Paris, supposedly presented a more accurate likeness of her than David's painting did.

Chapter 6

Lucien

Her name is Peace.
Lucien Bonaparte

On 9 November 1799, at the height of Lucien's passion for Juliette, Napoleon overthrew the Directory, which ushered in the period of the French Consulate. The coup d'état of 18 Brumaire, as it came to be called, involved Lucien and four others: The French Roman Catholic Abbé Emmanuel Joseph Sieyès; the director Joseph Fouché; speaker of the Council of Five Hundred Roger Ducos; and Talleyrand.

The coup began after three of the five directors were induced to resign, which meant no quorum was possible and so the Directory was practically abolished anyway. Lucien then falsely claimed a Jacobin plot was afoot to overthrow the Directory. For their supposed safety, Sieyès arranged for the Council of Ancients and the Council of Five Hundred to meet at the Palace of Saint-Cloud. In addition, the councils were told that Napoleon and his troops would protect them.

At Saint Cloud, Lucien, who had been elected President of the Council of the Five Hundred, chaired the meeting. A state of emergency had to be declared for the coup to succeed and for the Directory to be dissolved. Lucien put forth the suggestion, but his suggestion was not well received. In fact, the Council howled him down, being suspicious of his motives. Instead of dissolving the Directory, the idea was then generated that every deputy should swear allegiance to the constitution.

While that slow and laborious process was occurring, Napoleon was growing anxious and impatient. He marched into a meeting of the Council of the Ancients that was being held in a long gallery, the Gallery of Apollo. His intrusion was not well received and when he spoke, a heated exchange took place as a few deputies thought something fishy was happening. Those deputies protested and others challenged Napoleon, which put him on the defensive and had him declaring that he was no 'Caesar'. He then marched to the orangery, where the Council of the Five Hundred were meeting.

Orangeries are like conservatories, greenhouses, or hothouses into which delicate fruit trees can be moved outdoors during the warm months and indoors in winter so that they could survive the harsh weather. Thus, the November coup meant that the Council of Five Hundred were comfortably warm in the orangery when Napoleon intruded.

The orangery was a long narrow building that had been hastily converted to hold the Council of Five Hundred. It had a podium erected in the centre and its entrance allowed for only two deputies to pass through its doors at a time. It also had long narrow windows, under which the deputies stood, milling about, expressing their opinions and listening to one another.

Napoleon headed for the podium, but he faced a tempest of criticism and was jeered, denounced and physically attacked before he could reach it. In fact, he was howled down and guards helped him retreat safely outside. The council then turned on Lucien who, fortunately was able to calm them down.

Outside, Napoleon decided that his brother might be in danger and sent in guards to retrieve him. They were confused as to what was happening but got him safely out of the orangery. It was then that Lucien made a stupendous move.

He approached the guards and flat out lied with exceptional persuasion claiming that some of the deputies were conspiring with the English, that royalists were attempting to gain control and that an assassination attempt against Napoleon had just occurred. In addition, Lucien also maintained that most of the deputies were being held hostage inside. With all the drama that he could employ, Lucien then theatrically drew his sword from its scabbard, pointed it in a threatening manner at Napoleon's chest and swore that he would kill anyone, including his own brother, if he ever betrayed the Republic.

It was an inspiring moment. What Napoleon had been unable to achieve by stealth, Lucien did with dramatics. The guards were outraged and cleared the chamber, which effectively ended the reign of the Directory and ushered in the era of the French Consulate.

Exactly how the chamber was cleared has been debated. Some people claim it was a chaotic situation with deputies diving out of windows and hiding in bushes. Another version maintains that the event was much more orderly. In the end, however, the coup d'état of 18 Brumaire resulted in Napoleon serving as First Consul with two other consuls (initially Roger Ducos and Sieyès who were succeeded by Jean-Jacques Régis de Cambacérès and Charles-François Lebrun). Napoleon had supreme power with a council of state to advise him and after the new 'Constitution of the Year VIII' was created in December 1799, Ducos, Sieyés and Napoleon declared in the preamble:

> '[Frenchmen] a constitution is presented to you. … The constitution is founded on the true principles of representative government, on the sacred rights of property, equality, and liberty. … Citizens! the revolution is fixed on the principles which commenced it: It is finished.'[1]

Because Lucien helped with the coup d'état and it was successful, Napoleon promoted him to Minister of the Interior. In honour of his new position, Napoleon also held a fete for his brother sometime in the winter of 1799/1800. At the time, Lucien's wife Christine was ill and she did not attend, but Juliette and Jacques-Rose were obligated to appear and they did.

Juliette arrived decked out in her usual white wardrobe, a colour she now wore nearly every day and for every season. The only thing that varied in her selection of white was the style, the fabric, or the trimmings. Instead of sparkling diamonds, Juliette also preferred white pearls. Perhaps, she chose them because she 'found a certain feminine satisfaction in surrounding herself with objects whose dazzling whiteness was eclipsed by the brilliancy of her own complexion'.[2]

After Juliette's arrival at the fete for Lucien's promotion, she noticed two men standing in dim lights next to the fireplace in the salon. Juliette thought one of the gentlemen was Napoleon's oldest brother, Joseph, and, as she had met Joseph several times, she bowed to him. However, in doing so, she quickly realized she was mistaken as it was not Joseph but rather the First Consul, Napoleon. She had once again committed a faux pas in Napoleon's presence, but he nodded, even if he was surprised at her over-familiarity. Then he purposely said a few words to the gentleman standing next to him and made it clear to Juliette that he was talking about her. Shortly thereafter, the gentleman who had been standing next to Napoleon told Juliette that the First Consul thought she was charming.

Dinner was announced soon after this incident. Napoleon rose, did not offer his arm to any woman and strolled into the dining room alone. He took a seat in the middle of the table as guests began to arrange themselves around him. His mother took a seat on his right and there was an empty seat to his left, but no one dared sit there.

As Juliette entered the dining room someone mumbled something to her. She could not understand what was said and took a seat some distance from the First Consul and his mother. After she was seated, Napoleon brusquely turned to Pierre-Jean Garat, a French Basque singer standing nearby, and said, "Come Garat, sit down here!"[3] He then took the unoccupied seat next to Napoleon.

Dinner was brief. The First Consul barely ate and what he did eat, he ate quickly. He then rose and left the dining room. Most of the dinner guests also rose and left with him. Soon after, Napoleon approached Juliette. He first asked her if she had been cold and then asked why she had not seated herself next to him at dinner. 'She replied that she could not take such a liberty without having been authorised to do so. "You did wrong," said Napoleon; "the place was intended for you, and you ought to have known it."'[4]

After this admonishment, everyone proceeded into the music room where Garat performed a piece by Gluck, followed by performances from several other artistes. The First Consul then demanded Garat perform again. This time, his rendering from 'Orpheus,' surpassed his first. During this musical interlude, Juliette claimed she was transfixed on the music until she realized that whenever she raised her eyes, she found Napoleon's fixed gaze boring through her.

Soon after Lucien's promotion, his ever faithful and loving wife Christine died of consumption. It was around this same time that Lucien finally realized his pursuit of Juliette was doomed. She had made it clear that she thought of him more as a brother than a lover and, having received little satisfaction from pursuing her, Lucien decided to abandon the chase. He thereafter took comfort in the fact that for a short time he had enjoyed the status as Juliette's favourite.

Despite Lucien's pursuit of Juliette and his inability to remain faithful to his wife, he was inconsolable at his wife's death. He wrote Juliette a note and lavishly praised Christine. He also commented that his wife was flawless and stated that he been too much loved by her to ever love again. As a further declaration of his love for his wife, he erected a bronze and marble monument to her in the park of Du Plessis Chamont, near Senlis. It was inscribed: 'A daughter – wife – and mother – without reproach!'[5]

With his wife dead and with his pursuit of Juliette at an end, Lucien then decided that he wanted Juliette to return his love letters. Perhaps he wanted them back because they demonstrated his failed love for her or maybe he was embarrassed. Whatever his reason, Juliette refused to comply with his request. He asked for the letters several more times, supposedly becoming increasingly threatening each time and once even sending his good friend Sapey to retrieve them.

Despite Lucien's insistence and his unorthodox tactics to retrieve the letters, Juliette did not waver. She flatly refused to return them. Exactly why she would not give them up remains unclear. One suggestion is that after Lucien's first request for his letters, he complained to his friends about her and because he spoke harshly of her and her unwillingness to return them, Juliette dug in her heels and became even more adamant that she would not give them up. To make matters worse, at some point Juliette shared Lucien's passionate love letters with her friends. She read them aloud, pointed out his bad grammar and laughed at his misspellings. Moreover, she read and reread his amusing phrases aloud to her friends, who laughed and made things worse by indiscriminately repeating to others what they heard Juliette say.

Lucien, in the meantime, learned of Juliette's jests and ridicules. He grumbled to Napoleon and then wrote to his friends complaining of Juliette's behaviour. He said how cold she was and how she was causing a scene at his expense. Perhaps he even hoped that he might somehow obtain revenge against his once beloved Juliette, who was now making him look like a fool. Fortunately for Lucien, his moment for revenge came soon enough. A banker and millionaire speculator named Gabriel-Julien Ouvrard hosted a fete to which fifty of the most important people in banking were invited. Because of her husband, Juliette was one of attendees and because of her importance, Ouvrard seated her on his right side. His mistress, the gossamer clad Madame Tallien, also known to be a great beauty, was seated on his left.

As with any celebration, it was a gay affair with a bounty of food and plenty of good conversation. Wine also flowed freely and before long guests were drunk. Toasts to the host were soon offered up, along with toasts for a variety of other things. Then one drunk gentleman noted that it would be only fitting to toast to the beautiful women present.

At this suggestion, Lucien seized the moment. He lifted his glass and suggested everyone drink to *the* most beautiful woman. As he spoke, everyone's eyes naturally settled on Juliette, who fluttered her lashes, bashfully lowered her eyes and coyly blushed. Juliette must have felt that she had triumphed over Madame Tallien, and she must have thought Lucien's toast awarded her a smidgeon of satisfaction, despite their disagreement over his love letters.

Her satisfaction was short-lived as someone asked Lucien to provide them with the name of the most beautiful woman. He said, after pausing for dramatic effect, 'Well, gentlemen! … Her name is Peace, the peace we desire so much!'[6] Everyone but Juliette took his toast well. Lucien later remarked that he 'was amused at her discomfiture … and that he thought he had the right to humiliate her coquetry.'[7]

Chapter 7

Friendships

From that hour I was against him.
Juliette on Napoleon

Masked balls began in the fifteenth century and were a feature of the Carnival season. They remained popular throughout the Renaissance and stayed popular until around the beginning of the French Revolution in 1789. Later, these popular affairs emerged once again after the coup d'état of 18 Brumaire and the Bonapartists did all within their power to encourage them by holding many such social affairs.

Juliette attended the first masked ball given since the Revolution on 25 February 1800 at the Opera. She also attended many other masked balls that followed, and these events soon established her schedule of rising at 4pm, taking a bath, then dressing. In fact, anyone who arrived at Juliette's home before 5pm was greeted by the porter exclaiming, 'Madame's day has not yet commenced'.[1]

At the masked balls, women wore a variety of costumes that included Egyptian, Roman, French, Spartan, or Turkish themes. Jacques-Rose rarely attended them, so Juliette's escort was usually her married brother-in-law, Laurent Récamier. He was nine years older than her husband and went only because he felt that his sister-in-law must have someone to look out for her.

At these events, women wore masks, but generally not the gentlemen. Rather, they spent their time trying to guess the female behind the mask. Juliette, who was usually timid, conversed freely when wearing a mask, while her talkative friend Germaine reacted in just the opposite way, becoming quiet and withdrawn. It was also customary for the women to disguise their voices and use the more formal means of address – 'vous' rather than 'tu' as they normally would to those they knew – but as Juliette refused to do this, she was often recognizable.

Contemporaries maintained that Juliette was also the first person to hold a ball in a private house. Her ball was held at the Hôtel Jacques-Rose and it was a brilliant affair, as were all the events she held. Moreover, despite her youth, Juliette was the 'prototype' that many other Parisian women emulated.

One interesting story about a ball she held at her house comes from an English visitor named Henrietta Ponsonby, Countess of Blessborough. She was sister to William Cavendish's first wife, Georgiana Cavendish. On 25 December 1802, Henrietta wrote to her long-time lover Granville Leveson Gower stating:

> 'I must tell you, tho', a nasty and an indelicate story, how distress'd I was at Mad. Recamier's. We went there and found her in bed – that beautiful bed you saw prints of – muslin and gold curtains, great looking glasses at the side, incense pots, &c., and muslin sheets trimm'd with lace, and beautiful white Shoulders expos'd perfectly uncover'd to view – in short, completely undress'd and in bed. The room was full of men – M. de Narbonne, M. de Ségur, Camille Jordan, and others. After some conversation, knowing she had been in bed at her ball … I asked her if she was incommodée. She answer'd, quite aloud and very shortly, "Oh, non seulement, "and then explain'd to the whole company that she was not with child."'[2]

Other interesting stories about Juliette involved several flirtations that occurred at masked balls. One was with a Rhenish politician and statesman who served Austria, Prince Klemens Wenzel von Metternich. Their flirtation lasted a whole winter. Another romance involved the Prince of Württemberg. He had previously met Juliette but as she was masked, he did not recognize her. Accordingly, they began a conversation and, having no suspicion as to whom he was talking to, Juliette asked the Prince of Württemberg what he thought of Madame Récamier. He replied she was beautiful but boring and stated that he did not find her the least bit appealing. Piqued by his comment, Juliette proceeded to have an intensely interesting conversation with him.

The Prince was captivated by the sparkling conversation and begged the fascinating woman behind the mask to reveal herself. Juliette refused. Instead she gave him a ring and told him to meet her at an upcoming ball that was not a masked affair. She said he would recognize her when she came to claim it.

At the unmasked ball, the Prince of Württemberg realized his temerity when Juliette came seeking her ring. He begged for forgiveness in a letter addressed to her:

> 'It is to the most beautiful, amiable, but the proudest of women, that I address these lines, in returning to her a ring

> which she so kindly confided to me at the last masked ball. If my thoughtlessness was beyond conception, my punishment yesterday was very severe; and I am sure I shall profit all my life by the lesson.'[3]

A third flirtation involved George, the Grand Duke of Mecklenburg-Strelitz. He was brother-in-law to Frederick William III of Prussia, who had married George's sister, the beautiful Louise of Mecklenburg-Strelitz. George met Juliette at a masked ball, and they conversed the whole evening and he asked if he could call on her the next evening. She granted permission.

George arrived at her home at the appointed hour and left his carriage. He sneaked through a gate hoping to go unnoticed by Juliette's staff but unfortunately, a porter saw him and called after him. George quickened his pace, which made the porter suspect he was a thief. George then heard the porter's footstep as he was pursued and began to run. The porter cornered George outside Juliette's drawing room, so that when she heard the commotion and opened the door, she found him firmly collared by her porter.

Juliette quickly untangled George from the porter and proposed that they take a walk in the moonlit garden. As they left for the walk, an unexpected visitor called. He was ushered into Juliette's drawing-room and she was informed of his presence. She went to dismiss the unexpected guest but discovered it was the prominent French statesman Mathieu; he fixed his eyes on George's hat that had been forgotten on the table and asked if she was alone. She laughed and then told him the adventure of George and her porter.

Flirtation wasn't the only thing going on at masked balls. At one masquerade ball given by some Italian nobility, Juliette and Josephine's daughter, Hortense, embraced some shenanigans by deciding to wear the same costume. It was a white satin domino (a robe-like costume often with back pleats that had a cape and wide sleeves) trimmed with white pearls. The only difference was Juliette crowned herself with a wreath of roses while Hortense carried a bouquet of roses.

Throughout the evening, Hortense and Juliette passed each other and said a few words to arrange their plot. When the crowd was huge, Juliette suddenly left her escort's side and removed her wreath. At the same time, Hortense was on alert. She gave Juliette her bouquet and took Juliette's place, as Juliette occupied Hortense's former spot. Juliette noted that she was soon surrounded by representatives of foreign powers and mentioned that she was 'astonished' to hear political comments that are generally only spoken to a person in one's own political party.

Before they were found out, the two women switched again and resumed their original places. However, the first exchange had been so exciting, they repeated the switch again. Rumours soon began to circulate that Hortense and Juliette were wearing the same disguise and this roused some suspicions amongst the crowd as people became unsure who was Juliette and who was Hortense. After the ball Juliette wrote:

> 'The perplexity of those who accosted us, while they were not sure of our identity, prolonged for some time our pleasure in the joke. Everybody took it in good part, with exception of the Princess de Lieven, who never throws off politics, even at a ball, and who thought it a great evil that she should have been compromised by association with a Bonapartist.'[4]

While Juliette was enjoying herself at masked balls, Napoleon was busy with other things. In February of 1800, he and Josephine began setting up their household at the Tuileries Palace and, a month later, he took time out of his schedule to complain about Juliette's friend Germaine. From Paris he wrote to his brother Joseph denouncing her for living a life of luxury while her husband was 'destitute.' He noted:

> 'If you are still seeing her, couldn't you induce the woman to make her husband an allowance of 1,000 or 1,200 francs a month? … They may, indeed, judge Mme De Staël's conduct as though she were a man: but if man had inherited M. de Necker's fortune, had enjoyed for years the advantages of a famous name, and had then let his wife starve, while he himself lived on the fat of the land, he would be cut by all his friends.'[5]

By May, Napoleon was back in the saddle and leading his army across the Alps in the Second Italian Campaign. He then found himself fighting the Austrians at Marengo on 14 June. It was a hard-fought battle where he made some disastrous miscalculations.

Napoleon's 22,000 soldiers with their 20 guns were surprised by Austrian troops, 32,000 strong with 100 cannon. Moreover, he received poor battlefield intelligence that caused erroneous thinking on his part and he misjudged what the Austrian commander, Michel Melas, would do. When the fighting began, the French fought bravely and held their ground for three hours, despite being outnumbered and outgunned. However, by early afternoon, the Austrian had the upper hand and the French were on the verge of collapse when victory was snatched from the Austrians' hands:

> 'Three events turned certain defeat into smashing victory. Auguste Marmont, commander of the artillery, hastily assembled a battery of eighteen cannon whose deadly blasts disrupted the enemy ranks. Then musket volleys plus a vigorous charge by [Louis Desaix's] division into the Austrian front blunted and shocked its advance. Finally, a timely heavy-cavalry charge by four hundred horsemen under Francois Kellermann completed the enemy confusion and commenced their retreat and rout.'[6]

Napoleon won but did so by the narrowest of margins. As he converted a near loss into a win, Napoleon remarked, 'The fate of a battle depends on a single moment.'[7] Yet, that single moment was costly. Some 5,000 French soldiers died, as did Desaix, a man Napoleon held in great esteem and whose death caused him great anguish. Still, Marengo was a positive experience for Napoleon and it became a major turning point in his life.

Before Marengo, other French generals had been threatening Napoleon's power. However, none of the generals had accomplished any decisive victory. This meant Napoleon's win at Marengo allowed him to temporarily relax. Moreover, within 24 hours of the battle, negotiations were underway that resulted in the Austrians evacuating north-western Italy and suspending military operations there.

His win at Marengo also helped strengthen his position as First Consul. He could easily reject offers from Louis XVIII, who thought of the French Consulate as a temporary transition until his own restoration. Also, the vision Napoleon had of establishing his own rule now had a clear pathway which he adorned with mythological versions of the battle of Marengo published in army bulletins and in 'Official Reports'.

To further ensure his triumph would not be forgotten, Napoleon ordered the construction of a great pyramid at the site of the battle. On 5 May 1805, a foundation stone inscribed to Napoleon's greatness was presented to him on the field of Marengo. Josephine accompanied him and was there to oversee the military parade that followed. Unfortunately for Napoleon, his grand scheme to glorify himself and his conquests would be abandoned in 1815.

Napoleon was not just facing a threat from Austria. A mutual dislike had been growing between him and Germaine. Her initial troubles with him began after Robespierre fell and the Terror ended. It was at that time that she opened a new salon in Paris and began to receive Napoleon's younger brother Louis, who had bouts of mental instability. His visits to her salon made Napoleon uneasy, as did the fact that her salon soon evolved into a group of liberal resistors. According to Germaine, after the coup d'état of 18 Brumaire, she and Napoleon's older brother Joseph had the following exchange.

> '"My brother complains of you." "Why," said he to me … "does not Madame de Staël attach herself to my government? what is it she wants? … In short, what is it she wishes?" "Good God!" replied I, "it is not what I wish, but what I think, that is the question."'[8]

Napoleon and Germaine's mutual dislike for one another become even stronger when Germaine was unwilling to succumb to his influence and wrote a political essay titled *De la littérature dans ses rapports avec les institutions sociales* (The Influence of Literature Upon Society), published in 1800. It was about the history of literature but also touched on politics and Enlightenment ideals, which displeased him immensely.

Despite their dislike for each other, some people claim their mutual animosity did not become apparent until Napoleon was marching across the Alps on his way to Italy. It was then that Germaine's father invited the First Consul to breakfast. Germaine dined with them and wrangled a private audience with Napoleon afterwards.

Although there are variations about what really happened, one version claims that Germaine 'delivered a political lecture on her views … advised him in regard to his administration; and, finally, urged him to take [George] Washington for his model'.[9] Napoleon listened to her lecture on the art of governing and when she was finished, he complimented her on her mothering skills and then asked whether she educated her own children. He then glanced at his watch, stated that his army was waiting, and abruptly departed. His sarcastic behaviour stayed with Germaine and supposedly thereafter she made it her life's work to criticize and pursue him with her pen.

The biggest problem between the two was that they were just alike and that may have been exactly why Napoleon wanted to crush her. An opportunity to do so came in 1802 when she published a hugely popular novel titled *Delphine.* In it she praised Protestantism, liberalism and the

British. Napoleon quickly declared her novel anti-Catholic, anti-social and anti-French. In fact, he was so upset about it, he decided to banish her.

When Juliette heard rumours that Germaine might be banished, her feelings towards Napoleon hardened. Friendship, with its intimacy and sociability, was of great importance to Juliette and, over the years, she and Germaine had grown close. Germaine also appreciated their close friendship and considered Juliette her muse and a source of wonderful artistic inspiration.

Juliette understood Germaine's dislike for Napoleon. After all, she had suffered two unhappy experiences with him, so it was easy for her to sympathize with her friend's feelings. Hoping to comfort Germaine, she asked her to visit. At the time, Juliette was staying in a charming rented summer chateau at Saint Brice with sunny landscapes, rippling streams and delicious shady spots. When Germaine accepted, Juliette wrote:

> 'I received her at St. Brice, and was witness to her despair. She wrote to Bonaparte "You would be treating me cruelly! I should have a page in your history." I had a passionate admiration for Mme. de Staël, and this harsh and arbitrary act showed me despotism under its most odious aspect. The man who banished a woman, and such a woman, who caused her such unhappiness, could only be regarded by me as an unmerciful tyrant, and from that hour I was against him, against his elevation to the throne and the establishment of absolute power.'[10]

After spending several days without receiving any official word about the banishment, Germaine thought that perhaps the First Consul had reconsidered and might revoke her sentence. Then, at four o'clock one leisurely afternoon, a man appeared on horseback wearing a brown coat. Germaine wrote:

> 'He asked for me, and I went to receive him in the garden. In walking towards him, the perfume of the flowers, and the beauty of the sun particularly struck me. … This man informed me, that he was the commandant of the gendarmerie of Versailles, but that his orders were to go out of uniform, that he might not alarm me; he shewed me a letter signed by Bonaparte, which contained the order to banish me to forty leagues distance

> from Paris, with an injunction to make me depart within four and twenty hours; at the same time to treat me with all the respect due to a lady of distinction. … I proposed to him to accompany me to Paris, where I had occasion to pass three days to make the necessary arrangements for my journey. I got into my carriage with my children and this officer, who had been selected for this occasion … "You see," said I to him, "the consequence of being a woman of intellect, and I would recommend you, if there is occasion, to dissuade any females of your family from attempting it." I endeavoured to keep up my spirits by boldness, but I felt the barb in my heart.'[11]

If Napoleon had hoped to end Germaine's popularity by banishing her, it did not work. His dislike for her made her more fashionable than ever. It also resulted in the popular saying, 'There are three powers to be reckoned with in Europe – England, Russia, and Madame de Stael.'[12] Furthermore, the First Consul's dislike for Germaine ate at Juliette. How could he be so cruel to someone she loved?

Chapter 8

Intrigues and Assassination Attempts

Republicans are exiled, royalists die.
Michael Broers

Germaine's banishment was not the only disagreement brewing between Juliette and Napoleon. The two were also at odds because Juliette supported one of the boldest of liberals, Moreau, the French general who had visited her salon. He had arrested the Jacobin directors and commanded one of the forces that helped Napoleon win in the coup d'état of 18th Brumaire in 1799. In addition, a year or so later, on 3 December 1800, a few months after Napoleon's win at Marengo, Moreau achieved his own win. His decisive victory occurred at Hohelinden against the Austria and Bavarians and resulted in them suing for peace.

Nonetheless, before Moreau's thrilling triumph, he decided to settle down. He married a 19-year-old creole woman, Louise-Alexandrine Eugénie Hulot d'Oseray, who was born to a respectable family on 26 July 1781 in Port Louis, Mauritus. She was also an accomplished musician and piano virtuoso and was said to be socially ambitious.

Four months after his marriage, Moreau bought a home in the rue d'Anjou and immediately invested fourteen months in redecorating and renovating. It was at this home that Eugénie began giving celebrated balls, concerts and soirees, which were said to be as popular as any of those given by Juliette. Aiding Eugénie in her social ambition was her mother, Madame Hulot, whom critics described as jealous, narrow-minded and pushy. She had big ambitions for herself, her daughter and her son-in-law and she was good friends with Juliette's mother, Madame Bernard.

Although Napoleon might have been unhappy with Eugénie's social ambition, Madame Hulot bothered him more because among those friendly to her cause were two ex-lovers of Germaine's. The first was Mathieu. He came from the Montmorency line, which was one of the oldest and most distinguished families of nobility in France. He was born 10 July 1767 and was ten years older than Juliette, which was partially why she thought of him as a father figure. As a young man, Mathieu had served with his father in the American Revolution and because of this early service, he supported ideas of democracy. He also served on the Estates-General, joined the Third-Estate and became a member of the National Assembly, which at the time made him the youngest member, at only twenty-three.

Mathieu was also cousin to Adrien of Montmorency and it was Adrien who first met Juliette. He was a year younger than Mathieu and tall, slender and fair. He was also near-sighted and described as both elegant and awkward in appearance. He liked lively conversations and was extremely witty. Yet, because of a speech impediment, he did not always come across as such. Adrien also enjoyed reading and held moderate political views, but of the two cousins, Mathieu was the more passionate.

At the time, because families wanted to retain their bloodlines, intermarriage was common and so Mathieu married his first cousin, Hortense of Luynes, who was not known for her good looks! He would have preferred not to marry her as he was in love with another cousin; he was nursing heartbreak for her as she had died suddenly and that left him with no choice but to marry Hortense.

Mathieu was considered at the time of his marriage to be a fashionable, fun-loving person who always embraced the pleasures of the world and neither his marriage nor the birth of a daughter, Elisa, stopped him from continuing to do so. What did stop him was when his brother, the Abbé of Laval, was guillotined during the French Revolution. Mathieu was extremely attached to his brother and deeply grieved at his death. Moreover, he blamed himself, believing that his brother was implicated due to his support for the revolution. Germaine, whom Mathieu had a deep affection for and ultimately gave his heart to, tried to ease his suffering. Her efforts were to no avail and it was not until he found solace in religion that Mathieu, who had once been frivolous, fun-loving and impetuous, became a devoted, austere and sober Christian.

The second of Germaine's lovers who was friendly to Madame Hulot's cause was Narbonne-Lara. Described as handsome, mysterious and intelligent, he was brought up at Versailles, with the future Louis XVI as his godfather and Louis XV's daughter, Madame Adélaïde, as his godmother. Because Narbonne-Lara was a nobleman, he had the opportunity for an illustrious future, but at the time he met Germaine his accomplishments consisted of two illegitimate children, numerous mistresses and mountains of debt. However, their meeting changed his life and because of her, he was suddenly inspired to fulfil his dreams. Germaine even told a friend:

> '[When Narbonne-Lara saw me] he changed his destiny for my sake. He broke his attachments and consecrated his life to me. In a word, he convinced me that he could love me well enough, and that he would consider himself happy to possess my heart, but that if he lost it irremediably, he could not survive.'[1]

Narbonne-Lara always supported the king and hoped for a constitutional monarchy. He became maréchal de camp in 1791 and, through the influence of his lover Germaine, was appointed Minister of War under Louis XVI. In this office, he tried to impose his ideas and was supported by Talleyrand and others, but he lacked the capability needed and eventually resigned.

Madame Hulot's relationships with Narbonne-Lara and Mathieu exasperated Napoleon because he feared the two men might leverage the military jealousies among the French generals to further monarchist causes. Moreover, Madame Hulot taunted Napoleon by forming and heading a band of opposition composed of those who felt any discontent or dislike towards him. This greatly annoyed the First Consul and whipped up royalists. It also caused Napoleon to worry that Moreau might conspire against him and try to oust him from power.

The tipping point between the Bonaparte and Moreau families supposedly occurred on Easter Sunday, 18 April 1802 at the cathedral of Notre Dame, where a grand event was scheduled. According to one newspaper, chairs had been reserved for distant relatives of Napoleon, along with two chairs reserved in the front of the choir for Josephine and for Napoleon's mother, Letizia.

Just before noon, the pushy Madame Hulot and her ambitious daughter presented themselves at the cathedral door. After a discussion, soldiers let them pass, and the women entered and boldly took the two seats saved for Josephine and Letizia. Moments later, the Bonaparte women arrived and those present at the cathedral expected the worst. They did not have to wait long. Josephine both feared and intensely disliked Madame Hulot. So it was indeed a shock when she discovered Madame Hulot and her daughter sitting in their reserved spot.

A war of words ensued with 'delicate impertinences,' catty remarks and bitter remonstrances. Madame Hulot protested that to remove her was an 'affront! … Very well, she would complain to her son-in-law, and they would soon find out what sort of a man her son-in-law was!'[2] Eugénie, embarrassed by the squabble, felt faint. Letizia was fortunately in no mood to continue the fight and gave up her seat. One newspaper reported,

'Generale Moreau was allowed to keep her seat by the side of the Generale Bonaparte,'[3] during which time, Madame Hulot stared insolently at the First Consul, and he noticed.

Afterwards, in his private rooms, Napoleon's anger was barely contained. He supposedly railed with hostility, 'Very spiteful, that old Hulot! She keeps her son-in-law tied to her apron-strings, and leads so well that he'll break his nose! … What a plague, those two women! The mother, a corporal, the daughter a nut-cracker!'[4]

Shortly after Moreau's victory at Hohelinden, on Christmas Eve 1800, an assassination attempt was made on Napoleon's life. The attempt, known as the Plot of the rue Saint-Nicaise, which is also sometimes known as the Machine Infernale Plot, was planned by a group involved in various royalist uprisings during the French Revolution. This group was known as the Chouannerie or Chouans.

A Chouan officer, Pierre Robinault de Saint-Régeant, orchestrated the plot and a Breton politician, Georges Cadoudal, was also indirectly involved. Cadoudal had served as leader of Chouans during the French Revolution and was involved in several rebellions afterwards. In addition, he fought against revolutionaries, but ultimately found it impossible to continue fighting against them and became involved in conspiracies that supported Louis XVIII.

The *machine infernale* was a bomb. It was to be placed north of the Tuileries Palace in the rue Saint-Nicaise. The plan was to signal the bomb fuse to be lit when Napoleon left the Tuileries and approached the rue Saint-Nicaise so the explosion would kill the First Consul as he passed by. On Christmas Eve, the plotters readied the bomb and took it to the rue Saint-Nicaise in a cart with a big wine cask pulled by a mare. There, Saint- Régeant paid 14-year-old Marianne Peusol, whose mother was a food vendor, twelve sous to hold the mare. The person who was to give the signal took his place, as did Saint-Régeant, who was to light the fuse. However, when Napoleon's carriage reached the spot for the signal to be given, the person who was to give it panicked and thereby delayed the lighting by a few minutes.

After the fuse was lit, Saint-Régeant fled and the bomb exploded. But rather than killing Napoleon, who had by then passed by, it killed innocent bystanders – three women, a grocer, and, of course, 14-year-old Peusol. At least fifteen people were wounded and there was damage to at least fifteen houses. *Le Publiciste* reported on 26 December:

> 'All Paris has been curious to see the ruins produced by this terrible explosion. They are terrible. The windows of the castle

> of the Thuilleries, and of the house which surround the ground and the little Carousel, are shivered to pieces; the entire street of St. Nicaise, St. Thomas, Echelle, and Chartres, have been shaken, as by a violent earthquake. So great a shock, in this populous quarter, might have been fatal to a great many people. However, the number of victims is not so great as was at first supposed.'

That same day, another French paper, the *Journal des Defenseurs*, gave more details about the blast.

> 'The cask of powder which was blown up was hooped with iron, and contained a quantity of balls in such a manner, that the discharge must be a real discharge of cannister shot. The carriage on which it was placed blocked up the street at the time when the first guards of Bonaparte passed. – They made it draw off a second time, and thus there were two very remarkable movements. At that moment it was conjectured that the explosion, which was made by pulling the trigger of the gun with a string, these different movements altering the position of the carriage, prevented the cord from being sufficiently stretched in order to pull the trigger, and it was at that moment the coach of the First Consul, which drove rapidly, happily avoided the fatal blow.'

After the blast, Napoleon believed that extreme-left Jacobins had plotted his assassination. Police then arrested several Jacobins, who they accused of plotting the First Consul's demise. However, Fouché, the same man who had been involved in the coup d'état of 18 Brumaire and was now serving as Minister of Police, was sure the Chouans were the guilty party. He therefore attempted to focus on them.

Napoleon refused to listen, believing that it had to be the Jacobins who attempted to kill him. In the meantime, Fouché found strong proof against the Chouans. The man who made the *machine infernale* was also positively identified but Napoleon still would not listen. He insisted that it was the Jacobins who tried to kill him, no matter what evidence Fouché presented to him. Around this same time, 130 Chouans were exiled from France and, on 9 January 1801, four Jacobin conspirators were condemned to death for their supposed role in the assassination attempt.

As a sign of Napoleon's belief that it was the Jacobins who wanted him dead, he turned against his former Jacobin allies. A few days later, the Chouan bomb maker was arrested and he gave up the names of six fellow conspirators, including Saint-Régeant and Cadoudal. When the trial began, it did not go well for the conspirators. They were found guilty and Saint-Régeant was executed on 20 April at the Place de Grève. However, one conspirator escaped to America and Cadoudal fled to England.

On 25 March 1802, the Treaty of Amiens temporarily ended hostilities between France and Britain. It was signed in the city of Amiens, by Napoleon's brother Joseph and the British Army officer and colonial administrator Charles Cornwallis, 1st Marquess Cornwallis. Under the treaty, Britain recognized the French Republic and the British parliament dropped English claims to the defunct French kingdom. The treaty also marked the end of the Second Coalition (European monarchies led by Britain, Austria and Russia that included the Ottoman Empire, Portugal, Naples, various German monarchies and Sweden), which had waged war against France since 1798.

During this peaceful time, many Frenchman were eager to visit England. For instance, in 1802, the famous wax sculptress, Madame Tussaud, together with Paul de Philipstal, who had a phantasmagoria show, travelled to England. Philipstal wanted Madame Tussuad's waxworks to help enhance his shows and so she exhibited her waxworks at the Lyceum on the Strand under the name of 'Curtius' Grand Cabinet of Curiosities'. Juliette was also interested in visiting England and she arrived there with her mother in the spring of 1802, perhaps around the same time Madame Hulot and Eugénie were fighting with Josephine and Letizia over seats at Notre Dame.

In England, Juliette's international status was quickly confirmed and one admirer, the Countess Brownlow, remembered:

> 'The peace of 1802 brought, I suppose many French to England, but I only remember one, the celebrated Madame Recamier, who created a sensation, partly by her beauty, but still more by her dress, which was vastly unlike the unsophisticated style and poke bonnets of the Englishwomen.'[5]

Juliette also made friends with Georgiana Cavendish, Duchess of Devonshire, through introductions arranged by a former French ambassador. Georgiana then introduced Juliette to Lady Elizabeth Foster (known as 'Bess') whom Georgiana had met while on a retreat in 1782. At the time, Bess was destitute due to her separation from her husband and the two women grew close. Because Georgiana's husband, William Cavendish, the 5th Duke of Devonshire, was a cold, emotionally reserved man, the women's friendship blossomed and the needy Georgiana became emotionally attached to Bess.

Georgiana eventually convinced her husband to allow Bess to move in with them. Contemporaries reported that Bess took advantage of her friendship with Georgiana and began a sexual affair with William. At the time, it was common for upper class men to take mistresses, but it was uncommon for mistresses to live openly with a married couple. Georgiana was initially upset about the affair, but there was nothing she could do. William had complete power over her financially and over their children.

Georgiana eventually became complacent about the relationship and before long notorious gossip swirled about what was happening in the Devonshire home. Contemporaries of Georgiana and Bess began to speculate that the three were involved in a ménage à trois. No evidence existed at the time to prove anything other than an emotional relationship between Bess and Georgiana and a sexual relationship between William and Bess. In fact, during the time the three lived together, Bess had several well-publicized sexual relationships with other men.

During her affair with William, Bess also bore him two illegitimate children; a daughter, Caroline Rosalie St Jules, and a son, Augustus Clifford. When Georgiana died in 1806, Bess married William. He died five years later, on 29 July 1811. Bess never remarried and died in Rome in 1824. Upon her death, a locket with some of Georgiana's hair was discovered around Bess' neck and a bracelet containing another lock was discovered on the nightstand.

Of course, Juliette knew none of this when Georgiana aided her in her first public appearance in London. Her first outing was when Georgiana took her to see a play being performed at Covent Garden. Also, among the party was the Prince of Wales, who reportedly paid Juliette 'chivalric attentions'. However, the Prince was not the only one paying attention to Juliette.

Those attending the play had heard about the Frenchwoman's legendary beauty and were fascinated to see her up close. When Juliette appeared, every head swivelled and every opera glass focused on her. A buzz of curiosity also arose from the floor. Because there was so much attention paid to Juliette by theatre goers, the Prince of Wales decided it wise for Georgiana's party to leave before the play's conclusion. Georgiana agreed and the party rose early and discreetly exited into the vestibule, but to their surprise many people in the audience also flocked there, hoping to get a better look at the beautiful Frenchwoman. It was reported, 'So great was the crowd that poor Madame Récamier was nearly swept off her feet; but, fortunately, managed at length to reach her carriage in safety.'[6]

That was not the end of the English people's fascination with Juliette. The following day, Juliette and her mother appeared at Kensington Gardens. Both women were dressed in white and carried violet-coloured parasols. Within a turn and a half around the garden, Juliette was recognized beneath her white veil. Word of her being at the gardens passed from one person to the next with great excitement, and one newspaper later shared Juliette's appearance with its readers:

> 'They [the crowd] pressed on all sides upon her. Men kneeled down before her to peep up under her veil. Some absolutely seemed disposed to uncover her face. There was nothing but crowding, tumults, and squeezing – the delicacy of the fair objects felt this conduct an insult, and … they left the garden. Their situation outside was not less painful. Grooms and footmen with most insolent curiosity crowded around them. Gentlemen on horseback left the ride and rode up to join the admiring mob. The ladies became alarmed, and feared every moment that they should be crushed to death or trampled down by horses. Their servants could not penetrate the crowd to apprize them of the place where their carriage was in waiting. At length they reached it with great difficulty, but fortunately without receiving any other injury than a terrible fright.'[7]

Juliette had not been thinking about Moreau while in England, but upon her return from England, things began to heat up for him and the Chouan Cadoudal. He had earlier fled to England and remained there until he suddenly reappeared in France in August of 1803. His reappearance was due to conceiving another plot to kill Napoleon.

The new plot was called the 'Pichegru Conspiracy' or the 'Cadoudal Affair', and the planning of it began when Jean-Charles Pichegru contacted Cadoudal. Pichegru had defected to the royalist side in the early years of the French Revolutionary Wars and he knew Moreau because he had been his protégé. Cadoudal became involved and wanted revenge against Napoleon because he had killed his best friend, Pierre Mercier, and his brother, Colonel Julien Cadoudal.

The new conspiracy involved either kidnapping or assassinating Napoleon during one of his frequent road trips between Tuileries, La Malmaison and Saint Cloud. The plotters decided that once Napoleon was neutralized, Pichegru and Moreau could take control of the army until Louis XVIII arrived. Pichegru and Moreau met several times and Moreau listened because of the discord between his wife and Napoleon. Nevertheless, just before the plot was to go into effect, Moreau refused to cooperate because he discovered Cadoudal and Pichegru were completely disorganized and the plot lacked any real planning.

Although Fouché had been dismissed as Minister of the Police, he was the person who unravelled the plot after two of Cadoudal's conspirators were arrested in Paris and revealed Cadoudal's involvement. The police then watched Cadoudal and Pichegru for a short time hoping they would implicate Moreau, but that did not happen. In the meantime, Cadoudal learned his involvement had been revealed and he once again escaped. He evaded capture for six months but eventually, Moreau, Cadoudal and Pichegru were all arrested and brought to trial.

Some people claimed that Moreau was a potential rival against Napoleon, but historian Steven Englund claims that Moreau 'more exasperated Bonaparte than rivalled him'.[8] Because Moreau's involvement was questionable, Napoleon had to force judges to bring charges against him. Juliette supported Moreau, never believing that he was involved in the plot against the First Consul, but she also never planned to attend his trial. That changed when his wife Eugénie approached her and mentioned that her husband looked for Juliette among his friends in the crowd.

She then decided she must attend the trial and noted it generated such great interest that the courtroom was full of spectators on the day she attended. When she arrived, she raised her veil and Moreau, seeing her, rose from his seat and gave her a gentlemanly bow. She later wrote:

> 'I returned his greetings with respect and emotion, and hastened down the steps to take the seat reserved for me. … I was deeply touched to see this great captain, whose reputation was, at that time, so great and so untarnished, treated as a criminal. It was no longer a question of Republic and Republicans; it was … Royalist fidelity which struggled against the new power.'[9]

After the session, Juliette was escorted towards the door. However, this time she was to exit on the opposite side to the one through which she had entered. Moreau was being accompanied by two gendarmes and some other prisoners and at the same moment, she and Moreau passed each other, separated by only a railing. He took this opportunity to speak a few words of thanks to her for attending.

The next morning, Juliette received a message from Eugénie begging her not to attend the trial for Moreau's sake. Apparently, Napoleon had seen a report of the session, took note of who was there and saw Juliette's name. He then supposedly asked sharply, 'What business had Madame Récamier there?'[10] Eugénie heard of this and decided that any marked interest by the First Consul towards anyone in attendance might harm her husband's position and so Juliette attended no more.

Moreau was ultimately sentenced to imprisonment, but Napoleon, pretending to be lenient, commuted his sentence to banishment. After the verdict, Moreau and his wife immediately embarked for America. Napoleon ordered Moreau's home in the rue d'Anjou be seized, as well as another chateau he owned; the furnishings of these residences were removed to the royal chateau at Fontainebleau.

When Pichegru was tried, he refused to confess to anything and gave up no one. He also denied under examination that he, Moreau and Cadoudal had plotted anything or that he and Moreau had ever met. So, it was extremely mysterious when Pichegru was suddenly found dead in his cell on 5 April, having been strangled. An examination of his corpse on 16 April resulted in the following official report:

> 'The body had round the neck a black silk handkerchief, through which was passed a stick about forty centimetres (nearly sixteen inches) long, and from four to five (one and a half to two inches) in circumference, which after being twisted round in the handkerchief was stopped by the left cheek, against which one of its extremities rested, and which had produced a strangulation sufficient to occasion death.'[11]

A guard on duty during the evening that Pichegru died reported that he heard coughing and spitting coming from his cell and he supposed someone was suffering but thought nothing further of it. The following day when Pichegru was discovered, he was lying on his right side with his head having fallen back onto the pillow so that it compressed the stick and prevented the cravat from untwisting. The government claimed that Pichegru had strangled himself and their official report stated that he had committed suicide. Nonetheless, some people insisted that he had been murdered. They believed Napoleon had ordered Pichegru's death because he would not implicate Moreau, but there is no evidence to prove such allegations.

When Cadoudal went to trial, he made no effort to save himself, so it probably came as no surprise that the bold and energetic Chouan leader was condemned to death. Friends begged him to sue for pardon, but he would not and was executed along with eleven of his Chouan brothers in June 1804.

There was also one other person executed, the youthful aristocrat Louis Antoine de Bourbon, Duke of Enghien who had been living in Baden. There had been some talk that after Moreau helped overthrow Napoleon, he was to be replaced by a mysterious nobleman noted only as 'Lieutenant General of the Kingdom'. Napoleon decided Enghien fitted the bill as the mysterious nobleman because he feared him and thought that his ties to the British and to another French general who had defected made him a threat.

Napoleon then took great delight in hunting him down. However, in so doing, French dragoons crossed an international border without permission, violated Enghien's rights and kidnapped him. He was taken to Paris and imprisoned at the royal fortress, Chateau de Vincennes. A military commission of French colonels then hastily convened and, despite a lack of evidence that Enghien conspired with Pichegru or Cadoudal, the commission condemned him that same evening. They did so primarily because Anne Jean Marie René Savary had orders to kill him; he was shot on 21 March 1804 and buried in one of the ditches at the chateau.

François-René, Vicomte de Chateaubriand, was among the royalists alienated by Napoleon's execution of Enghien. Chateaubriand had been appointed secretary of the legation to the Holy See by Napoleon and accompanied Napoleon's uncle Fesch to Rome. However, after Chateaubriand and Fesch quarrelled, Chateaubriand was appointed minister to Valais in Switzerland. While in that position, he heard of Enghien's death:

> 'This voice fell upon me like thunder; it changed my life, as it changed the life of Napoleon. I returned home; I said to Madame de Chateaubriand, "The Duke of Enghien has just been shot." I sat before a table and began to write my resignation.'[12]

Chateaubriand was not the only person appalled by Napoleon's behaviour regarding Enghien. It turned the whole of European royalty against him, or at least that is what Chateaubriand claimed. Englund put it this way:

> 'The outburst against Bonaparte in the royal and aristocratic families of Europe would be hard to overestimate. Prince de Condé reviled Bonaparte as "the new Robespierre" and "the booted Jacobin," but the epithets contain an important political truth: with this act, redolent of regicide, the First Consul branded his regime(s) for all time with the mark … of the Revolution.'[13]

It was also true that Tsar Alexander I of Russia was particularly alarmed and decided Napoleon's power needed to be curbed. Historians and memoirists have since characterized Napoleon's role in Enghien's death as either a blunder, a crime, or a vengeful murder. However, Napoleon's contemporaries saw him in a different light. They knew that he would rule by fear and retaliate against anyone whether they be friend or foe as his tactics were simply: 'republicans are exiled, royalists die'.[14]

Chapter 9

It's Business

Since when has the council of ministers been held at Mme. Récamier's house?

Napoleon

Due to the many attempts on Napoleon's life, it was decided there needed to be an institution that would survive him and thus the idea of a monarchy was re-born. Between Pichegru's strangling and Cadoudal's execution, Napoleon was proclaimed Emperor of the French by his hand-picked Senate, known as the *Sénat conservator.* The hereditary title was given him on 18 May 1804, with his coronation following immediately afterwards. In addition, a referendum was presented to French citizens to elevate Napoleon to Emperor and confirm the change. The results of the referendum were nearly unanimous because when announced, of the 7 million called to participate, less than half abstained, over 3.5 million voters favoured the change and a mere 2,569 voted against it.

Napoleon's coronation was held Sunday, 2 December 1804 and from the beginning problems arose. One of the first issues involved Pope Pius VII, who was not inclined to perform the traditional consecration or anointing because of how the church had been mistreated and decimated during the French Revolution. Even though the Pope's consecration was nothing more than a symbolic gesture, it was important and so Napoleon appealed to his uncle, who was now a Cardinal. Fesch acted as an intermediary with the Pope and Napoleon exerted pressure, threatened and cajoled until the Pope finally agreed to perform the consecration. That also meant he had to meet with Napoleon's timeline and hurry, which the Pope declared was unsuited to his dignity.

Another problem was Napoleon's and Josephine's civil marriage. The Pope was offended when he learned that the couple had been living together in 'deadly sin,' and the consecration could not go ahead without the couple being married according to the rites of the Church. To accomplish that, Fesch once again stepped in and arranged a secret and hasty marriage ceremony for 1 December 1804, the day before Napoleon's coronation.

A clash of egos within the Bonaparte family was another hurdle Napoleon had to overcome. None of the Bonapartes liked Josephine. When Napoleon's sisters (Elisa, Pauline and Caroline) learned that they were to carry Josephine's massive velvet train, they adamantly refused, and their brother Joseph backed them. Napoleon then threatened that they would lose their titles and so they quickly, but unhappily, agreed to participate.

Also, Letizia boycotted the ceremonies, unhappy over the new title that Napoleon had bestowed on her. The title she received was 'Madame Mère de Sa Majesté l'Empereur' (Mother of His Majesty, the Emperor), which everyone shortened to Madame Mère. In addition, since her son Lucien was also not attending, she travelled to Rome to be with him. He was absent because he was living in exile due to his marriage on 26 October 1803 to the widow Alexandrine de Bleschamp, better known as Madame Jouberthon.

The coronation ceremony was to be held at Notre Dame, which had been newly painted for the occasion. The pews and galleries were also adorned, and two thrones were placed at the end opposite the entrance on an elevated platform facing the choir. The Pope's pontifical throne was in the choir, beside the high altar. The French writer Laure Junot, Duchess of Abrantès, attended Napoleon's coronation and reported:

> 'Who that saw Notre Dame on that memorable day can forget it? I have witnessed … the celebration of sumptuous and solemn festivals; but never did I see anything at all approximating in splendour to the coup d'oeil exhibited at Napoleon's coronation. The vaulted roof re-echoed the sacred chanting of the priests, who invoked the blessing of the Almighty on the ceremony about to be celebrated, while they awaited the arrival of the Vicar of Christ. … Along the ancient walls of tapestry were ranged, according to their ranks, the different bodies of the State, the deputies from every city; in short, the representatives of all France assembled to implore the benediction of heaven on the sovereign of the people's choice. The waving plumes which adorned the hats of the Senators, Councillors, of State, and Tribunes; the splendid uniforms of the military; the clergy in all their ecclesiastical pomp, and the multitude of young and beautiful women, glittering in jewels, and arrayed in that style of grace and elegance which is to be seen only in Paris – all together presented a picture which has perhaps rarely been equalled, and certainly never excelled.'[1]

The Pope's train left at 9am headed by a squadron of dragoons and near its end was the gilded Papal carriage with a triple crown on the roof supported by four gilded doves. Josephine had previously used the carriage but to ready it for the Pope, it was refurbished. Eight enormous windows made it easy to see the Pope dressed in white sitting upon a white upholstered velvet seat with gold embroidery. Pulling the carriage were eight dappled-grey horses with plumed crests headed by grooms and outriders dressed like the coachman in yellow livery trimmed with gold lace.

Napoleon, Josephine and their procession departed from the Tuileries Palace about 10am and their departure was announced with salvos of artillery. The procession consisted of 152 horses drawing 25 carriages and 6 cavalry regiments. Like the Pope's procession, security was tight with some 80,000 soldiers in uniform, three rows deep on either side of the route. The procession proceeded slowly with the widest streets chosen wherever possible. There were several stops along the way, partly because of confusion and partly because of several small accidents.

Napoleon and Josephine's carriage was near the middle. Napoleon was decked out in Spanish dress of purple velvet, glittering with gold and precious stones. To his left sat Josephine in a robe and mantle of white satin embroidered with gold and silver.

> 'The body of the carriage was all gilt and decorated with a frieze of medallions, representing the Departments of the Empire, and linked with a chain of palm-leaves. On the doors were the grand armorial bearings. Four allegorical figures upheld the roof, which was covered with green velvet embroidered with branches of olive and laurel, and surrounded by a garland of gilded bronze laurels fastened with golden eagles. … The inside was upholstered in white velvet embroidered with gold. On the ceiling was a winged thunderbolt surrounded with a double crown of olives and laurels. On the floor and in front were branches of laurels round a coroneted N. On the lower parts of the doors under the windows was a garland of oak enclosing a crown of sixteen stars, with the star of the Legion in the centre stamped with an N. Everywhere were laurels and swarms of bees. … The eight livery bay horses with white plumes, their manes plaited, decked with rosettes and cockades of red and gold, were harnessed with red morocco leather, and the bronze-work on the pole was carved and gilded. They were

> driven eight-in-hand by a coachman … stout and prosperous with gold lace on all the seams of his long green coat. An outrider was mounted on one of the leaders, a groom was at the head of each pair. Behind the coachman's seat and behind the carriage were knots of pages – as many as there was room for.'[2]

Upon arriving at their destination, Napoleon and Josephine changed into State robes. His purple mantle was lined with ermine and covered with embroidery. Hers was a similar velvet mantle but 20 ells (approximately 9m) long with 1,600 francs of embroidery and 10,300 francs worth of ermine fur. To ensure her breast area remained uncovered, the immense mantle was fastened only to her left shoulder and secured by a clasp to her belt.

It was a quarter to twelve when Napoleon, Josephine, and their procession finally entered the cathedral. As they entered, they found the galleries full of spectators, who, upon seeing their leader, cried out with great enthusiasm, 'Vive l'Empereur!' Josephine's sisters-in-law were to carry her mantle and did so 'as little as possible; in return for their submission each had an officer of her household to act a train-bearer.'[3]

The procession eventually reached the altar, and as Napoleon had requested, the unction, the blessing and the bestowal were accomplished unseen with only a brief glimpse given of him crowning himself. During the coronation, Napoleon wore two crowns. The first was a golden laurel wreath meant to invoke memories of the Roman empire and the second was a replica of Charlemagne's crown, since the original could not be obtained from Austria. Napoleon initially placed the laurel crown on, then the replica of Charlemagne's crown, which he also touched to the head of the Empress.

Later, there were comments about the Empress' enthronement. After she 'mounted the first five steps, … the weight of her mantle, no longer upheld by the Princesses, who remained at the bottom of the steps, brought her up with a jerk, and almost made her fall backwards. She had to put forth all her strength to recover herself and continue the ascent.'[4] Some people may have thought the princesses were getting revenge, but apparently Napoleon also staggered, recovered, and mounted the steps.

After the enthronement, the Pope kissed the Emperor's cheek and declared, '*Vivat Imperator in* æternum' (May the Emperor live forever). The orchestra began to play, offerings were given, and the Mass followed its stately course. At its conclusion, Napoleon removed one of his gold embroidered gloves, placed his hand on the Gospel and took the oath, thereby becoming the new recognized leader of the French.

Estimates are that over two million people were in Paris to celebrate his coronation. When the procession left Notre Dame around 5:00pm, the Emperor and Empress were greeted by people holding flickering torches or candles and upon reaching the boulevard they found that two rows of lamp stands, other illuminations, and wreaths of coloured lights lit their pathway. The ensuing celebration was intense and festivities lasted two weeks. Hundreds of church bells chimed, fireworks were set off, and several formal dances were held. It was a costly event, paid for by the crown and state treasuries, that totalled about 8.5 million francs.

Two months prior to the coronation, Napoleon contacted David, the artist who had started Juliette's portrait but failed to finish it. Napoleon wanted him to capture his coronation and, to enable him to do so, he told him to choose a convenient spot at the coronation where he could see the 'whole ceremony, and draw it with exactness. The place selected was above the chief Altar, so that the painter could see perfectly the choir of the church. … Immediately after the ceremony, … David, full of his subject, went home and sketched out the design of his work.'[5] In addition, although his mother was absent, Napoleon ordered David to include her in the scene.

Despite her dislike for the Emperor, Juliette remained friends with his sisters and hid her feelings about Germaine's banishment and the outcome of Moreau and Cadoudal's trials. Everything appeared normal at her salon because she continued to receive both friend and foe with no thought of political affiliations. Part of the reason for her pretence of neutral ground had to do with her husband's extensive business dealings. She knew she had to dole out politeness and guarantee that every guest was greeted cordially so as not to damage his business.

One of the more prolific visitors to her salon at the time was the intelligent and crafty Fouché. Napoleon had created and given Fouché the hereditary title of Duke of Otranto after he stationed naval ships in Otranto harbour beginning in 1804. However, although Napoleon admired Fouché, he never fully trusted him.

Fouché had been born in a small village near Nantes, and from an early age he showed an aptitude for literary and scientific studies. He wanted to be a teacher and was sent to Paris to accomplish that goal. Because of his intelligence and abilities, he was soon performing tutorial duties and was subsequently initiated into Freemasonry, where he met Robespierre.

In 1790, Fouché became a leader in the Jacobin Club. He left the Jacobins for a time and supported the Girondists but returned to the Jacobins and favoured the death of Louis XVI. Fouché was not considered a radical Jacobin until after the Convention issued a declaration of war against Britain and later Spain. Then, he was sent to crush the royalist revolt in Brittany and La Vendée, and he did so with such vigour that he became quite infamous.

In 1793, he became involved with the dechristianization movement. He also helped established the Cult of Reason, a state sponsored atheistic 'religion' that was intended to replace Roman Catholicism. To drive home his support for atheism, he suppressed any signs or emblems of religion in public places. In fact, it was Fouché who had inscribed over all the gates of every French cemetery the words, 'Death is an eternal sleep'.[6]

During the Reign of Terror, he was ordered to Lyon, the home of Juliette's birth. There he carried out reprisals sanctioned by the Convention because the Lyonnais had revolted. He and another Frenchman, Jean-Marie Collot d'Herbois, also formed a Temporary Commission for Republican Surveillance and began to terrorize and purify Lyon. The zeal and happiness Fouché felt in doing so was displayed in a letter he wrote to d'Herbois on 19 December:

> 'Let us show ourselves terrible: let us annihilate in our wrath, and at one blow, every conspirator, every traitor, that we may not feel the pain, the long torture, of punishing them as kings would do. We this evening send two hundred and thirteen rebels before the thunder of our cannon. Farewell my friend! tears of joy stream from my eyes and overflow my heart.'[7]

Fouché accomplished this punishment by chaining 213 men together. A firing squad of soldiers then blasted them with grapeshot resulting in the victims falling to the ground mutilated or severely wounded but not always dead. As the wounded begged for death, Fouché's soldiers finished them off using their bayonets, sabres, or the butts of their muskets. The dead were then unceremoniously dumped into the Rhone.

Unfortunately, over time, so many bodies were dumped into the river that they washed up back onto its banks. The putrid stench and possible contagion from the rotting corpses compelled Fouché and Herbois to have all the dead bodies interred, which they turned to their advantage by ordering the graves of the condemned to be dug by the nearest female relatives, such as mothers, sisters, or wives.

After their deaths, the condemned were stripped naked and plundered by a band of women said to be in the pay of Fouché's revolutionary judges, called the furies of the guillotine. Stories about such atrocities at Lyon were published in newspapers, and one story that appeared was about the wife of a man, Danois, who had been condemned to death. As was customary, his wife was sent to dig his grave the night before his execution, even though she was pregnant.

> 'In being dragged to the place of execution she miscarried and was taken home senseless. When Daunois was taken to be shot the furies of the guillotine had Fouché's orders … and among other things told him that his wife was … to be married to his executioner, whom they pointed out. And in fact Fouché put her in requisition for this man, but she expired at the sight of him when presented Fouché's orders.'[8]

The brutality undertaken by Fouché in Lyon resulted in him acquiring the nickname of the 'Executioner of Lyon'. However, when the Convention learned of his sadistic and unorthodox tactics, they halted the grapeshot executions, which were then replaced with normal firing squads that resulted in the death of about another 1,800 people.

In July 1799, the Executioner of Lyon was appointed Minister of the Police by Napoleon. The position only lasted a few years because after Napoleon attempted to establish the Consulship for life, Fouché opposed it. Napoleon dismissed him on 15 September 1802 and his duties were transferred to the Grand-Judge, Claude-Antoine Régnier. However, despite his dismissal, Fouché kept abreast of illegal and secret events and continued to rely on his spy network to ferret out plots. It was because of such contacts that he was able to unravel the Pichegru plot when Régnier and his people knew nothing about it. Therefore, Napoleon realized Fouché's importance, reconstituted the Ministry of Police, and reinstated him on 10 July 1804.

In the summer of 1805, Fouché was paying Juliette regular visits and during one of them, he requested a tête-a-tête with her. He then warned her against showing the Emperor any hostility, citing the case of the Duchess de Chevreuse. She had been cold to Napoleon and in return, he had sharply reprimanded her and threatened the confiscation of her wealth. Juliette was startled by Fouché's advice and thanked him. However, she protested that she had no interest in politics and made a point of mentioning that she was loyal to her friends and would not abandon them. As far as Juliette was concerned, that was the end of the conversation.

A few days later, Fouché reappeared. He and Juliette went for a walk in the gardens of Clichy and he asked for Juliette's 'true sentiments' regarding Napoleon. Juliette was surprised but mentioned the persecution that her family and friends had endured. She further expressed her unhappiness over the banishment of Germaine and Moreau. Juliette was also bothered by the arrest of her father in 1802, while he was serving as Postmaster-General. At the time, secret correspondence between royalists was circulating in the south and authorities were unsure how such correspondence was being transmitted. As Monsieur Bernard was the head of the administration at the time, fault soon focused on him and he was arrested.

Juliette, her mother and three gentlemen guests were dining with the younger sister of Napoleon, Madame Elisa Bacciocchi, when Juliette learned that her father had been arrested. The group had just finished dinner and were about to enter the drawing room when a note was handed to Madame Bernard. Fearing the worst, she glanced at it and promptly fainted. After being restored to consciousness, Madame Bernard handed the note to Juliette, who then hastened to appeal to Napoleon. Due to her solicitations, her father was not tried; however, Napoleon was unwilling to immediately dismiss the charges and Juliette's father remained imprisoned for some time. He was finally released through the efforts of her friend Jean Bernadotte (the future King of Sweden and Norway), who, like other men, was smitten by her. In fact, he once penned the following message to Juliette:

> 'When friendship, tenderness, and sensibility inflame a loving heart, all that it expresses is profoundly felt; but though bound to love you for ever, I have not dared to fatigue you with letters. Adieu! If you sometimes think of me, remember you are my principal idea, and that nothing can equal the sweet and tender sentiments I shall ever feel for you.'[9]

Fouché was not necessarily interested in Juliette's complaints and without listening to her 'true sentiments,' he boldly broached his purpose in meeting her. He proposed that she request a position at Napoleon's court as it would be immediately granted. She was shocked by the suggestion and felt immediate disgust, but she recovered herself and quickly cited a litany of reasons why she must decline.

Fouché was oblivious to her disgust and ignored her reasons. He then suggested that a woman of her charms could exert her influence over the Emperor. Furthermore, he stated of Napoleon:

> 'He has not yet … met a woman worthy of him; and no one knows what the love of Napoleon might be, if he attached himself to a pure person. Assuredly, he would allow her to exert an influence that would be entirely beneficent.'[10]

Juliette was invited some time later to visit Napoleon's younger sister Caroline Bonaparte. She was better known as Madame Murat after having married Joachim Murat in a civil ceremony on 20 January 1800 that was solemnized in church two years later. On 18 May 1804, Napoleon made his brother-in-law Marshal of France and a year later named him 'Prince of the Empire'. Of Madame Murat, Juliette once said:

> 'Of all the sisters of Napoleon, Caroline was the one who most resembled him. She was not so regularly beautiful as his sister Pauline … but she belonged distinctly to the Napoleonic type; she was of a marvellously rich colouring; her intelligence was quick, her will imperious, and the contrast of the girlish grace of her face with the decision of her character made her a very attractive person.'[11]

In 1805, the Murats were residing at the Château of Neuilly, a vast estate that included a 170-hectare park. When Juliette arrived to visit, she was surprised to find Fouché also there. He, Madame Murat, and Juliette breakfasted together and afterwards shared light conversation. Eventually, however, Fouché again asked Juliette to serve in a position at the Emperor's court. Madame Murat was delighted and, whether out of ignorance or not, she became Fouché's advocate and ally. She felt that such an arrangement would place Juliette on equal footing with the Empress, and, later that same day, as Juliette was departing, Madame Murat remembered her great admiration for the French actor François Joseph Talma and offered her box at the Théâtre Français. The next day, 14 October, word reached Juliette in the form of a note that read:

> 'Her Royal Highness, the Princess Caroline, informs the managers of the Théâtre Français, that, from this date, until a

> new order be given, her box is to be open to Mme. Récamier, to those she brings with her, or those to whom she gives an order.'[12]

From the box, Juliette could see Talma's every expression, but she only used the box twice. Both times, she found Napoleon was present. Moreover, to her dismay, he persistently pointed his opera-glasses her way. Courtiers noted his singular and marked attention to her, and rumours began to swirl that she was on the verge of being 'highly favoured.'

Meanwhile, every time Fouché met her, he implored her to accept a position at court. Each time she coyly provided an excuse and escaped any commitment. Finally, however, one day he arrived and blurted out, 'Well now you will have no more excuses, for the emperor has sent me expressly to offer you the place of lady in waiting.'[13] Juliette could no longer be coy and gracefully declined the request. Her refusal offended Fouché as he considered it a great insult to Napoleon. 'He changed countenance, and, carried away by his anger, broke out in reproaches … He indulged in a philippic against *the old aristocracy*, to whom he added, the emperor showed a *fatal indulgence*; and he left Clichy never to return thither.'[14]

Now that Juliette's opposition to Napoleon was no secret and she had blatantly spurned him, she found herself engaged in a struggle. He put her salon under surveillance and after hearing that three ministers had visited her salon, he was furious, yelling at his council, 'Since when has the council of ministers been held at Mme. Récamier's house?'[15]

Chapter 10

Losses

Every cabinet earnestly wished the overthrow of Napoleon.
Louis Antoine Fauvelet de Bourrienne

Rumours about the Récamiers facing financial problems had been circulating since Juliette's falling out with Lucien in 1800. At that time, Royalists had been whispering that Napoleon's policies had caused the bankruptcies of many rich bankers whom he feared might conspire against him. If it was true, Jacques-Rose did not seem affected until one Saturday in the autumn of 1806 when he dejectedly approached his wife.

He confided in her that because of a series of unfortunate circumstances, his banking house was suffering a 'state of embarrassment'. His problems were partly caused because his bank took on too much risk and partly because it relied heavily on international trade, which was affected by Napoleon's attempts to defeat Britain using embargoes to isolate them economically. Jacques-Rose told his wife that all their problems might be resolved if the Bank of France would advance his banking house the money he needed, but if refused, then on Monday, the banking house would have to suspend all payments.

The Récamiers had planned a banquet on that Sunday. To cancel at the last moment would arouse suspicion, which Jacques-Rose wanted to avoid at all costs, even if his optimism had completely deserted him. He decided the best plan was for Juliette to host the banquet while he left for the country. It all depended on the Emperor's decision; if it was favourable, he would return immediately, and if unfavourable, he would stay in the country until the fallout had settled. In the meantime, he would rely on his wife to put on a brave face and appear as if everything was normal.

Although Juliette was momentarily shaken by the news, she agreed and on Sunday, when the banquet was held, nobody suspected anything amiss. She smiled and delighted her guests as usual, all the while disguising her agony. She later stated that she felt the evening was a nightmare, 'and that her mental suffering was so great, that natural objects assumed, to her disturbed imagination, strange and fantastic shapes'.[1]

When Jacques-Rose did not return, Juliette knew the advance had been refused. She accepted her change of fortune calmly and without complaint. She knew deep down that the Emperor's personal resentment towards her was a partial cause of the refusal. On Monday, the banking house suspended payments, Jacques-Rose gave everything to his creditors and Juliette sold off her jewels and plate. Additionally, smaller houses connected to Jacques-Rose's banking house also folded.

With no money, the fairyland house in the rue du Mont Blanc was advertised for sale, but being so costly, it was not easy to find a buyer. The Italian Prince Pignatelli was willing to rent the grand suite if furnished, so Juliette gave up her apartment and moved to the ground floor, taking a room where the windows opened onto the garden. Finding a buyer took several years and it was not until 1 September 1808 when the house finally sold to a M. Mosselmann.

If there was any sadness associated with Juliette's new financial situation it was her inability to continue to do good. For instance, her husband's ruin resulted in the discovery that Juliette had paid for the education and training of twelve orphaned girls, who upon reaching the age of fifteen would be 'fully prepared'. Moreover, for those who saw her carriage pass by and thought she was going to 'Leroi's or … the Petit-Dunkerque, [they] were often surprised to see it stop at the door of some obscure house, where this amiable lady would alight to administer succour to some infirm old man, or give a packet of child-bed linen to some distressed woman'.[2] In addition, one story that appeared about Juliette and her financial difficulties stated:

> 'She has renounced entirely all society, and in solitude applied herself for her new situation of life. Even the brilliant offer of princess Louis Bonaparte, to be governess of her children, has been declined in a modest letter: in which she says – "that though her education and capacity might be sufficient for the instruction of children of citizens, they were not calculated for the education of the children of princes." – She adds, "that the unavoidable dissipation of courts would besides prevent her from fulfilling her first duty, that of a wife."'[3]

Amidst the Récamiers' crumbling fortune, there was more bad news. Juliette's mother, Madame Bernard, became ill and, despite her intense suffering, Juliette was blinded to the seriousness of her condition because her mother dressed nearly every day in some fashionable gown and received visitors after being carried from her bed to her chaise longue. Perhaps Madame Bernard thought such behaviour would shield her daughter from the truth or that it would give her daughter hope that she might recover. However, even Madame Bernard did not believe such a thing could happen as she required around-the-clock care.

The pretence that she might recover ended on Tuesday, 20 January 1807, when she passed away in Paris. Juliette had rarely been separated from her mother and her grief was overwhelming. She sent a couple of brief notes to the father-like figure Mathieu and her dear friend Germaine. Both responded quickly. Mathieu's note of condolence was dated 22 January 1807 and remarked on the depth of Juliette's heartache and her desire for solitude. Germaine's note came two days later and though brief, came right to the point:

> 'Dear Friend – How much I feel for your grief! How much I suffer from not seeing you! Is it not possible then to see you, and must my life pass thus? I know of nothing to say. I embrace you, and weep with you.'[4]

Juliette's mournful isolation lasted for the next six months. She cried alone, went nowhere and did little. Ultimately, however, she realized her mourning was ruining her health and to help her recover, she finally consented to visit Germaine at Coppet in Switzerland.

As Jacques-Rose and Juliette faced financial ruin, the beautiful Queen Louise of Prussia was promoting war and pushing her husband, the weak-willed and vacillating Frederick William III, to face Napoleon. She was determined to achieve her goals and finally her husband listened. Prussia soon joined with Russia, backed financially by Britain. Now, with Russian support, the Prussian king ordered France to evacuate all of Germany.

Although the Prussian army was large, it had poor leadership and was old-fashioned, disorganized and slow. However, that did not stop the Prussian king from advancing on Napoleon's forces without his Russian allies in August of 1806. When the Prussians met the French, it was disastrous for them. Napoleon was by far the more skilful strategist and had a superior army. In the end, he beat his enemy at the twin battles of Jena and Austerädt.

After defeating the Prussians, Napoleon continued to plot against his arch enemy, Britain. The Berlin Decree of November 1806 instituted the Continental System, which was intended to destroy Britain's ability to trade and cause economic collapse so that France could easily invade them. Britain had issued embargoes against military shipments to France, and Napoleon's Continental System retaliated against those embargoes by ordering all European nations and all French allies to stop corresponding and trading with Britain. To ensure trade with Britain stopped, Napoleon ordered all ships leaving Britain to stop at a French port.

Besides the British and Prussians being unhappy with the French, so were the Russians and that unhappiness would culminate in the Battle of Eylau. It was a hard-fought two-day battle that began on 7 February 1807 when Napoleon's exhausted soldiers faced Russian troops commanded by Count Levin August von Bennigsen, a German general in the service of the Russian Empire. The battle was fought in the freezing cold between approximately 67,000 Russians and Napoleon's 45,000 soldiers. When the fighting began, Napoleon expected reinforcements, as did Benningsen.

The first battle was for control of the German city of Eylau, now in Russia and called Bagrationovsk. A blizzard obscured visibility, although it couldn't hide the red blood in the snow as the soldiers fell. Inch by inch, foot by foot, and yard by yard the soldiers battled for dominance until by the end of the day, the French proved triumphant and captured the city. That was fortunate for Napoleon's tired troops who then enjoyed a good night's rest, warm beds, and shelter.

The next day proved to be a continuation of the previous day's vicious and close quarter combat. Napoleon's enemies were determined to wrest Eylau away from him, but French troops were equally determined to achieve victory. Fighting proceeded to the point where Napoleon's enemies almost captured his headquarters. Fortunately, they did not realize their advantage, and it slipped away.

As the battle raged on, it appeared as if the Russians would be victorious, and things became calamitous for the French when Bennigsen's reinforcements began to arrive without any sign of French reinforcements. Then, Napoleon's brother-in-law Murat made a brave move and saved the day. His cavalry courageously charged through the centre of the Russians while another French Marshal repulsed them and sent them scurrying to the left. However, before any clear gain could be achieved, darkness fell and fighting ended.

An eager Napoleon awoke the next morning to face his enemy. Instead, he discovered Benningsen and his troops had withdrawn. The engagement that Napoleon hoped would provide a solid victory proved inconclusive as both sides lost at least 25,000 men. Napoleon's only consolation was that he remained on the battlefield and thus he claimed victory.

A few months later in June, in the aftermath of his decisive win at Friedland, the Emperor met Tsar Alexander I of Russia and the Prussian king, Frederick William III in the town of Tilsit. The historic meeting took place on the River Niemen on a raft placed equidistant from the shores with their troops patiently waiting on their respective side of the river. The raft was richly decorated and carpeted with a covered pavilion rising from its centre. At 1pm, thunders of artillery roared as the imperial figures, accompanied by a few choice officers, stepped onto a boat from shore and headed to the moored raft.

Napoleon arrived first and crossed the raft to greet the blue-eyed, brown-haired Alexander. The two leaders cordially embraced. Napoleon had never thought much of the impetuous and ambitious Russian Tsar, but this time when they met, they warmed to each other and talked for three hours. Alexander impressed Napoleon and the young Tsar found himself entranced by the enigmatic older man. Perhaps for that reason, the Emperor's terms for 30-year-old Alexander were lenient, even if he demanded Russia join the Continental System, withdraw from Walachia and Moldavia and give France the Ionian Islands.

Napoleon did not grant Prussia the same leniency. Although Napoleon had soundly defeated Frederick William III, Frederick hoped the appearance of his pregnant wife might induce Napoleon to be merciful to them and so he convinced her to travel there. Queen Louise had every reason to dislike Napoleon as he had previously attempted to ruin her reputation by questioning her marital fidelity. In response, she had called him a 'Monster', but now she put those negative feelings aside and praised him, spoke of his greatness and lauded his wondrous genius.

Napoleon refused to make any concessions to Prussia and it did not matter that the queen fell to her feet begging and offering herself to him if he would allow Prussia to keep Magdeburg. The Emperor already believed she was 'meddlesome' and later wrote to Josephine stating that 'the queen of Prussia … is really charming and full of coquettishness toward me. But don't be jealous … it would cost me too dearly to play the gallant'.[5] He took half of Prussia's territories and gave the new 1,100 square mile kingdom of Westphalia to his brother Jérôme to rule.

The ultimate effect of the Treaties of Tilsit was that Napoleon's treatment of Prussia caused bitter feelings to fester and Alexander I's pretence of friendship caused the Emperor to completely underestimate his Russian counterpart. Yet, the treaties did briefly give Napoleon a reprieve from war. They also allowed him to return home after more than 300 days away, which he noted in a short letter to Josephine dated 18 July 1807.

> 'My dear: I got to Dresden yesterday at 5 p.m., feeling very well … I am staying here with the King of Saxony … So you see I am more than halfway back to you. One of these fine nights I may turn up at Saint-Cloud in the role of the jealous husband; I give you fair warning. Good-bye my dear. It will be a great pleasure to see you. All my love.'[6]

The controversial Napoleon fascinated the people of Britain, and it was probably no surprise they considered him a cause célèbre. The famous wax sculptress Madame Tussaud, who arrived in London in 1802, realized his exasperating allure and began displaying his wax figure and relics associated with him while she was touring in the early 1800s. With no way for people to know for sure what Napoleon looked like, Madame Tussaud's wax displays brought their mortal enemy to life. Later, because his spellbinding appeal proved so profitable, she dedicated two rooms in her museum to him where intrigued visitors could linger and mingle.

Besides visiting Madame Tussaud's, the English could also buy items that prominently featured Napoleon. Pricey items like snuffboxes containing his image could be found for sale, like the one created by the Parisian goldsmith Pierre-Andre Montauban. He made one in 1797 that relied on a portrait of Napoleon created by David. Other treasures with the Emperor's likeness available for public consumption included tokens, prints, medals, medallions and miniatures. Commoners were not the only ones buying such things as most aristocrats or nobles also possessed some sort of Napoleonic trinket.

English caricature artists Thomas Rowlandson, James Gillray and George and Isaac Cruikshank also produced thousands of cartoons of the man they called 'Boney', 'the Usurper', or the 'Corsican Ogre'. Their caricatures depicted him in the most unflattering light and their visual assaults portrayed him as a spider, a tiger, or even the devil. Moreover, caricaturists also regularly depicted him as short, despite him being 5ft 7in tall, which was taller than the average Frenchman.

British parents also took advantage of Napoleon's fierce reputation to keep their children in line. Tales abound that he was some sort of bogeyman and Betsy Balcombe, the daughter of a minor official for the East India Company living in St. Helena noted the terror and dread she felt when she learned that Napoleon was aboard the *Northumberland* and sailing to the island. In her childish reflections, she knew something awful would happen:

> 'The earliest idea I had of Napoleon was that of a huge ogre or giant, with one large flaming red eye in the middle of his forehead, and long teeth protruding from his mouth, with which he tore to pieces and devoured naughty little girls, especially those who did not know their lessons.'[7]

All the bad press, insults, and libellous caricatures took their toll on Napoleon's reputation. He became so upset that he complained vehemently to the British government, but they did little to stop the tide of negativity because it whipped up support for their cause. Napoleon finally attempted to mobilize French caricature artists against Britain's King George or his court, but instead of getting even with the British, French caricatures concentrated on improving Napoleon's image.

Later, when Napoleon's triumphs declined, British caricature artists were overjoyed. They did everything humanly possible to destroy whatever shreds of reputation he had left. For instance, after his divorce from Josephine, sexual innuendo about his inability to produce an heir was rampant. His failed Russian Campaign also allowed British caricature artists to embrace themes showing him betraying the lofty ideals of the French Revolution.

Caricature artists did not necessarily need to skewer Napoleon. The damage he caused himself and France because of the Berlin Decree and the Continental System cannot be underestimated. Britain had retaliated against France by banning all trade with them except through Britain and even the United States decided to get into the act by banning all trade with western Europe. 'Britain's exports to northern Europe fell from £10 million to £2 million in the space of two years. With the country in the middle of an industrial revolution, it was massively overproducing and desperately needed markets. The warehouses were overflowing … Mills and factories closed and unemployment soared'.[8]

France was even worse off than Britain. Industries that relied on overseas markets declined or closed. Napoleon also refused to grant anything that would help the enemy, even if it would benefit his own people. He believed Britain would ultimately suffer more, not realizing that because of that country's immense wealth and commercial abilities, she could endure deprivation much longer than France.

Napoleon's Continental System ultimately failed. A thriving black market of smugglers developed, prices soared, and beggars were found everywhere throughout France. 'At the same time sixty thousand tons of coffee lay in the London warehouses, unsalable at sixpence a pound, while the price on the Continent was from four to five shillings, and in places even seven shillings.'[9]

Bourrienne had met Napoleon when they were both eight while attending the Military School at Brienne. He was now serving as a diplomat in Hamburg and tasked with carrying out the measures of the Continental System. Because he was unhappy with the measures, he secretly relaxed restrictions to favour merchants who plied him with *douceurs* (bribes) and even once procured military cloaks from England for the Emperor as that was the only expeditious way to obtain them. So, when orders were given to burn all British manufactured goods, there could not have been anyone as melancholy as Bourrienne, who wrote:

> 'Persons who at this epoch were living in the interior of France can form no idea of the desolation which so savage a measure spread through countries accustomed to living by commerce. What a spectacle offered to peoples impoverished and lacking everything, to see the burning of articles the distribution of which would have been an alleviation to their sufferings! … There was already an understanding from one end of Europe to the other; every cabinet earnestly wished the overthrow of Napoleon, as the people also wished, with at least equal ardour, a state of things less stifling for their industry and trade. Despite the terror inspired by Napoleon's name, there was, side by side with that terror, the damnable Continental System … it was necessary either to fight or to succumb. The people of the North were under an imperious necessity to break the yoke of lead, which made the custom house the prime agent of the governments of Europe.'[10]

Chapter 11

Love is in the Air

One has only to see you in order to love you.
Prince Augustus of Prussia to Juliette

The year 1807 was more than fighting battles or being victorious for Napoleon. He had adopted Josephine's children, but together they had none of their own so doubts about whether he could sire his own children weighed heavily on him since their marriage. Fortunately, in mid-December 1806, his illegitimate son Charles Léon Denuelle with Louise Catherine Eléonore Denuelle de la Plaigne was born, thus ending the debate.

The new year also brought other developments, such as an affair with a 20-year-old Polish beauty, who captured Napoleon's heart and who was married to 71-year-old Count Anastase Walewski. The Count was the starosta of the Warka district, a once-chamberlain to the last Polish king, and a Polish patriot. His patriotism was supposedly why he encouraged his wife to develop a relationship with Napoleon.

Her name was Marie Walewska, and exactly where and how Napoleon and Marie met is shrouded in mystery, with various versions that contradict one another. However, once they met, Napoleon invited her to go with him to a ball, which again involves controversy. Some people claim she went willingly, others maintain she did not, still others allege that Talleyrand procured her for Napoleon's pleasure.

For the 71-year-old Count and other Polish patriots, there was no question that they thought Napoleon could help their country become an independent state, thus, it is likely that Marie's husband and others encouraged her to advance their cause with the Emperor. Marie evidently took the Polish cause seriously, maybe too seriously. The two fell in love, and everyone noticed that Napoleon's passion for her was hard to contain. For instance, after the Battle of Eylau, he established his headquarters in the Kamieniec-Finkenstein region at the Finkenstein mansion, built in 1706. He then spent more than two blissful months romancing Marie. It was a delightful time and one of the happiest periods in his life. Moreover, just as he had earlier written to Josephine, he sent passionate letters to Marie:

> 'Marie, my sweet Marie, my first thought is of you, my first desire is to see you again. You will come again, won't you? You promised you would. If you don't, the eagle will fly to you! I shall see you at dinner … I want you to accept this bouquet: I want to be a secret link, setting up a private understanding between us in the midst of the surrounding crowd. We shall be able to share our thoughts though all the world is looking on. When my hand presses my heart, you will know that I am thinking of no one but you; and when you press your bouquet, I shall have your answer back! Love, my pretty one, and hold your bouquet tight!'[1]

Josephine became aware of Napoleon's relationship with Marie, but there was little she could do. Moreover, almost immediately after their marriage she had been unfaithful to Napoleon. When he departed for Italy, she was swept off her feet by the young and dashing staff officer, Lieutenant Hippolyte Charles. She was so in love with him that she avoided joining Napoleon for some time and when she finally did, she brought Hippolyte with her as her aide.

For a time, Napoleon kept his domestic problems to himself and ignored the fact that his wife was having an affair. That changed during the Egyptian Campaign when one of his Generals showed him a letter detailing Josephine's and Hippolyte's relationship and others told him that the relationship was common knowledge throughout Paris. That awareness, coupled with Josephine's extravagant spending, resulted in a livid and depressed Napoleon writing to his brother Joseph. Napoleon was planning to divorce Josephine when he returned to Paris and his unhappiness was evident in his letters.

> 'It is melancholy business, when all the affections of one's heart are wrapped up in a single person. I want you to arrange to have a country place ready for me when I return … I am counting on spending the winter there, and seeing no one. I am sick of society. I need solitude, isolation. My feelings are dried up, and I am bored with public display. I am tired of glory at 29; it has lost its charm and there is nothing

> left for me but complete egotism. I mean to keep my Paris house — I shall never give that up to anyone. I have no other resources.'[2]

Napoleon's plan to divorce Josephine at that time never came to fruition; that would take a few more years. Instead, he became involved with a blonde femme fatale while he was still in Egypt. Her name was Pauline Fourès and she was married to one of his lieutenants. Napoleon undeniably hoped word would reach Josephine that he was involved because he and Pauline, or as he called her, Cleopatra, were anything but discreet. Moreover, when he left Pauline in Egypt in the autumn of 1799, a cavalcade of relationships followed until he finally fell in love with Marie in 1807.

The same year that Napoleon found love in the arms of Marie, Germaine was staying in Coppet, a cosy municipality situated about nine miles north of Geneva. Germaine wanted Juliette to visit, but she could not travel alone, so she travelled with a male companion, Count Elzéar of Sabra, along with several servants.

Along the way, one of their carriage wheels was wrenched off when the postilion misjudged the edge of the roadway. It caused the coach to overturn and resulted in everyone and everything ending up in the ditch. Two of the four horses were killed but the postilion escaped unhurt, as did the footman who jumped free of the accident just in time. The postilion and footman then came to the aid of the injured travellers. The Count and servants were bruised, and Juliette's foot was hurt. Help was sought in a nearby village and once everything was set right and repaired, the travellers were back on their way and their trip concluded without further incident.

The centre of the village of Coppet was quaint. It had been created from numerous buildings during the thirteenth century, along with the gothic Maison Michel that dated from the fifteenth century, and a sixteenth century building called the Maison de Ville. At the time, the village had a population of just over 450 people and Juliette's mid-summer arrival at Germaine's chateau with its colonnades of oaks, sycamores and elms, added one more to the number.

Another traveller to the area was Prince Augustus of Prussia. His father was brother to Frederick the Great (Prince August Ferdinand of Prussia) and his mother was Margravine Elisabeth Louise of Brandenburg-Schwedt. She was niece to her husband and described by one nineteenth-century English visitor in the following unflattering terms: 'I never saw such a formal, stiff, disagreeable old woman; *vieille cour outrée*, and she frightened me to death. I was glad to get away.'[3]

Although not disagreeable like his mother, Augustus was brusque and frank. He was described as distinguished and a man of formal bearing. He was also young and passionate and referred to in Prussia as a Don Juan. Other descriptions of Augustus ranged from giddy, frivolous and thoughtless to someone who was infatuated by his own accomplishments and successes.

He was also said to be a fervent and devoted patriot of his country who enjoyed a fast-advancing military career; he had earned the rank of captain by the age of eighteen, became a major by 1803 and received the rank of lieutenant colonel just three years later. In late 1806, Napoleon's army had killed his older brother Prince Louis Ferdinand. Augustus had fought with fervour but been captured and held prisoner by the French until 1807.

Having just been released by the French, Augustus' travails, misfortunes and heroics were on everyone's tongue and because he was the talk of Germaine's salon, she invited him to visit Coppet. He accepted her hospitality for a few days and happened to appear there at the same time as Juliette was visiting. The two had never met before but when they did, sparks flew.

Augustus had of course heard of Juliette but never seen her. She spied the 27-year-old, a dashing, handsome man who cut a fine figure, for the first time as he was escorting Germaine into the salon. One historian provided the details of their first meeting:

> 'Her elegance, the dazzling brilliance of her beauty, prevented the Prince from recognising her, for he had formed a far different idea. He had imagined a woman renowned for her charms, proud of her success, with a self-assurance and confidence that celebrities usually enjoy. [Instead] he saw a young and timid woman advance with an air of embarrassment, and many blushes.'[4]

Juliette supposedly dictated her version of this meeting to Germaine, who then later provided the following extract:

> 'After dinner, Juliette entertained those gathered by playing her harp and singing. The Prince was ravished. When she ended, he looked at her with eyes full of inexpressible trouble, crying, "What talent!"'[5]

Cupid's arrow had hit its mark as both were smitten. Juliette's charms caused Augustus to delay his departure and she, nearing 30, was completely love struck. She was so enamoured that she could only think of him and he was the only man she wanted. Bourrienne who served as Napoleon's secretary, later a diplomat and writer of Napoleon's memoirs, noted that he thought one of the commonalities that brought Augustus and Juliette together was that they both thought of themselves as victims of Napoleon and developed a 'common hatred' of him. Whether or not it was true, Juliette was so infatuated, Lieutenant Général Vicomte de Reiset declared, 'Mme Récamier always said that Prince Augustus was the only man who had been able to make her heart beat for him'.[6]

Coppet was the perfect spot for their love to grow. It was romantic with its fresh summer breezes, blooming fragrant flowers and hazy moonlit nights. Three months of merry-making and starry-eyed passion ensued. Augustus made their time together romantic, providing trips to Lake Geneva where he rowed leisurely along the shore and waxed eloquently about life, love and their future together.

Augustus' wooing of Juliette also soon turned his thoughts to marriage. Despite Juliette already being a wife, Augustus saw no obstacle to them getting married. He had a mistress, Karoline Friederike Wichmann, with whom he had lived openly since 1805, but he was single. Unlike Juliette, who was Catholic, Augustus was Protestant and in Prussia, divorce was possible in both civil and church law. Therefore, he was unconcerned about Juliette's relationship with Jacques-Rose or her getting a divorce.

Germaine was a romantic at heart and love was always on her mind, so it was easy for her to become Augustus' unswerving advocate and sway Juliette to the idea of marrying him. Germaine had also just published a romance novel titled *Corrine, or Italy*. The novel was about the torment a Scottish peer named Lord Nelvil underwent when faced to choose between love and duty; his dead father had desired him to marry an English girl, but he was in love with an Italian poetess named Corinne. Germaine was not necessarily thinking about Nelvil or Corrine but rather about the love her good friend Juliette might share with Augustus and so she gave him all her support.

With Augustus' passion and Germaine's support, Juliette was easily swept up in the deliciousness of romance. Here was a prince proposing that she become his princess bride. The thought was irresistible, it made her heady and she did the only thing she could do. She denounced her marriage vows with Jacques-Rose and accepted Augustus' proposal. Thus, inspired by love, she wrote to her husband requesting their marriage be dissolved.

Napoleon's father and mother, Carlo and Letizia.

Napoleon Bonaparte at 23 years old as a lieutenant-colonel of a battalion of Corsican Republican volunteers by Henri Félix Emmanuel Philippoteaux.

Pasquale Paoli.

Napoleon's oldest brother Joseph Bonaparte, by Luigi Toro.

Juliette Récamier in 1801 by Jean-Baptiste Augustin.

Empress Josephine in her coronation robes as painted by François Gérard, circa 1807-1808.

Mathieu of Montmorency-Laval.

Napoleon's brother, Lucien Bonaparte.

Nineteenth-century portrait of Charles Maurice de Talleyrand-Périgord by Pierre-Paul Prud'hon.

Titled 'Portrait of Mme de Staël' showing Germaine in her turban, which she became famous for wearing. By Marie-Éléonore Godefroid after François Gérard.

Jean-Victor-Marie Moreau in 1810.

Above: Jacques-Louis David's version of Juliette in 1800 that was never finished.

Right: François Gérard's version of Juliette in 1802.

Joseph Fouché, Duke of Otranto by Claude-Marie Dubufe.

Josephine's daughter, Hortense de Beauharnais painted by Anne-Louis Girodet de Roussy-Trioson in 1808.

François-René, vicomte de Chateaubriand circa 1828.

Napoleon's sister and Joachim Murat's wife Caroline, by François Gérard.

The flamboyant Joachim Murat as King of Naples by François Gérard.

Napoleon with Tsar Alexander I, Queen Louise, and Frederick William III of Prussia in Tilsit in 1807.

Napoleon's mistress Marie Walewska, by François Gérard.

Portrait painted by Franz Krüger of Prince Augustus of Prussia with François Gérard's portrait of Juliette in the background.

Benjamin Constant.

Napoleon's second wife Marie Louise, by François Gérard in 1810.

Self-portrait in 1792 by the Italian neoclassical artist and sculptor Antonio Canova.

Lithograph in 1848 of Juliette's beloved Pierre-Simon Ballanche.

Above: Napoleon's retreat from Russia in this 1866 painting titled, 'The Grande Armée Crossing the Berezina' by January Suchodolski.

Left: Arthur Wellesley, 1st Duke of Wellington, circa 1815-16, by Thomas Lawrence.

General Count Adam Albert von Neipperg.

Engraving of Marshal Michel Ney.

Napoleon on his death bed by Horace Vernet, 1826.

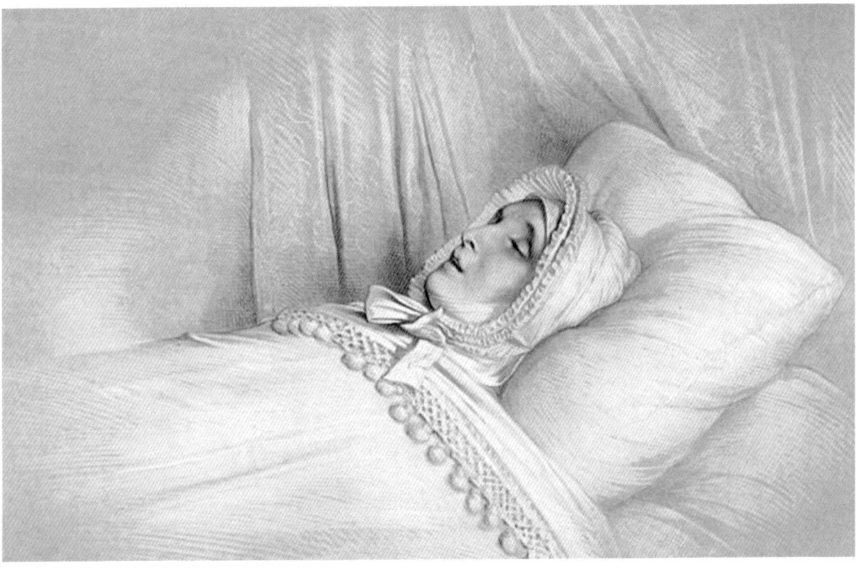

Juliette on her death bed.

About the time she sent off her letter asking for a divorce, Augustus left Coppet on 28 October 1807 on pressing business. Before he departed, he gave Juliette a gold bracelet and a chain with a ruby heart and, on the day he rode out, his gift was followed up with a romantic note in which he poured out his heart:

> 'I eagerly take advantage, my dear Juliette, of the time while the horses are being changed to tell you again of the intense grief that our separation causes me. After a lucky chance had given me the happiness of sending nearly three months in your company, a cruel obligation compels me to leave you. One has only to see you in order to love you, but one must have had the opportunity of knowing the sweetness and nobility of your character, your winning modesty, the inexpressible charm of yourself and your ways in order to feel the passionate affection with which you have inspired me. You alone, my dear Juliette, have made me know what true love is, the love which excludes every other sentiment and ignores the limits of time.'[7]

Augustus continued to express his love for Juliette in note after note and as she basked in the glow of his love, her husband replied to her request for a divorce. His reply was as unexpected as it was tender, dignified and paternal. He stated that if Juliette truly wanted a divorce, he would consent. However, he appealed to her goodness and requested that she recall the care and affection he had showered on her since the beginning of their marriage.

There was more. He also asked that she remember how he had loved and cared for her since childhood. Then, he added that if she still found herself wanting a divorce, he would agree, but there was one caveat. He did not want the divorce to occur in Paris, or even in France. He told her that he would meet her anywhere else to have the divorce arranged and finalized.

Jacques-Rose's letter touched Juliette and she was filled with remorse and compassion. She remembered her childhood and her husband's kindness. She recalled how he gratified her every request and how she had lived in luxury for so many years. Doubts began to creep in and these were reflected in her fears associated with the scandal of divorce, concerns related to her religion and worries about leaving her homeland for good.

Other worries soon crowded Juliette's mind. She thought about Jacques-Rose, old, poor and alone. The very idea of it, of divorcing or even abandoning the man who had cared so long for her, seemed impossible. The more she reflected, the greater her desire grew to refuse Augustus' marriage proposal and thus, by autumn, she convinced herself that she had no choice but to stay with her husband.

Augustus was unaware of how Juliette was feeling. She kept her doubts, reflections and decisions to herself. Instead, her replies to him became less frequent. She hoped that a slow withdrawal and her absence might soften the blow. Meanwhile, he continued to imagine a golden future for them, and he strived to obtain his family's blessing for their union. Along these lines, he also continued to faithfully write to Juliette expressing his hopes and dreams. In fact, the first hint for him that there might be a problem was when he received her letter refusing to meet him in the Rhine as promised. It prompted him to write:

> 'You refuse … in spite of my earnest entreaties, to undertake this journey, to come a distance of four hundred leagues and to give up the most brilliant entertainments and the most interesting society that has existed in Europe in order that we may see each other again for a few days. In spite of this you do not speak to me in your letters of the incertitude that the future seems to have for you. Nevertheless, all these proofs of your indifference for me have not destroyed a friendship which, unfortunately for me, has taken too deep a root in my heart … It is cruel to remind me of past happiness and to paint the future in such seductive colours if you will never realize these hopes.'[8]

At Coppet, all of Germaine's guests left around mid-November, including Juliette, so that by December, the chateau was empty. Germaine went to winter in the south of Germany where her son would attend school. However, she was sorrowful about her separation from Juliette, even though the two women made plans to meet again the following summer. They also agreed that until their reunion, Germaine would write two letters to every one of Juliette's and as promised Germaine kept her word.

Napoleon was thinking about Augustus, just as Germaine was leaving Coppet. In that regard, he sent a letter about his earlier capture to the Ministerial Secretary of State, Monsieur Maret. The letter dated 6 December 1807 stated:

> 'Let it be also said … that the Prince Augustus of Prussia, who was taken prisoner … and who has been for some time at … Coppet, where he paid his court to Madame de Stael, appears to have imbibed there some very bad principles … This prince is as big a blusterer as the other officers of his nation, and events do not seem to have corrected him. He accuses Prince Hohenlohe, the Duke of Brunswick, General Blucher, the Prussian army, the King: everybody has done wrong except himself. All that one knows about him is that he was captured in a swamp. He has neither intellect nor generosity. He is a youth without experience, and has no proof to substantiate his outcry against old soldiers who have been the victims of the imperious circumstances of war. We are far from blaming Prince Augustus because he was made a prisoner. Such a fate arrives to the bravest. But when this happens without a wound it calls for justification and not a general accusation embracing, unknown and misunderstood events. The young prince should seek the advice of his worthy father and his dignified mother. It would be of more profit to him than the bad lessons and bad propositions he has listened to at Coppet.'[9]

Despite Napoleon's continuing dislike for Germaine and his poor assessment of Augustus, Augustus remained preoccupied with his love for Juliette. His obsession for her continued even after he returned to Berlin and discovered his country was occupied by the French army. Imprudent as it was, he continued to write to her despite her being under active surveillance by Napoleon. The outcome of the surveillance was not lost on Napoleon and Augustus' 'matrimonial project' was mentioned years later while Napoleon was on Saint Helena.

As for Juliette, when she returned to Paris, she sent Augustus her portrait, the same portrait painted by David's student Gérard in 1802. Augustus immediately responded with a note dated 24 April 1808.

> 'I hope that you have already received my letter No. 31, wherein I could but feebly express the happiness that your last letter gave me; but still it will give you some idea of my sensations at receiving it, and getting your portrait. I looked for hours on the enchanting picture, dreaming of a

> happiness that must surpass all the most delicious dreams of the imagination. What fate could be comparable to that of the man whom you will love?'[10]

Juliette then decided to be frank. She sent him an agreeable but carefully worded letter, refusing to pursue their relationship any further and depriving him of any hope of marriage. Augustus was dumbstruck and responded that her words were a 'thunderbolt' to his heart. He was unwilling to accept her decision and insisted that they meet again.

Chapter 12

War, Marriage, and Exile

One is almost dead when one is exiled.
Madame de Staël

Napoleon was intent on enforcing the Continental System and, as he was unhappy with Portugal's defiance, he negotiated a secret treaty with Charles IV of Spain. He then sent French troops into Portugal in October of 1807, which turned into a six-year struggle known as the Peninsular War. In addition, because there was discord among the Spanish royal family and court, Napoleon sent his brother-in-law Murat with 120,000 troops to mediate between all the political factions.

At the time, Napoleon's brother Joseph was serving as King of Naples and Sicily. He was extremely popular with the people and it was an idyllic post. Nonetheless, Napoleon persuaded him to leave Naples, which he reluctantly did and on 6 June 1808, Napoleon appointed him King of Spain. In addition, Napoleon appointed Murat to the post vacated by Joseph and so, on 1 August, Murat became King of Naples.

In Spain, Joseph ended the Spanish Inquisition and began to institute Napoleon's reforms. The Spanish intelligentsia supported his actions, but the peasants did not. They were ultra-religious, extremely conservative and liked the ways of the old Catholic Church. In addition, they disliked Joseph because he was a foreigner and belonged to the Masonic lodge.

Ultimately, the Spanish turned against France and, when they rose against Napoleon's forces, the warfare term 'guerrilla' became popular. Guerrilla strategy involved unequal opponents fighting against one another, and guerrilla fighters used unconventional methods that might include strategies such as taking advantage of the terrain, hit-and-run tactics, destroying infrastructure, achieving public persuasion through propaganda and using ambushes, sabotage, or raids.

The battle of Bailén was fought on 16 July 1808. General Pierre Dupont de l'Étang commanded the French troops and the largely raw and inexperienced Spanish army was under the leadership of Generals Francisco Castaños and

Theodor von Reding. Despite being disadvantaged, the Spanish soundly trounced the French and the Napoleonic army suffered their first open field defeat, which gave Spain hope that they might succeed against France.

The defeat also caused Napoleon to realize that he was personally needed in the Iberian Peninsula as an allied force composed of Spain, Britain and Portugal had formed against him. Napoleon also realized that he needed Russia's support against Spain and against any possible conflict that might erupt with Austria. So, in October, at the Congress of Erfurt, which was intended to reaffirm the alliance previously resolved by the Treaties of Tilsit, Napoleon worked hard to keep Russia as an ally and that country reconfirmed its status.

Napoleon returned to France, prepared for war and crossed the Ebro River with his Grande Armée. He inflicted a series of punishing defeats on Spain and triumphantly entered Madrid on 4 December. However, Napoleon would eventually leave Iberia to deal with Austria. As the Peninsular War raged on without him, Lieutenant General Wellington (later the Duke of Wellington) left Cork on 12 July 1808 heading to Iberia. He would participate in what would become a complex deadlock of warring parties attempting to gain the upper hand through brutal guerrilla warfare tactics that resulted in horrible atrocities on both sides.

Meanwhile, the Récamiers' Mont Blanc home finally sold in September of 1808 and Jacques-Rose and his wife moved to No. 32 rue Basse-du-Rempart with Juliette's father and his childhood friend, Monsieur Simonard. Juliette travelled to Coppet to reunite with Germaine a year later in the autumn of 1809. The next year, in the summer, the two women met again at the tenth century Château de Chaumont, near Blois.

Germaine had been tirelessly working on a literary and philosophical novel, *De l'Allemagne,* that contained historical and contemporary observations by her, and she would continue to work on it for the next two years. Part of her tirelessness had to do with a love interest she had made years earlier in 1794 with Henri-Benjamin Constant. He was a Swiss-French activist and writer of politics and religion who quickly became enamoured with Germaine.

At the time of their first meeting, Germaine was still married but having an affair with Narbonne-Lara, who was her first love. As her passion for Narbonne-Lara continued to grow, his passion for her began to fizzle. When she learned he had been unfaithful, she was so distraught she declared she would swallow poison rather than live without him. The threat did not work and their relationship ended.

Like Narbonne-Lara, Constant's meeting with Germaine was fateful, but from the start, a relationship between the two seemed unlikely. Although they shared a Swiss background and belonged to the Protestant faith, Germaine found him unattractive. He was not dashing like Narbonne-Lara and in fact she wrote that he was 'outstandingly ugly'. To make matters worse, he was said to be half blind and wiry with a pot-belly. He also had shocking red hair that was either worn in falling curls at his neck or braided and held up by a comb. He was also endowed with a caustic tongue, freckled face, blue-grey eyes, a nervous tic and poor posture.

Although Germaine found him extremely intelligent, the two were also opposite in nature. Constant was weak, Germaine was strong; he was cold, she was warm; he was calculating, she was sympathetic. Their childhoods were also different. Constant's angelic and sweet mother died when he was born and he was raised by a timid but brusque father and two grandmothers who spoiled him.

It was while separated from his wife that Constant met Germaine. Initially, he thought of her as a friend and described her as talkative, active and imprudent. He also noted that she was clever and a wonderful listener. However, his liking increased over time because the more he was around her, the wittier he thought she was and then he began imagining a relationship with her.

Unfortunately for him, Germaine's impression remained the same. Several people noted that she received his attentions 'coldly'. Moreover, after her break up with Narbonne-Lara, she became interested in pursuing a relationship with a Swedish count and politician named Adolph Ribbing. It was to Ribbing that she wrote the following:

> 'M. Constant … I think, has conceived a passion for me that is beyond description, he is at death's door and overwhelms me with so much misery that it deprives of his one charm – a very superior mind – and inflicts on me a kind of compassion that both wearies me and reminds me that my Adolph perhaps never, never loved me so deeply.'[1]

Despite Germaine's coldness to him, Constant became part of her trusted inner circle and when not with her, he busied himself by writing to her, sometimes sending as many as five letters a day. He also embraced some strange ideas about how to demonstrate his passion for her. One idea involved him once smashing his head against her chimney when she asked him to leave her room; another time, he attempted suicide to prove his love for her.

He may have been so taken with Germaine in part because she inspired him just like she had inspired Narbonne-Lara. She also praised and encouraged him, and it was heady for him to receive such compliments from an accomplished author like Germaine. With her help, he also became focused and it was because of her that he began writing about political affairs, which she then promoted.

When Napoleon gained fame with his whiff of grapeshot, Germaine was visiting in Paris. She was then ordered to leave, but, fortunately, protests by her husband and some friends resulted in that order being rescinded. However, Germaine decided to leave anyway and cited health reasons for her departure. She then headed to the healing thermal waters of Forges-les-Eaux in Normandy with Constant following her. After a brief return to Paris, they then left for Coppet, where they remained until December of 1796.

While at Coppet, Germaine and Constant both wrote, but he left periodically to return to Paris. It was during one return trip that he won Germaine's heart when the French journalist Louis-François Bertin de Vaux wrote an article and called him a 'terrorist'. Constant cried libel and challenged Vaux to a pistol duel. The two men met at dawn in the thickly wooded forest of Bois de Boulogne. Germaine received word about the duel even before Constant sent her a note informing her of it and leaving her his papers, a ring, his house and his estate of La Chablière.

Germaine had always been a romantic at heart, loving and wanting love. The idea that Constant might die in a duel was a passionate fairy tale come to life. She loved his courage. She loved his passion. She loved his heroics. Fortunately, no duel occurred because Vaux and Constant reconciled before either were shot, but Germaine's heart was bursting with such love that she could hardly wait for Constant's return.

Their love survived but became rocky after Germaine's father died at Coppet on 9 April 1804. As Germaine's father had been her best friend, she felt rudderless without him. Overwhelmed with grief, Germaine needed continual attention and the lack of it from Constant caused continual fights and endless reconciliations. As their relationship deteriorated, he stated, 'I am deeply attached to all at Coppet, but this continual activity, this perpetual distraction, fatigues and unnerves me. I lose my strength and I ask myself bitterly, "When will this end?"'[2]

As the relationship was in its death throes, Napoleon made the most of the year 1810. He conquered Austria and knew that a new Franco-Austrian alliance was needed if war was to be avoided. One way to avoid warfare and strengthen his dynasty was for him to divorce Josephine and marry the Holy Roman Emperor Francis II's daughter, the Austrian archduchess Marie Louise, who was also the great niece of Marie Antoinette. So, on 30 November 1810, Napoleon told Josephine he wanted a divorce. Her cries and shrieks reputedly reverberated throughout the palace before she collapsed onto the floor and had to be carried to her apartments.

As Germaine added the final touches to *De l'Allemagne*, Napoleon celebrated his marriage to Marie Louise. He would later say that although he loved her when he married her on 2 April 1810, he loved Josephine more and would have never left Josephine if she could have given him a son. But he did leave her.

To celebrate his new nuptials, a fete was hosted by Prince Joseph Schwarzenberg, a loyal subject of Francis II. It was held on 1 July at the Austrian Embassy on the Chausée d'Antin. It was an elegant affair and to properly accommodate guests, a spacious timber-planked ballroom 'was erected, of very slight frame-work … and protected by a cloth awning [gauze, muslin, and other light stuffs] richly covered over'.[3] Furthermore, to light the area, there were an immense number of 'lustres' suspended from the ceiling, and, in addition, candles were sprinkled about to increase the illumination of the happy affair.

Hungarian Prince Esterházy opened the ball around ten o'clock in the evening. He was followed by Prince Schwarzenberg and his wife, the Princess Pauline, who was mother to nine children. Besides Napoleon, his new Empress and other royalty, many other impressive guests attended. By midnight, between 1,200 to 1,500 guests appeared and the ball-room and its approaches were filled beyond capacity with those celebrating the marriage. It was a glorious fete described as follows:

> 'Some singers, representing the Muses, sang a joyous chorus. Napoleon and the Empress then walked on to a cascade; harmonious sounds issued from a subterraneous grotto which led to a vine-clad arbour, ornamented with mirror, monograms, flowers and wreaths. Then a concert partly German partly French took place, and Their Imperial Majesties continued to wander about the garden till they came to a Temple of Victory and the muse Clio and Fame, where trumpets pealed, followed by songs of triumph; the whole are loaded with perfumes burning on gold tripods, and a beautiful ballet was danced on the lawn, which was intended

> to recall Luxemburg, that favourite resort of Marie Louise's. Their Majesties then returned by the wooden gallery to the ball-room.'[4]

Then midnight struck! A wax candle accidentally tipped. It lit one of the garlands that decorated the walls, and it in turn caught a gauze curtain on fire. Attempts were made to pull down the blazing curtain, but before that could be accomplished the fire spread, setting everything that was nearby ablaze. The fire spread stunningly fast and gave no one time to think.

An alarm was raised, but firemen did not respond immediately and, as the danger increased, Napoleon was informed. He had just been introduced to the Princess Schwarzenberg's daughter and was across the room from the Empress when he learned the news. He then rushed to Marie Louise and led her safely back to the Tuileries Palace.

As the Emperor was taking his new wife to safety, panic spread among the guests, who only now discovered the fire. In their flight to escape, passageways quickly became choked with people rushing in all dirctions. Moreover, the fire had now nearly engulfed the entire timber-planked ballroom and because of the crush of people trying to flee, escape became more difficult.

As the burning structure fell in on those remaining in the ballroom, no firemen appeared. When at last they did, there were only six, several were drunk and they were completely unprepared as their engines had no water. Fortunately, with other aid and quick thinking by guests, the fire was eventually extinguished.

Napoleon heard about the deadly consequences of the fire the following morning while he was at St. Cloud. Among the revelations was that numerous victims were burned, some victims suffered hideous scars and a dozen or so people died, among whom were several women, including the Princess Pauline Schwarzenberg. She had escaped the blazing structure but became so worried about her daughter, she foolishly returned. She was consumed by fire and her jewels were the only remains indicating she had been there.

Two other women also died. One was Madame Touzard, the wife of a general officer of the artillery. She had been caught up in the blaze and killed. There was also the Countess de la Layen, wife of the Russian consul-general. She died several days later due to her wounds. She, like the Princess Schwarzenberg, had returned to find her daughter and became a victim of the fire when the blazing structure fell on her.

In mid-September, the last volume of Germaine's three-volume *De l'Allemagne* was ready to be published in Paris. Napoleon's censors had the proofs for it and had already approved the first two volumes. Unexpectedly, however, Germaine received news that the Minister of Police had been directed to seize the proofs and she was being ordered to leave the country. On 30 September, Germaine wrote to Juliette, as she was one of the only people who could console her:

> 'Dear Friend, I have fallen into a state of frightful sadness. … I was counting on the effect of my book for keeping me up. There are six years of work, study and travelling as good as lost … the two first volumes which had already been passed by the censor were the ones that were seized … and so I am sent forty leagues away because I have written a book which was approved by the [Emperor's] censors. That is not all … I should never finish, my dear friend, if I were to discuss this subject.'[5]

Napoleon resented Germaine and *De l'Allemagne*, which he declared to be anti-French and anti-patriotic. The printing shops that produced it had their plates destroyed on 11 October 1810 and the proofs were destroyed a few days later. Additionally, copies in circulation that could be located were seized and destroyed.

Germaine was heartbroken, but she could do nothing more than protest Napoleon's harshness and resume living in exile. She had been hoping to return to France and had applied through the Austrian minister Klemens von Metternich, believing that Napoleon would allow her to do so. Unfortunately for her, the request went nowhere as Napoleon was having none it. He viewed her as a threat and said to Metternich:

> 'If Madame de Staël would be, or could be, either a Royalist or a Republican, I should have nothing to say against her; but she is a machine in motion which will make a disturbance in the *salons*. It is only in France that such a woman is to be feared, and I will not agree to [let her return].'[6]

Germaine's loneliness was exacerbated by a permanent end to her relationship with Constant. He had decided the only solution was complete emancipation from her. It was difficult, though, because years earlier they had drawn up a document swearing eternal fidelity. They had also pooled their resources and money. Moreover, Germaine had enormous sway and power, so that in 1811, when Constant said a final goodbye, he found himself forever indebted to her.

In the meantime, Juliette was heartbroken over Germaine's exile, but there was little she could do. In fact, her own loyalty was being questioned and Napoleon's agents were watching her as he was greatly irritated about her ongoing friendship with Germaine. It was also difficult for Juliette to suffer the constant begging by her friend to come and see her. It did not help when Germaine wrote the following: 'One is almost dead … when one is exiled. It is merely a tomb where the post arrives'.[7]

Germaine's sad words finally caused Juliette to decide she must risk everything. She made plans to see her friend and on 23 August 1811, she departed for Coppet on a mission of 'heroic devotion'. To ensure Germaine knew, she also wrote to her telling her of her intention to see her. However, to confuse Napoleon's agents who might be watching, Juliette announced she was going to the watering hole of Aix-en-Savoie and acquired her passport for that place.

Amidst Juliette's trip, Germaine sent her a note using her now 21-year-old son Auguste de Staël as the courier. He had become enamoured by Juliette's plentiful charms and was in fact spellbound and passionately in love with her. However, his romantic feelings created a touchy situation for Juliette because she knew she could not displease him without displeasing his mother.

Before Juliette arrived at Germaine's on 30 August, Napoleon gave orders to locate Juliette and tell her that she had been banished. However, before official word arrived, other sources told Juliette that she had been exiled. She still decided to follow through with her trip to see the lonely Germaine but spent just one night at Coppet. Mathieu was also there visiting, having received his own letter of banishment from Napoleon a few days earlier.

It seems that the Emperor was upset with anyone who supported Germaine and he was willing to punish them. Juliette still hoped to protect herself and avoid exile, so she stayed but one night and started back to Paris the following day. Regrettably, on 3 September, while at Dijon, she received official notification of her banishment and learned that she must remain forty leagues away from Paris.

Unable to remain in Paris anymore, Juliette chose Châlons-sur-Marne for her exile as it was precisely forty leagues away. However, before going there, she returned incognito one last time to Paris. She stayed for two days and when she left for Châlons, she was accompanied by her niece, 7-year-old Amélie Cyvoct, whom she had adopted a few weeks earlier.

Juliette knew that her correspondence was being monitored and she had been warned not to see any of her friends while living in exile. However, nothing stopped Germaine's son, Auguste, from visiting her. Germaine also continued to write, and the two women made plans to see each other in Germany if measures against them were not soon revoked. In the meantime, Juliette, unlike Germaine, prudently forbade her friends from coming to Châlons to visit. She feared that if they did, they might be banished also.

Chapter 13

Juliette's Exile

Those days in Rome are gone to return no more!
Ballanche to Juliette

Prince Augustus had not forgotten Juliette. He had continued to think of her since they parted, and he continued to imagine a life together. He finally obtained a promise from her that she would meet him at Schaffhausen, Switzerland, in the autumn of 1811. Augustus was so excited that he set out for the Swiss city without obtaining a proper leave of absence and was cruelly disappointed when Juliette failed to appear.

His unhappiness was relayed to Germaine: 'At last I hope that I am cured of a foolish passion that I have cherished for four years'.[1] However, his letter to Juliette was much more subdued. He asked her why she did not wish to see him and why she would cause him to undertake a 'useless' journey when she had no intention of being there.

> 'After four years of absence, I hoped at last to see you again, and this exile seemed to furnish you with a pretext for coming to Switzerland; … What I cannot comprehend is, that, not being able or not wishing to see me, you did not condescend to tell me so, … I leave to-morrow for the mountains of Oberland and the Petits Cantons. The wild nature of these countries will be in harmony with my sad thoughts, of which you are the sole object.'[2]

Despite his sadness, Augustus continued to correspond with Juliette during the time she lived in Châlons, an area where the most remarkable thing was a magnificent estate nearby called La Rouchefoucalds Doudeaville. It was owned by close friends of hers, the Duke and Duchess of Doudeaville, who had a son, Sosthènes, who was married to Mathieu's only daughter.

Despite the nearness of the estate, the Duke and Duchess could not visit Juliette too often without incurring the Emperor's displeasure and so Juliette found herself frequently lonely and bored. Part of her boredom was due to the lack of public entertainment in the area and the few guests willing to visit her besides her husband, cousin, father and her father's friend, Simonard.

To staunch the boredom, Juliette decided to befriend the organist of the local parish and thereafter she played the organ at high mass every Sunday. Eight months passed in this dull and boring fashion with the only break in the monotony being an infrequent visit by someone or an occasional letter brought by Auguste from his mother. It was in one of these letters that Germaine suggested Juliette go to Lyon stating:

> 'You are without relations as you are without an equal. Leave a spot where every thing is noticed, because there is nobody there.'[3]

Juliette finally decided her friend was right and took her advice, leaving in June 1812 for Lyon, a city in east central France where the Rhône and Saône rivers converge south of it. Historically, the city made a name for itself in the late 1400s when it became the first city to have a printing establishment and produced books written in Greek, Latin, Hebrew, Italian and French. The Lyonnais revolted during the French Revolution and it was d'Herbois and Fouché who cleansed it.

Because of the revolt, on 12 October 1793, a leading member of the National Convention proposed certain houses and buildings in Lyon be destroyed and the city lose its name. It thus was renamed *Ville-Affranchie* (Liberated or Liberty City), and on the ruins a commemorative plaque declared: 'Lyon made war against Liberty — Lyon nor longer exists'.[4] However, about ten years later Napoleon ordered the rebuilding of the city and it once again became Lyon.

In comparison to Châlons, there were many things for Juliette to see and do there. The Museum of Fine Arts of Lyon opened in 1803 and a university was established there in 1808. There were also numerous charitable foundations and benevolent institutions, along with a library that offered a commanding view of the Rhone. One of the supposedly handsomest buildings in Europe existed there, the Hotel de Ville, built in 1647 and there was a bustling population of over 100,000 people, including Juliette's relatives and the Récamier family.

Another person of interest was the elegant Madame Chevreuse, who had been exiled and had established her residence there in 1808. Her problem with Napoleon began after she was pressured by her mother-in-law, the

Duchess of Luynes, to become part of his court by insisting Madame Chevreuse accept a position as lady of honour to the Empress. This Madame Chevreuse did, but was extremely unhappy. The Emperor tried to appease her for having forced the position upon her, but it did not matter what he did because she brought with her 'all the disdain and haughtiness of the old régime'.[5]

Of course, her implacable attitude displeased Napoleon and things soon got worse. After the royal family of Spain was arrested and taken to Fontainebleau, Napoleon decided Madame Chevreuse should be the one attached to serve (or rather guard) them. When she discovered his plans, she replied that she would not be their jailor and would rather serve as a prisoner herself. Thus, he complied by exiling her.

Madame Chevreuse had always been delicate in health and therefore extremely spoiled. Yet, despite her ill health, she was known for her wilful personality, fabulous wit and striking red hair. Napoleon once decided to punish her because of her uncooperative attitude and thinking that her red hair was a sore point, said:

> '"What shocking red hair you have, Madame de Chevreuse." The lady courtesied deeply, and answered with great quickness, – "I may very possibly have red hair, but your Majesty is the first gentleman who ever told me so."'[6]

Juliette, Madame Chevreuse and Mathieu's mother-in-law, the Duchess of Luynes, soon formed a warm friendship. The Duchess had a masculine aura with hard features and a coarse voice. She also tended to dress in masculine fashion and when she did try to pull off a feminine style, she looked peculiar because she wore a large, ample gown with two pockets and a high cap. Yet, for all her masculinity, it was impossible not to recognize her as a woman of noble standing.

Besides the friendship with Madame Chevreuse and the Duchess, Juliette also became acquainted with others from Lyon. For instance, two guests were visiting her when a Lyonnais gentleman, known only as M.G. de B., stopped by after learning Juliette was staying at the Hôtel de l'Europe. He had met her when he visited Paris and had been well-received by the Récamiers. Now he wanted to return the favour.

Unfortunately, he had not yet heard that Juliette had been exiled and so he invited her and her two guests to a fete. She hesitated, but he insisted, and as he would not accept her refusal, Juliette and her guests reluctantly agreed to attend. Delighted at his great luck, M.G. de B. then began proclaiming to anyone who would listen that Juliette was attending his fete, but when he learned that she had been exiled, he despaired and knew he must make her visit as short as possible.

On the appointed day, Juliette and her guests appeared at his gate. To their surprise, it was open and after inquiring, they learned their host was in the garden. When they reached the garden, they discovered him:

> '[He was] astride on the balustrade of a ring-game of which he was counting the strokes. When he saw the three guests whose society he had so obstinately solicited, he did not condescend to get down, but gave them a patronizing little nod, and went on marking the points. Such visitors were not in the habit of being thus treated: they exchanged looks of astonishment, went back to their carriage, and returned to Lyon.'[7]

Initially, Juliette and her guests were offended by their host's behaviour but later they found the situation laughable and amusing. As for M.G. de B., word of his odd behaviour became the talk of the town only because he repeated the story to several people. It was also reported that 'his frankness and stupidity were so complete, … he did not even make an apology'.[8]

While in Lyon, Juliette's niece and adopted daughter Amélie claimed that she first saw the famous shawl dance that had inspired Germaine in 1807 when she wrote *Corinne or Italy,* a fictional narrative and travelogue that discusses the issues of artistic creativity of females in England and Italy. According to Amélie, Juliette had become bored one day and decided to demonstrate it:

> 'With a long scarf in her hand, she went through all the poses, wherein the light tissue becomes in turn a girdle, a veil, and a drapery. Nothing could be more graceful, more decorous, or more picturesque than this succession of harmonious attitudes, worthy to be perpetuated by the pencil of an artist.'[9]

Juliette found Lyon better than Châlons as she had plenty to occupy her time, but her goal of reuniting with her friend Germaine failed. Germaine did not visit, although Auguste did. Apparently, the reason she failed to appear was because she was madly in love with a new man. He was a young Swiss officer, twenty-three years her junior, remarkably handsome, noble in character, and named Albert Jean Michel de Rocca. Juliette didn't know about this romance and in 1811, the same year that Marie Louise delivered Napoleon's son, Napoléon François Charles Joseph Bonaparte called from birth the King of Rome, the lovers secretly married. Juliette was also unaware that Germaine delivered Rocca's son, Louis-Alphonse Rocca, a year later, on 7 April 1812.

Mathieu arrived in Lyon at the close of January 1813 and encouraged Juliette to travel to Rome. She took his advice and left with her maid and Amélie. When they arrived in Turin, she stayed for a few days before travelling to Rome.

One of the first places she visited in Rome was the workshop of the most celebrated artist in Europe, the Italian neoclassical sculptor Antonio Canova, who had also been hired to make a bust of Napoleon in 1802. Juliette found his workshop delightful, admired his marble sculptures and gave her name to an attendant hoping to meet Canova personally and praise him. The sculptor was impressed and immediately appeared.

While in Rome, Juliette also received a note from the Duchess of Luynes about the precarious health of Madame Chevreuse and the fact that her illness was such there was little hope of recovery. The first note arrived on 10 June and stated that her daughter-in-law was extremely weak, haemorrhaging, and had swollen hands and feet. The next letter, dated 3 July, stated she was swollen from her feet to her waist and had difficulty swallowing and finally, on 18 July, news arrived that she had died.

Around the time of Madame Chevreuse's death, Pierre-Simon Ballanche arrived in Rome. Like many men before him, when he met Juliette, he was immediately fascinated by her. He called upon her the next day as she was embroidering and although their conversation was stilted and boring at first, it soon turned to the interesting topics of philosophy, literature and politics.

Juliette became captivated by their conversation but also noticed a horrible odour and realized it was coming from Ballanche's new leather shoes. The smell finally overcame her discomfort and she timidly confessed that his shoes were producing an unbearable, foul stench. Ballanche immediately excused himself and returned moments later in stockinged feet. When some new visitors called and spied Ballanche's feet, he matter-of-factly announced that his leather shoes had bothered his hostess so much he removed them.

Ballanche was not a handsome fellow. Some people even called him ugly. This was because of a frightful facial disfigurement which had occurred after he experienced excruciating headaches and went to a charlatan hoping to cure them. Instead of a cure, the remedy made things worse and resulted in him suffering a chronic problem known as caries of the jaw-bone. To solve that problem, surgery was required, the consequence of which was that a portion of his face was thereafter severely swollen, as if he had a toothache.

Over time, Ballanche became one of Juliette's most intimate friends. She admired his sentiments and she was kind to the point that Mohl declared, 'he expanded like a drooping plant in the sunshine of her presence'.[10] Historian and writer Hugh Noel Williams wrote of their interesting relationship:

> '[Juliette] led this shy, retiring, austere thinker into a new world; she taught him that there were more things in heaven and earth than were dreamed of in his philosophy; she inspired his best efforts, and encouraged him to accomplish work which, otherwise, he would have been too modest even to attempt.'[11]

With Juliette's encouragement, Ballanche, who had lived through the cleansing of Lyon, would go on to become a celebrated poet and counter-revolutionary philosopher. His philosophy was an original system based on a theology of progress achieved through ordeals. His ideas also embraced change based on expiation and involved sanctified suffering. He did not remain long in Rome and when he left, he expressed his sentiments to Juliette in a note dated 10 July 1813:

> 'I am between Rome and Lyons. It seems to me I am entirely out of my element. I find no resources within myself, not even enough to aid me in passing the time. What a poor sad nature is mine! Those days in Rome are gone to return no more! Oh that I could live them over again, or at least, if I could know that you are in a state of repose, taking an interest in life and smiling at vexations! But I have too much reason to think that you also lead an irksome life. I think of you on the doleful terrace of the doleful palace where you live, – a veritable exile's home.'[12]

In August, the weather became hot and stifling and as malaria was a real possibility, Canova invited Juliette to go to Albano, an area about 12 miles southeast of Rome. It was also the site of the seventeenth-century Papal Palace of Castel Gandolfo that served as a summer residence for the Pope.

Juliette accepted and for the next two months, as Canova worked, every morning Juliette and Amélie took a leisurely stroll along verdant pathways called galleries that bordered Lake Albano.

Juliette also made the acquaintance of the local organist and just as she had played for the congregation every Sunday in Châlons, she began playing for the congregation in Albano. One Sunday when she was returning home after mass, she saw a crowd around a doorway and when she inquired as to why, they told her a local fisherman had been accused of complicity with the English. At that precise moment, the prisoner's confessor appeared. He asked Juliette to intervene with French authorities, as they were the ones who would determine the fisherman's fate.

Without knowing exactly how, Juliette found herself at the prison's cell door. There she found a prisoner clapped in irons who appeared to be in great fear and who begged her to save him from certain death. As his execution was slated for the next morning, Juliette had no time to lose and immediately ordered her carriage. Unfortunately, despite visiting several French authorities, she received no satisfaction and in fact she was chastised for interfering as she was an exile with no standing.

The next morning, the fisherman was executed. He stood with his eyes transfixed towards Rome and hoped that Juliette would appear on the horizon to save him. Although Juliette was unable to do so, she later claimed to have found comfort in that fact that she had given the poor man some peace because he rested well the night before his execution, ate a good breakfast the following morning and had no fear up until the last few moments of his life.

Chapter 14

The Russian Campaign

Horrible day! 27 degrees. An immense number of soldiers remained dead on the road.
Boniface de Castellane

In the same month that Juliette reached Lyon, the Grande Armée crossed the Neman (sometimes spelled Nieman) River in June 1812. Napoleon had decided that war with Russia was inevitable and his official aim was to liberate Poland from the threat of Russia, which for legitimacy he named the Second Polish War. However, the unofficial and real reason for Napoleon's Russian campaign was that he was tired of Tsar Alexander's boldness, insults and contempt. Napoleon hoped to compel the Tsar to stop trading with Britain, which would thereby cause Britain to sue for peace.

Some months earlier, the 'Great Comet of 1811' supposedly portended success for Napoleon and encouraged him to invade Russia. It was discovered on 25 March 1811 by Honoré Flaugergues and was visible for 260 days, making its brightest appearance in October. Napoleon viewed it as a sure sign of success and as a guiding star for his destiny. Some of his advisors also saw it as a favourable sign for his invasion and Europeans began referring to the dazzling light in the sky as 'Napoleon's Comet'.

Even without its appearance, Napoleon had grand plans to defeat the Russian army using the divide-and-conquer approach. He expected it to take twenty days and to help him accomplish this goal, he had somewhere between 500,000 to over 600,000 soldiers, about twice the size of the Russian forces. Also accompanying him were camp followers consisting of unarmed men, some soldiers' wives and their children. He believed that his army would easily crush Russian forces.

From the start, the Emperor, who admired the Roman leader Julius Caesar and emulated him, appeared unlucky in what came to be known in France as the Russian Campaign. As the Grand Armée was marching to war, somewhere near the Neman River in the early morning hours, Napoleon abandoned his carriage to reconnoitre the area from horseback. Near a bank and without warning, his horse suddenly threw him to the ground. Being highly superstitious, he supposedly exclaimed, 'This is a bad omen. A Roman would recoil'.[1]

Napoleon's signal for his soldiers to attack was given in the dead of night and after they made their move, they quickly discovered that the banks of the Neman River were undefended. There was no fight at the border because there was but one single Cossack who was highly surprised when they appeared.

More back luck followed when the Russians proved uncooperative with Napoleon's strategy. Instead of fighting, they kept retreating, which greatly disappointed the Emperor and prevented him from engaging the enemy in any decisive battle. Furthermore, it caused him to continually pursue them. His aide-de-camp, Philippe Paul de Segur, who was present at the time when the French invaded Russia recounted the scene:

> 'Napoleon hastened to plant his foot on the Russian territory. This first step towards his ruin he took without hesitation. At first he stationed himself near the bridge, encouraging the soldiers by his looks. They saluted him with their accustomed acclamations as they passed. They appeared, indeed, more animated than himself; whether it was that he felt oppressed by the weight of so great an aggression, or that his enfeebled frame could not support the effect of the excessive heat, or that he was astonished at finding nothing to conquer.
>
> 'At length he became impatient; all at once he dashed across the country into the forest which girt the sides of the river. He put his horse to the extremity of his speed, and in his eagerness he seemed desirous to come singly in contact with the enemy. He rode more than a league in the same direction, surrounded throughout by the same solitude. … In a short time the sky became overcast, the wind rose and brought with it the inauspicious mutterings of a thunder-storm. That menacing sky and shelterless country filled us with melancholy impressions. There were even some among us who, enthusiastic as they had lately been, were terrified at what they conceived to be a fatal presage. To them it appeared as though those combustible vapors were collected over our heads, and descending upon the territory we were approaching, to prevent us from entering.'[2]

Despite all the bad omens, Napoleon's troops pressed on, pursuing the Russian army and hoping for battle. As the monstrous army moved forward it did so slowly and experienced difficulties sending communications and supplies to the front. However, a major battle did occur in western Russia at the city of Smolensk in August and although the French won, the Russian army slipped away as the city burned.

Napoleon had underestimated his opponents. The size of his army caused the Russians to decide it would not be wise to attack. Their scorched-earth policy also caused Napoleon problems, because his plan for his men to forage proved unfeasible and forced them to rely more heavily on their own supply system than had been intended. Thus, almost from the beginning, supplies were being overused and he would soon be incapable of feeding his monstrous army of soldiers.

On 7 September, Napoleon's army, now consisting of about 130,000 men, caught up again with Russia's 154,000 soldiers in the town of Borodino, located about seventy miles west of Moscow. It was the Russians' last chance to stop the French before they entered the city. The battle of Borodino that unfolded resulted in staggering casualties numbering 77,000, the bloodiest single-day of action in the Napoleonic Wars. The higher death count of 44,000 went to the Russians while the French lost 33,000. Fortunately for the French, they were considered to have narrowly won, but they hardly had time to enjoy their victory as the Russian army withdrew the following day.

Napoleon's Grand Armée was once again marching and once again pursuing the Russian Army as it retreated to Moscow. A week later, cheers erupted when Napoleon's soldiers came within sight of the glittering and colourful sun-streaked city. However, when the French trudged in, they found it desolate and quiet, as most Muscovites had already evacuated under orders from the governor, Count Fyodor Vasilievich Rostopchin.

The Emperor thought he might find supplies in Moscow, but he instead found enormous quantities of hard liquor and little food. Moreover, the evening after his arrival, small fires were set around the city by Russian patriots under orders of Rostopchin. The French could not put out the flames as all the firefighting equipment had been removed. Thus, the fires leapt from one building to the next until about 80 per cent of the city was engulfed in flames. All Napoleon could do was flee the Kremlin, take up quarters at the Petrovsky Palace and helplessly watch the city burn.

Encamped near Moscow, Napoleon hoped the Tsar would sue for peace, but as Napoleon's position grew worse with each passing day, he found the stubborn Alexander had no intention of negotiating. After waiting a month,

Napoleon ordered his troops out of Moscow on 19 October. The arduous and difficult retreat that followed lasted until December with the defeated French army unravelling along the way. Over the course of the campaign, the French would succumb to desertion, typhus, suicide, starvation and exposure.

Desertion by French soldiers had begun early in the campaign. Some soldiers left before they crossed the Neman River and others disappeared soon after they marched into Russia and found themselves hungry and facing disease. At the time, France never acknowledged deserters and so they did not count those who did, but there may have been as many as 30,000 deserters roaming and pillaging the countryside.

Lice was a more serious issue than desertion as they were a wingless enemy that appeared soon after the soldiers crossed the Neman. This obligate parasite lived on warm-blooded hosts and survived by feeding on skin and debris or by piercing the host's skin and feeding on blood and other secretions. The lice fed on fever-ridden humans and once having ingested the pathogen for typhus, known as rickettsia, the insect's gut ruptured resulting in the disease being present in their faeces. Humans then infected themselves by scratching or rubbing the faeces into their skin or mucous membranes.

Suicide was another problem. When Napoleon entered Russia, the heat, typhus and food shortages quickly began to take their toll. Famished soldiers became unreasonable when searching for food and sometimes when they discovered a cottage and descended on it, they would accost and molest innocent residents or inflict unfair or abusive punishments upon the inhabitants and then, ashamed of their barbarous behaviour, they committed suicide. Segur noted:

> 'Some there were who actually destroyed themselves rather than proceed to such extremities; others, after having done so; and these were chiefly the youngest … placed their foreheads on their muskets and blew out their brains in the middle of the highway.'[3]

Starvation was a problem throughout the campaign and worsened as it neared its end. Retreating soldiers found their hunger all-consuming, and the starving men could think of nothing else but self-preservation. Hungry and starving soldiers ate all the horses that were dying in droves by attacking them like a pack of wolves, tearing them to pieces the minute they fell or broiling them while still warm and bleeding. Segur wrote:

> '[F]amine … detached every man from his neighbour, isolated him, and centred him utterly within himself. We did not exhaust ourselves in provocations – not even complaints – we marched silently, husbanding all our resources against the hostile climate; diverted from every reflection by incessant action and incessant suffering.'[4]

When the horses were gone, the soldiers were so desperate that they ate their dead comrades. If that was not bad enough, they also faced freezing to death. The cold was intense and as Napoleon had only planned on being in Russia during the summer months, the soldiers lacked the proper clothing and footwear necessary to survive Russia's bitter winter.

Segur's description of what he saw is indicative of how badly the soldiers suffered. He stated that soldiers were dressed like 'spectres covered with rags, women's pelisses, bits of carpet, or with dirty cloaks scorched and burnt by the fire of the bivouacs, and with feet wrapped in the most wretched tatters'.[5] In addition, Boniface de Castellane, who had left Paris in 1812, served as aide-de-camp to Germaine's one-time lover, General Narbonne-Lara, and then worked in Napoleon's personal protection detail, provided another description of the poor state of Napoleon's army. In his daily diary he penned:

> 'Horrible day! 27 degrees. An immense number of soldiers remained dead on the road. We saw many corpses of the Neapolitan division. The soldiers fall; a little blood comes to their lips, and all is over. When they see this sign of approaching death, their comrades often give them a push, throw them on the ground, and take their clothes before they are quite dead.'[6]

The French public knew little of the details even though, as in other campaigns, Napoleon published propaganda bulletins containing war news. The bulletins were republished for the general public's consumption by the government's official mouthpiece, the *Moniteur.* Napoleon's exaggerations (and sometimes outright lies) in the bulletins eventually resulted in the phrase 'to lie like a bulletin.'

The twenty-ninth bulletin was published on 16 December and discussed the cold, the ice, and how cavalry, artillery and baggage horses had perished by the thousands. Nevertheless, it ended on an upbeat note with the final line reading, 'The Emperor's health has never been better'.[7] While the

Emperor's health may have been of great importance to his French subjects, the bulletin neglected to mention the hundreds of thousands of soldiers who died in the disastrous Russian Campaign.

The last obstacle Napoleon faced when getting his army out of Russia was the Berezina River, a tributary of the Dnieper River in Belarus. Napoleon's plan was to cross the frozen river, but upon his arrival at Studzianka, instead of a frozen river that would be easy to ford, he was faced with a partially thawed flow of huge chunks of ice.

Napoleon had to act quick to solve this crisis. That is when Nicolas Charles Oudinot, who was wounded 34 times in battle, suggested a plan to outwit the Russians by sending stragglers down river to make it look as if the French might cross to the south. The stragglers' actions caused the Russian military leader and naval commander Admiral Pavel Chichagov to move his army accordingly.

As Chichagov and most of his troops were being drawn off, Napoleon busied his engineers, ordering them on the night of 25 November to build two 300-foot bridges. They had the expertise and equipment to do so and those employed in the task were courageous enough to brave icy waters that could kill them very quickly. Twenty-first century historian Robert Harvey provides the details:

> 'The bridges were erected some 200 yards apart, supported by twenty-three trestles. They were connected by sappers doing fifteen-minute shifts during the freezing night in the icy waters, which was all they could sustain; many were swept away and drowned or died of exposure. Only forty of the 400 "*pontonniers*" who built the bridge survived. … They worked all night, standing up to their shoulders in ice-cold waters.'[8]

At 1pm the first bridge was completed for the use of the infantry and the cavalry and at 4pm a heavier second bridge was finished to accommodate equipment, artillery and horses. As the French crossed, four Swiss infantry regiments acted as their rear-guard. About the time French forces were arriving safely on the other side, Chichagov realized he had been tricked.

Around midday on the 27th, after Napoleon and his Imperial Guard crossed, they swung back to protect the Swiss rear-guard, who had suffered extreme losses but whose bravery saved most of the French troops. Later that same afternoon, stragglers and civilians were given orders to cross that night, but instead, they sheltered at Studzianka.

The following day, the armies commanded by Mikhail Kutuzov and Peter Wittgenstein converged with Chicagov and they launched a brutal attack against the French rear-guard. As fighting was underway, stragglers, refugees and civilians crossed the bridge, but disaster soon struck when one span broke:

> 'The column which was in the act of crossing this narrow passage tried in vain to retreat. The crowd which pressed on from behind, unconscious of the disaster, and deaf to the cries of those before them, pushed forward and precipitated them into the chasm into which they were soon thrown in their turn.'[9]

This disaster was followed by a worse pandemonium when everyone flocked to the other bridge. Large lumbering caissons were also being urged to cross quickly by their drivers and in so doing, they crushed or ran over any unfortunate wretch among the thick mass of human beings that were also attempting to cross. Ségur again provides the nightmarish details:

> 'Whole ranks of men driven in desperate terror by these conflicting obstacles got entangled with them, were thrown down and crushed by other ranks who rushed on to the same fate in frightful and ceaseless succession. Thus, did the fearful torrent roll on, wave over wave; – nothing was heard but cries of rage, and agony, and despair. … The most fortunate gained the bridge, but not without trampling on still breathing heaps of wounded, of women and children thrown down and half suffocated. … In the column of desperate beings who crowded upon this solitary passage for escape, there now arose an infernal struggle; the weak, and those whose footing was insecure, were pushed into the river by the strong who, lost to every thing but the mere instinct of self-preservation, pushed furiously onwards to their end, … indifferent to the curses of rage and despair with which they were followed by their comrades or their officers, whom they sacrificed.'[10]

At 9pm, Claude Victor-Perrin, ordered the retreat of his own soldiers. Many stubborn stragglers and French civilians were still on the wrong side of the river, unwilling to cross because it was too cold or because they refused to abandon their luggage. In a last effort to get them to cross, their possessions were set on fire, but many still refused to leave until it was too late.

At half-past eight in the morning, as the Russian army approached, the bridges that had been taking the French to safety were set on fire to prevent the Russians from crossing. Wagons, carriages, several thousand men and some women and children were left behind to suffer their fate. The November crossing in 1812 had cost the lives of about 10,000 Russians, 20,000 French soldiers and 35,000 civilians. Afterwards, in France, the word 'Berezina' would be used to describe a catastrophe or disaster.

Napoleon had thought the end was near at Berezina, but he and his soldiers had survived. Now he turned his thoughts to Paris. Word had spread that he had been killed and based on that unsubstantiated rumour an unsuccessful coup had been launched to overthrow his government. He knew that he was needed at home to stop the rumours spreading further and to prevent another coup attempt, so he made all haste, leaving his army on 8 December and sending more bulletins about his good health.

While the Emperor may have been lauding his health, the result of his Russian Campaign was undeniable loss. He lost half a million good men, hundreds of thousands of reliable horses and an immeasurable number of cannons, equipment and supplies. However, his greatest loss was his invincible reputation. It took a significant blow as it was now completely clear to his enemies that he could be defeated.

Chapter 15

Rome, Naples, and Paris

Circumstances have led me to renounce the French throne.
Napoleon

Juliette remained living in exile during the Russian Campaign and, after a lull in the fighting during the winter of 1812-1813, a new coalition formed against Napoleon. Prussia declared war against France on 13 March 1813 and was joined by Russia, Britain and Sweden. The coalition later included Austria, Portugal and the rebels in Spain who were already at war with France in the Peninsular War. Napoleon suffered a disastrous defeat at the hands of the coalition, at the Battle of Leipzig in mid-October of 1813.

About a month and a half later, on 10 December, as Danish forces fighting for the French were victorious at the Battle of Sehested, Juliette completed her Italian tour by travelling to Naples to see Napoleon's sister, Madame Murat and her husband, whom Napoleon had named King of Naples on 1 August 1808. Travel to Naples was a dangerous undertaking because brigands frequently attacked travellers and so, as an extra precaution, Juliette travelled with an Englishman, Sir John Coghill, a famous antiquity collector.

Almost from the start, their journey seemed lucky as they continually made better time than expected, because at every relay, their carriages, postillions and horses were prepared and waiting. They could not believe their luck until around the last relay when they discovered why fortune had blessed them. Apparently, a courier riding ahead of them was ordering everything to be in readiness, but it was for another person and they had accidentally profited because of mistaken identity.

After learning this, Juliette was completing her toilette when she heard bells, horses and cracking whips. She glanced out the window and saw two carriages supplied with the same number of horses that she and Coghill had been using and realized it must be the traveller whose carriage they had so consistently taken. A few moments later she heard an angry man crying, 'Where are those insolent people who stole my horses on the whole route?'[1]

Juliette recognized the voice and when she opened the door, she could not help but laugh. There stood Fouché. He had been ordered to Rome and thence to Naples, to watch the movements of Napoleon's brother-in-law, Murat, and he had been the person the carriages were readied and ordered for by the courier. Although the last leg of Juliette's and Coghill's journey was somewhat slower, she must have taken great satisfaction in knowing that she had got the better of Fouché, if only for a time.

In Naples, Juliette had barely settled into her rooms when a note arrived from Madame Murat and her husband. They proclaimed their delight at her presence and requested that she make her appearance as soon as possible. Accordingly, the following morning, she presented herself.

Murat had long, curly hair and a well-proportioned figure. He was also described as strong, gallant and well-mannered and dressed flamboyantly, making him a dashing figure. However, he was also someone who lacked political ability. He wanted to honour his subjects, but after the disastrous defeat at the Battle of Leipzig, he now just hoped to save his throne and be assured the Kingdom of Naples would remain his. An opportunity to do so appeared but relied upon him going against his brother-in-law and signing a treaty with the English and the Austrian Empire. His defection on 11 January also cost him 35,000 men whom he supplied to his new allies.

On the same day that the treaty was to become publicly known, he approached Juliette in the hopes of getting her approval for his actions. She responded by telling him he owed his allegiance to France. He threw up his hands, claimed he was a traitor and pointed to the English ships sitting in the harbour. His sorrow was obvious, but his wife supported his decision, even if it went against her brother. Murat's subjects also supported his actions and thus, a couple of days later, he rode out of Naples with his troops to threaten Eugène de Beauharnais, Napoleon's regent in northern Italy.

In Murat's absence, Madame Murat acted as his regent. She was not as striking as her older sister Pauline, but she was still beautiful with fair hair and dazzling white skin. She was also intelligent, clever and prudent. Napoleon's one-time Foreign Minister Talleyrand thought highly of her abilities and intelligence and once remarked, 'She has Cromwell's head on the shoulders of a pretty woman'.[2]

Shortly after Murat left Naples, Juliette appeared at Madame Murat's luxurious apartments that had a spectacular view overlooking the bay. Juliette was ushered into Madame Murat's private bedroom, a room hung with white tulle and lined with pink satin. She was sitting in bed busily signing papers, a habit she had acquired long ago while living in Paris.

When Juliette arrived, Madame Murat's minister was standing dutifully next to her as she was reading a document. She paused and then noted that her position as regent was nothing to be envied as she was about to sign a death warrant. Juliette interceded, remembering the poor fisherman who had lost his life and asked if she could not grant the accused prisoner a pardon. Her questions resulted in Madame Murat having a short discussion with her minister and then ruling in the prisoner's favour, thereby providing Juliette with some compensation for the execution of the Albano fisherman.

While Madame Murat made decisions in her husband's stead, 1814 did not bode well for Napoleon. In Paris, Talleyrand, who had resigned as Napoleon's Foreign Minister in 1807, had thereafter come to believe that Napoleon might destroy the French empire and he secretly began working against him and accepting bribes from hostile powers. Now he was causing political unrest. Juliette's one-time admirer Wellington had also left Spain and was successfully fighting the French on French soil and Britain's economic blockade was taking effect and weakening France. Nonetheless, despite the success of Great Britain's and Napoleon's enemies, they were unsure what to do next as they had no intention of crushing or destroying France.

The coalition had offered Napoleon peace terms in November 1813, when the Austrian minister Metternich designed the Frankfurt proposals with the goal that the War of the Sixth Coalition would end peacefully. The terms allowed for Napoleon to continue as Emperor of France, but France's borders would be reduced to its 1799 'natural frontiers'. Napoleon delayed too long, and the offer was rescinded.

Napoleon anticipated war and returned to Paris where he prepared for the coalition's attack. He organized Parisian defences and reconfirmed that his wife would act as regent to their son, hoping that by doing so his hereditary rule would survive even if he did not. He also hoped that he could turn the tide in the war and, after appointing his brother Joseph to be in charge in Paris, Napoleon departed to re-join his troops on 25 January 1814.

At about the time he left Paris, he learned Murat had turned against him. It was a blow to have his brother-in-law abandon him. Fortunately for Napoleon, soon after, he experienced a series of victories between 10 and 15 February. This period became known as the Six Days Campaign and many historians believe it was his finest success.

He was desperate for victory and realized speed was required to achieve it. With dazzling strategy (and some ineptness by the Coalition) the next four engagements resulted in victory for the French when Napoleon's army of 30,000 inflicted over approximately 17,000 casualties on Prussian commander Gebhard Leberecht von Blücher's army, which was approximately four times larger. In addition, the Coalition undertook a second negotiation to stop the war around this time, but the terms presented to Napoleon were even harsher. France's borders were to be reduced to the 1792 boundaries, something neither Napoleon nor the French could accept.

Although Napoleon had been victorious for a short period, it was not something that he could sustain. Firstly, he could not be everywhere, and, secondly, his marshals and generals were unable to succeed without him, which caused some to lose hope and desert him in his hour of need. On 7 February, Napoleon sent a letter to the Minister of Police telling him that he was announcing that 'every tenth deserter will be shot'.[3] Napoleon also realized that the only way to save his throne came down to whether he could beat the Coalition to Paris and so he set off with all haste, hoping to be the first there.

As the Coalition's invasion continued, news soon reached Parisians that the enemy was near. Joseph ordered Marie Louise to leave with the King of Rome and, against her will, she and her son left. Talleyrand supported their departure because he did not want Napoleon's son on the throne. In fact, Talleyrand worked behind the scenes to install a Bourbon as Napoleon's replacement because he believed a Bourbon ruler would be most beneficial to him.

Coalition forces marched into Paris on 30 March, four hours ahead of Napoleon's arrival, and Paris surrendered. Napoleon had left specific orders that nobody was to greet or negotiate with the enemy. The ever-deceitful Talleyrand refused to obey, greeted the enemy and declared that he spoke for France. Later, when Tsar Alexander arrived, Talleyrand invited him to stay at his home.

In the meantime, having failed to prevent Coalition forces from reaching Paris, Napoleon and his troops went to the Palace of Fontainebleau to wait for news. The Emperor thought that perhaps he might somehow rally his soldiers and continue his fight against the Coalition, but it was a pipe dream. A few days later, he was deposed when his marshals refused to support him and forced him to abdicate in favour of his son. Napoleon was reluctant but did so on 4 April.

Tsar Alexander originally did not object to putting Napoleon's son on the throne or having Marie Louise act as his regent. He would have been willing to do so, but that was not what Talleyrand wanted. Moreover, Talleyrand had the Tsar's ear and used all his persuasive powers to make sure that the Tsar would not allow it. Talleyrand then ensured that Napoleon had no ability to wage war and no leverage to negotiate when he met with the Austrians. Thus, the Emperor abdicated unconditionally on 11 April and signed the Treaty of Fontainebleau the next day, making it official.

On the surface, things appeared favourable for Napoleon. Although he was no longer to be the great Emperor of the French, he would be the Emperor of Elba, a small island off the coast of Italy that is about 50km (30 miles) east of the island of Corsica. He was also not going to be a prisoner there as he could leave the island if he wished, as nothing in the Treaty of Fontainebleau stipulated that he had to stay there. In addition, he was to receive a pension, possess a military guard and his family members would keep their titles.

The one thing missing was his wife and child. When Marie Louise heard about his abdication, she tried to re-join her husband. But many among the Coalition feared what would happen if Marie Louise and Napoleon reunited, as her connection to the Emperor of Austria could prove dangerous if he joined forces with Napoleon. Thus, Metternich convinced her to see her father first, and she never saw Napoleon again.

Having lost his wife, his son and the French throne, Napoleon feared for his future and that of France. He was in a dark place at 4 in the morning on 13 April when he asked his valet, a man named Hubert, for his dressing gown.

> 'Hubert, after placing the light on a table, helped the Emperor to put on his dressing gown, his trousers with feet, and his slippers. Having done this, the valet uncovered the fire and fed it. … the Emperor rose and went toward the chest of drawers opposite the fireplace …
>
> 'On this chest of drawers there were usually two glasses on a plate, covered with a napkin, a little teaspoon, a sugar bowl, and beside it a carafe full of water. But by chance the sugar bowl was not there … While Hubert was listening in order to answer the Emperor, he heard water being poured into a glass and then the noise of the little spoon which was being stirred about in order to melt something. Knowing that there

> was no melted sugar in the glass, Hubert could not imagine what it was that the Emperor was stirring, but after a moment's consideration he thought that the Emperor … had taken some sugar out of his dressing case.
>
> 'When the Emperor had stopped stirring the glass there was a moment of silence, after which the Emperor came to the door and told Hubert to send for [some gentlemen and] … when these gentlemen arrived he told them that not being able to survive the dishonour of France, he had yielded to the weakness of taking poison.'[4]

Fortunately, the doctor was immediately called, and he administered an antidote that caused Napoleon to vomit. The poison ingested was one that he always carried and was old and weak; it was believed if it had not been, it would have caused instant death. Moreover, the poison caused no real effect because Napoleon's gentlemen friends reported that he had by 6am recovered enough to walk in the interior gardens with them.

A sad Napoleon said adieu to his Imperial Guard on 20 April 1814. According to rumours, it was an emotional scene after he descended the stairs from his rooms at Fontainebleau. He walked past where the travelling carriages waited and stopped in front of his guard, who had formed a series of straight lines. He then signalled for quiet and a hush fell:

> 'Soldiers of my Old Guard, I bid you farewell. During twenty years you have been my constant companions in the path of honour and glory. In late disasters, as well as in the days of our prosperity, you invariably proved yourselves models of courage and fidelity. With men such as you, our cause could not have been lost: but a protracted civil war would have ensued, and the miseries of France would thereby have been augmented. I have, therefore, sacrificed all of our interests to those of the country. I depart: you, my friends, will continue to serve France, whose happiness has ever been the only subject of my thoughts, and still will be the sole object of my wishes. Do not deplore my fate: if I consent to live, it is that I may still contribute to your glory. I record the great achievements which we have performed together! … Farewell, my comrades! I shall wish to press you all to my bosom: let me, at least, embrace your standard!'[5]

One of his generals then advanced with a flag. Napoleon received the general and kissed the flag as some of those witnessing the pathetic scene sobbed. Napoleon checked his emotions and offered the soldiers another heartfelt goodbye. 'Farewell, once more, my old comrades! Let this last kiss be impressed on all your hearts!'[6] With that he entered a carriage and left Paris the same day.

On the road, 'he met violent hostility … and, to escape the anger of his former subjects, was reduced to leaving his coach and riding a horse dressed as a postillion.'[7] Despite the close call, he arrived safely on Elba on 3 May, having written a note on his way to the island's commissioner. It stated:

> 'Circumstances having led me to renounce the French throne, sacrificing my rights to the welfare and interests of my country, I have reserved for myself the sovereignty and proprietorship of the island of Elba, with the fortresses of Porto-Ferrajo and Porto-Longone; and the powers have agreed to this arrangement. I am therefore sending General Drouot, so that you may make over the island to him without delay … Announce this new order of things to the inhabitants, and tell them that I have chosen the island for my residence because I know the kindness of their character and the excellence of their climate.'[8]

Word that Napoleon had abdicated reached Juliette in Naples. Although she had not received any formal revocation of her sentence with his downfall, she was ecstatic. She knew she would no longer have to live in exile and she began to make immediate plans to return home, a trip of over 1,600km (1,000 miles). Moreover, she could hardly believe it when she learned that Napoleon's empire had been reduced to the tiny island of Elba with 12,000 inhabitants.

Before setting off for Paris, Juliette returned to Rome and visited Canova at his studio where she found a mysterious curtain. When drawn back, she saw two plaster casts, one plain and the other veiled. Canova had created two busts from memory in the likeness of Juliette, whom he considered the ideal beauty. However, according to one of Juliette's friends, Canova 'had not attempted to copy [Juliette's physical] features so much as to embody the lineaments of her soul'.[9]

Unfortunately, Juliette disliked both of Canova's renditions and Canova, who was highly disappointed, immediately dropped the curtain.

The plain bust never appeared again and no one seems to know what happened to it. As to the veiled one, Canova transformed it and added a crown of olives. He called it the 'Beatrice of Dante' after Dante's muse. This marble bust he sent to her after his death and it became one of his most famous sculptures.

Juliette's trip home also included a brief stop in Lyon, where her good friend Ballanche was impatiently awaiting her arrival. While there, she attended several fetes, including one given in honour of the restoration of the Bourbons, who would now rule France. Germaine had also sent a note, having already returned to Paris:

> 'I am ashamed … to be in Paris without you, dear angel of my life. After so many trials, the sweetest prospect that lies before me is that of seeing you, for my heart is always devoted to you.'[10]

Juliette joyously re-entered Paris on 1 June 1814. She had lived in exile for nearly three years. During that time, she had spent many dreary months alone and missed the whirlwind and vivid excitement Paris offered. Now she was home and determined not to miss a thing.

The Paris she returned to was starkly different from the one she had left behind. Besides France's borders changing, the Bourbon restoration allowed the man who loved oysters, Louis XVIII, to be placed on the throne. He was now the supreme head of the state and would rule by hereditary right as a constitutional monarch. Moreover, the Catholic Church was poised to regain power and become a major player in French politics.

Just as Louis XVIII was restored to his throne, Juliette was also soon restored as the city's reigning queen of beauty, fashion and social good taste. It almost seemed as if she had never left Paris. She also reclaimed her mother's fortune and further good news awaited her in that Jacques-Rose had recouped some of his monetary losses. Moreover, Matthieu had returned to the capital city, because like Juliette and Germaine, he too was delighted with Napoleon's downfall and no longer had to live in exile.

Juliette was delighted to be reunited with Germaine. In fact, it was through her that Juliette had long ago met the hero of the day, Arthur Wellesley, who was being lauded for his fresh victories relating to the Peninsular War and had been made the Duke of Wellington on 3 May 1814. He was greatly charmed by Juliette, and Germaine advised her that she could gain influence over him. Unfortunately, Juliette did not find Wellington particularly 'animated or interesting'. He on the other hand was so enamoured by her that he began paying homage to her by calling frequently. One letter details his interest:

> 'I confess, Madam, that I do not much regret that business will prevent me from calling on you after dinner, inasmuch as every time I see you I leave you more penetrated with your charms, and less disposed to give my attention to politics. I will call on you, however, tomorrow … nothing withstanding the effect which these dangerous visits produce on me.'[11]

Chapter 16

Elba and One Hundred Days

An astounding piece of news arrived yesterday.
We learnt … that Bonaparte had landed.
Louis XVIII's Bodyguard

Napoleon arrived off Elba on 3 May and disembarked the next day. The British decided to remind him why he was there and used the island's commissioner, Colonel Sir Neil Campbell, to loosely watch him. Although the exiled Emperor's wife and son were not on the island, he was not without family. His mother came to visit, and his sister Pauline moved there to be with him. She also acted as his hostess at social gatherings and, as people remained fascinated by him, many were eager to call, including many British visitors.

Old friends also occasionally made appearances. These included Marie Walewska, who arrived with Napoleon's illegitimate son, to whom she had given birth on 4 May 1810. Marie had divorced her husband in 1812 after her brother admitted he had forced her to marry. As a settlement, she and her oldest son by him received half of her husband's estate, which made her a wealthy woman. Because she was a free woman, she now offered to stay with Napoleon on Elba, but he refused, worried that her presence might cause a scandal, so she stayed only two days.

Perhaps he also thought that Marie Louise and his son might appear, but he would never see either of them again because a confidant of Metternich's, General Count Adam Adalbert von Neipperg, was in the process of seducing her. Neipperg had fair curly hair, refined features and polished manners. He was also pleasant and had a zest for life. In addition, despite having just turned forty, he possessed youthful features, though his appearance was supposedly somewhat unusual. He wore a large patch of black silk over the upper part of his face to cover the loss of an eye and an oblique scar he obtained in the Netherlands whilst spying in 1794.

He met Marie Louise after her father instructed him to accompany his daughter to the spa town of Aix-les-Bains in southern France in the summer of 1814. However, Neipperg's real goal was to prevent Marie Louise from joining Napoleon on Elba, and he took his duty seriously. She fell in love with Neipperg during the trip and, as her love for him grew, her letters to Napoleon faded until they stopped, just like her desire to join him on Elba. When news leaked out that Neipperg and Marie Louise were a couple, neither the French nor Austrian public received it well.

The absence of Napoleon's wife and son become more bitter for him when, a month after he arrived on Elba, Josephine died. At the time Napoleon was alone. His sister had not yet arrived on the island and neither had his mother come to visit. Moreover, Josephine's death was completely unexpected. She thought she was suffering from a cold when she took a carriage ride in damp weather into the woods with Tsar Alexander and her children. However, despite rest and various remedies, she continued to worsen. The Tsar finally became so concerned for her that he ordered his physicians to attend her. Even they could not save her from pneumonia. She died around noon on 29 May with Eugène and Hortense at her bedside.

Napoleon and Josephine purportedly still loved each other immensely and, according to legend, Napoleon was the last name on her lips. At the very least, they remained friends after the divorce and regularly corresponded. When Napoleon received word of her death, he was said to have been inconsolable. He shut himself up and mourned uninterrupted for two days and later, he lamented, 'I ought not to have allowed myself to be separated from Josephine … no, I ought not to have been divorced from her; that was my misfortune!'[1]

Prior to his arrival on the island, Napoleon read books about Elba and thus decided to focus on infrastructure and improvements upon arriving. He also introduced some of the same measures and improvements he had made in France by revising the island's tax system, introducing social reforms and updating legal codes. Unfortunately, life on Elba was nothing like the freewheeling lifestyle he had been living in Europe. He soon got bored on a tiny island that he could cross in a couple of days.

Napoleon also came to believe that the Coalition was up to no good as he idled his time away. He knew he remained popular and everyone wanted to visit his new court. The British press also continued to plague him. They attacked him at every opportunity and there was also the troublesome Talleyrand. When a meeting of ambassadors for the European states gathered at the Congress of Vienna to provide a long-term peace plan for Europe, Talleyrand served as France's representative. Napoleon had no idea what Talleyrand might be up to or how he might influence the congress.

Napoleon's spies were also busy doing their job and reporting their findings to him. The reports were not good, as rumours persisted that he might be moved from Elba and sent to St. Helena, a remote, volcanic, tropical island in the South Atlantic Ocean that was thousands of miles away from Italy where the people supported him. In addition, rumours circulated that he might be assassinated if he wasn't sent to St. Helena.

The more time Napoleon spent on Elba, the more lethargic he seemed and the more harmless and less threatening Campbell came to regard him. When visitors called, they expected to see the once vital man they remembered, but that was not the case because a completely different man greeted them:

> '[He was] a thick-set corpulent, little man, with the profile of an Italian Polichinello, and nostrils stained with snuff, sharing a bouillabaisse cooked in their saucepans on the beach with the tunny-fishers, and apparently enjoying it. Or they espied him in his garden-plot at [Villa] San Martino, absorbed in quoits with the worthy dames of the Elban bourgeoisie ... The lorgnettes of the astounded tourists discovered the Emperor running after his fowls in the vineyard, or playing innocent games in the field with the same good ladies and their daughters.'[2]

The news Napoleon received from his spies worried him, and he knew that even if he appeared harmless, the Coalition, the Congress of Vienna and Talleyrand did not think of him in that light. Yet what made Napoleon the most nervous, was when Louis XVIII decided that he would disregard the Treaty of Fontainebleau that obligated him to pay Napoleon two million francs a year, along with other huge sums owed to the Bonaparte family. A bored and anxious Napoleon, having no wife or son at his side and now fearing a questionable financial future, was not about to sit around and wait for the axe to fall. If he couldn't live out the remainder of his life in comfort, then he decided he needed to take matters into his own hands.

He had no idea what the future held, but he knew that if he could resume power, he wouldn't be imprisoned, he wouldn't be sent to St. Helena and he wouldn't have to worry about money. Rumours that he was planning to leave Elba began as early as June 1814. By the end of the year, his supporters, advisors and family liked the idea of having him back on the throne, so he hatched a plot to regain it and set it in motion when the commissioner, Sir Neil Campbell, set off on a lengthy trip to Italy in his frigate.

On the evening of 26 February 1815, Napoleon set sail for France, but his dream of returning to power almost didn't happen because he nearly drowned. The seas were rough and after boarding a boat being rowed by sailors, they all found themselves being forcefully pitched back and forth on the sea. Suddenly, it was discovered the Emperor was missing, as he had apparently fallen overboard.

Napoleon was not a good swimmer and dressed in full uniform with a sword at his side, he was at a further disadvantage. Fortunately, a fisherman was nearby and as the Emperor struggled against the waves, the fisherman's dog, thought to be a Newfoundland, jumped into the water. This canine hero kept the Emperor afloat until the sailors returned and rescued him.

Ever since Napoleon's exile to Elba, he had been allowed a guard of men and a small navy. This small fleet provided him with the means to sail away, which did not happen until after midnight. He was aboard the *Inconstant* and had six other ships: a French merchant brig called the *Saint Esprit*, the *Étoile*; the *Caroline*, the *Saint-Joseph*, the *Fly*, and the *Bee*. Aboard were 1,000 soldiers, 4 cannons, and some 40 horses. His objective was to resume ruling France and his plan was to do so without firing a shot. He believed that his victory would be assured if enough people supported him, but he also understood that the French people were not universally supportive of him.

The Emperor had devised a plan to gain the people's backing, increase his presence and show that he could use force if necessary. He also planned to obtain momentum by acquiring more soldiers, equipment and horses after landing in France and he strategized how to avoid the royalist areas that were unsupportive. In addition, he prepared bulletins to remind the people that treachery had defeated him, and he reassured his enemies that he only wanted to rule France. His appeal read:

> 'Soldiers! In my exile I have heard your voice; I have arrived in spite of all obstacles and perils! Your General, called to the throne by the choice of the people, and raised upon your shields, is restored to you; come and join him!'[3]

Napoleon landed without opposition on the French Mediterranean coast and anchored in Golfe Juan on 1 March, which ushered in the period known as 'One Hundred Days'. Upon disembarking, local guards captured a small detachment of his troops and took them to Antibes. However, Napoleon remained free and insisted his men fight if necessary. It was also around this same time that he suddenly paid a great tribute to Germaine, the woman who had caused him to fear her because she had created a salon that opposed him and influenced Narbonne-Lara and Constant against him. Napoleon said to his brother Lucien: 'I was wrong; Madame de Staël made me more enemies during her exile than she ever would have done in France'.[4]

Germaine always thought of Napoleon as 'dangerous' even if she did feel some sympathy for him after he was sent to Elba in 1814. Despite her many attempts to influence him, she never succeeded, and when she learned that Napoleon had landed on the French coast, she was afraid and fled to Coppet. Others also feared the consequences of Napoleon's 'supposed' escape from Elba. This was noted by an officer in the king's bodyguard at Tuileries when he penned in his diary on 5 March:

> 'An astounding piece of news arrived yesterday. We learnt, by telegraph, that Bonaparte had landed at Cannes, near Fréjus … The King, who is very unwell, is at present suffering from an attack of gout, which principally affects his hands, so much so that he had great difficulty in opening the envelope. Having read the contents he remained silent, then spent several moments with his head in his hands, deep in thought.'[5]

As Napoleon marched northward from the French coast to Paris, over 900km (600 miles), the Congress of Vienna received news of his latest escapade. To say the least, they were furious. Other reactions to the Emperor's return varied. Some people were pleased, others confused and still others alarmed, like Louis XVIII. Although Napoleon possessed no massive military might like Louis, the king immediately sent his troops to intercept Napoleon with orders to capture or kill him. However, the Emperor's spies had already reassured him that the king's soldiers were highly unlikely to do either as Napoleon had once served as their commander and they had not forgotten him.

Two days later, on 7 March, a detachment of Napoleon's men met a battalion of the king's soldiers near Laffrey, south of Grenoble. Napoleon was informed of their presence and quickly proceeded to the spot with his guards following; as they had no intention of attempting anything, their arms were reversed. Still the situation was tense when Napoleon stepped in front of the battalion. Complete silence fell and then Napoleon bared his chest and called out a challenge:

> 'What! my friends … do you not recognize me; I am your Emperor; if there is a soldier among you who would kill his general, his Emperor, let him do so; I am here!'[6]

The battalion's commanding officer took that opportunity to give the order to fire upon Napoleon, but not a single soldier obeyed. Instead of gunfire, the troops responded with cries of 'Vive L'Empereur!' and then they abandoned the king's service and joined Napoleon's forces. Later that same day, more of the king's men defected, causing the Emperor's forces to swell.

Momentum was building, and when Napoleon next set his sights on Grenoble, it did not matter that his enemies locked the city's gates or that they refused to open them. Napoleon's men were whipped up with enthusiasm as were the Grenoble inhabitants that came to greet him. They could barely restrain their delirious joy at the sight of the Emperor. The people then pulled down the gates, carried Napoleon in on a wave of glory and took him to the Hôtel des Trois Dauphins where they presented him the gates as his reward.

Many soldiers were unsure what to do and faced a dilemma of loyalty. One soldier, Colonel Girod de l'Ain, who heard about Napoleon's return, decided he had to take up his old post and support General Curial, the principal colonel of the Infantry Chasseurs of the Old Guard. L'Ain then left on horseback for Paris and reported:

> 'As well can be imagined, the whole country was in turmoil. I travelled in uniform, but I took the precaution of providing myself with *two* cockades, one *white,* the other *tricolor*, and according to which colour flag I saw flying from the belfries of any town or village we passed through, I hurriedly adorned my hat with the appropriate cockade. Such a precaution was by no means needless, because on the stretch of road as far as Dijon, and particularly at Dôle, we were subjected to questioning by the makeshift and exceedingly zealous authorities, whom we encountered at every step and who were all on the lookout for suspects of one or other colour, depending upon whether they had adopted the tricolor cockade again or had kept to the white one.'[7]

As Napoleon continued his march to Paris, the Bourbons worried and fretted. The Congress of Vienna, described as the 'greatest diplomatic extravaganza ever mounted',[8] was at the same time meeting in Vienna. Napoleon's timing couldn't have been worse because if the Congress had not been together, they couldn't have agreed so quickly to arm themselves against the man they called the 'Corsican Usurper'. To counter their concerns, Napoleon continued to publish bulletins promising that he did not want war and that his only goal was to put himself back on the throne of France. He also began to represent himself as the 'soul of the Revolution', promised to protect Frenchmen and republicized all the advancements that had been made since the Bastille fell in 1789.

Napoleon was proving unstoppable and his northward march became christened 'The Flight of the Eagle'. Louis XVIII feared Napoleon and wanted him stopped, so he sent more troops. Unfortunately for Louis, whenever and wherever his troops met Napoleon, they soon fell under the Emperor's spell. For instance, Marshal Jacques Macdonald, who had served under Napoleon, attempted to stop him at Lyon but failed once his soldiers defected to Napoleon's side. The fearless and red-headed Marshal Michel Ney was also ordered to fight against his old leader, but when he discovered his troops were having none of it, he abandoned the king, joined Napoleon and encouraged his troops to follow suit. Thus, Napoleon's army grew bigger and bigger the closer it marched to Paris.

News of Napoleon's growing army was on everyone's tongue and the excitement was palpable as his journey turned into 'one long ovation'. At the time, Juliette was spending time with Napoleon's step-daughter Hortense, who, at Napoleon's request in 1802, had married his youngest brother, Louis Bonaparte. When Juliette learned that Napoleon was heading to Paris, she was concerned and feared that she might be sent into exile again. Hortense was understanding and reassured her that if necessary, she would intercede on Juliette's behalf with the Emperor. Hortense also promised to receive her if she appeared at court, but Juliette saw the offer as perilous and cleverly declined, stating that she would not appear anywhere if any of her friends continued to be persecuted.

Everything looked as if it was lining up well for Napoleon. The only thing that continued to be a problem was the unwillingness of the Congress of Vienna to allow him to rule. Fears about Napoleon had not subsided, and the Congress of Vienna did not want Napoleon back in power. That was a problem, because England and Austria had earlier signed a treaty with France that they could not break. The only thing they could do was declare war on Napoleon and brand him *hors la loi* (outlaw) and so, for the first time in history, war was declared on a person not a country.

As the Seventh Coalition formed, Napoleon's march continued, and Germaine's unstable and one-time lover, Constant, began thinking about Juliette, through no fault of hers. In addition, Murat had been worried about his kingdom after the Congress of Vienna began to meet. They were discussing how to manage Europe's new balance of power. To ensure that things would go his way and that he would keep his kingdom, he wrote to Juliette asking for recommendations for a publicist and she suggested Constant.

Working with Murat, she then held a two-hour interview with Constant, who fell madly in love with her. In fact, throughout the winter of 1814-1815, he acted like a passionate love-sick fool. A debate soon sprang up as to whether Juliette encouraged his affections or not. Some people allege that Juliette flirted outrageously with him. Others maintain he received no encouragement from her but was suddenly inspired and in love. However, the following excerpt from his diary seems to suggest he thought she encouraged him.

> 'Madame Récamier takes it into her head to make me fall in love with her. I am forty-seven years of age. Rendezvous which she gives me under the pretext of some business relating to Murat. Her manner to me that evening. 'Dare to make love to me!' says she. I leave her house madly in love. My whole life is *bouleversée*. Invitation to Angervilliers. Coquetry and cruelty of Madame Récamier. I am the most wretched of men. My frightful mental sufferings prevent me from writing a line of common sense. I am beginning to lose money at play, because I can think of nothing but Madame Récamier.'[9]

Amidst Constant's crisis of love, Napoleon landed on France's shores as Juliette continued to meet with Constant to aid Murat. However, he soon realized that the Congress of Vienna had no intention of allowing him to continue ruling Naples and he deserted his allies, issued a proclamation to the Italian patriots in Rimini and declared war on 15 March 1815 against Austria, hoping to help Napoleon by removing the Austrians from Italy.

Four days later, when Napoleon was practically at Louis' door, the king abandoned Paris and fled to Ghent. The tricolour flag was hoisted in his absence and was seen floating over the Tuileries Palace when Napoleon entered Paris the next day. The excitement at the Emperor's arrival could not be contained. Thousands of cheering people shouted the name of the man they thought of as a hero. He had accomplished his goal and had made it all the way to Paris without firing a shot.

It was around this time that Juliette received a note from his sister Madame Murat. The note reassured her that she was thinking of her and that she was unsupportive of her brother's actions:

> 'I have just received most alarming news, – that Paris is in revolt, – the king lost, – every thing overturned in fact. Do not forget that you, your family, your friends, have friends here who will be happy to receive you. … We are very tranquil here. The state of France and of all other countries where the old monarchs have returned, has done us great good. The people love us, and we love them sincerely. … Every thing promises us, therefore a tranquil future. … It will be very sweet to me to do something to prove to you, and to your friends likewise, the extent and strength of my attachment.'[10]

There would be no tranquil future for Caroline or for her husband. Murat was embroiled in the Neapolitan War that ended five days after it began. On the same day that Napoleon entered Paris, Murat found himself defeated in his bid to keep his throne and he fled to Corsica. He hoped he could regain his throne by fomenting an insurrection, but he failed again. On 13 October 1815, guards took him to a room in the Pizzo Castle at Calabria, Italy, where he was imprisoned:

> 'Twelve soldiers, who perhaps had served under him, awaited him, drawn up in two lines. Murat saw them load their muskets, refused to let his eyes be bandaged, and himself, as an experienced captain, chose the post where the bullets could best hit him. … He fell, holding in his hands the portraits of his wife and children.'[11]

Back in Paris, the same night of Murat's defeat, Napoleon's battalion bivouacked at the Place Carrousel and at around 9pm, their leader entered the Tuileries Palace under thick fog and drizzling rain. A crushing crowd of enthusiastic officers received him. After being embraced and lauded, he was carried to his apartments where he greeted Hortense, along with other dignitaries. One can only imagine the pleasure he must have felt at being home, but the following day, he was back at work reviewing his troops and giving a rousing speech:

> 'Soldiers, … The glory of that which we have done appertains to the people and to you! … the throne of the Bourbons was illegitimate, since it had been raised by foreign hands, since it had been proscribed by the wish of the nation expressed in our national assemblies; finally, since it guaranteed alone the interests of a small number of arrogant men whose pretensions are opposed to our rights. Soldiers! the Imperial throne can alone secure the rights of the people, and especially its greatest interest, that of our glory.
>
> 'Soldiers! we are about to march in order to drive from the territory these auxiliary princes of the stranger; the nation will not alone second us with its vows, but will follow our impulse. The French people and myself rely upon you. We do not wish to interfere with the affairs of foreign nations, but woe to those who meddle with ours!'[12]

Although Napoleon may have wished there would be no war, he soon saw that it was inevitable. As he prepared for it, the opposition against him grew. Many people were tired of war and they did not want to support him. Napoleon understood his popularity was fragile and to maintain power, he also realized he needed reforms. Liberals had been unhappy with his rule and he knew that if he was to succeed, he had to win them over.

That is when he came up with an ingenious plan to write a new constitution and to employ Juliette's love-sick Constant. He was an outspoken liberal and one of Napoleon's harshest critics, but because he led the liberal opposition, he was also the one person who could gain their support.

Napoleon was apparently desperate enough that he even wrote to Germaine asking her to offer 'constitutional ideas'. The woman who had argued that he had created a tyrannical government which 'rested upon three principal bases – to satisfy men's interests at the expense of their virtues, to deprave public opinion by sophisms, and to give the nation war for an object, instead of liberty',[13] provided a sharp reply. She said as he had no need for a constitution or for her for over twelve years, she could not imagine why he should suddenly require either one.

In the meantime, Constant joined with the Emperor. He also wrote Germaine that he thought a liberal constitution would be established and that some change had miraculously come over Napoleon. However, shortly thereafter, he had second thoughts about his participation and wrote to Juliette offering to resign if that was her wish. How she responded is unknown, but in the end, it was because of Constant's efforts that the new French constitution was ratified on 22 April.

Chapter 17

Waterloo

Believe me, nothing except a battle lost can be so melancholy as a battle won.
Duke of Wellington

Napoleon left Paris at midnight on 11 June 1815, having earlier dined with his mother, brothers, and Hortense. Some historians also say he slept one last time with Marie Walewska. He did not look healthy when he rode out of Paris. He was no longer young, thin and active. Instead, he had a bloated face, large belly and round, fat legs. He was also suffering from irresistible sleepiness, which when linked to a lack of mental power, would make victory for the 45-year-old that much more unlikely.

There were other problems. He had difficulty obtaining the best and brightest to help him. Firstly, some of his best men had retired and secondly, there were those who had little or no confidence in his ability to survive and therefore could not be recruited. He had always selected the right person for the right job, but ironically, now when he needed to do so, he made inappropriate decisions. For example, he left Louis-Nicolas d'Avout behind as military governor of Paris instead of taking him into the field. He would have been invaluable in battle as he was one of Napoleon's most capable commanders and, moreover, his trustworthiness and obedience to the Emperor were absolute.

Another major faux pas involved Napoleon's selection for chief of staff. He appointed Marshal Jean-de-Dieu Soult, who did not have the temperament or experience to be successful in such a position, partly because he left too much strategy to his subordinates. Soult got the job because Napoleon's previous chief of staff, Louis-Alexandre Berthier, was now dead.

Berthier had always proven indispensable to Napoleon because of his diplomatic and organizational skills and he had been the one person who could understand, clarify, and relay Napoleon's orders in minute detail to subordinate officers. Unfortunately, after escorting Louis XVIII to Belgium,

Berthier supposedly somehow fell out of an upstairs window on his estate. Whether he was pushed, purposely jumped, or was a victim of an accident continues to be debated by historians.

In Paris, Napoleon learned that the new allied powers were amassing their troops, and, near the end of March, news came that they had acquired 600,000 men in total. That was much more than Napoleon could ever raise and so he decided to forgo gathering more troops or using a defensive strategy because he worried that the French people might rebel if his campaign lasted too long. He also realized that to fight such a massive foe, his best tactic would be to use a divide-and-conquer approach. He had used that tactic successfully before and he hoped it would work again by fragmenting and demoralizing his enemy.

Napoleon's peace overtures had been rejected, and he decided that his best option was to launch a surprise attack against the British and Prussian troops who waited just over France's northern border. By June, he had acquired about 300,000 troops. He knew that his enemies were spread over the Belgian frontier for about eighty miles and that if he made a surprise attack, it would take them several days to assemble. He could do a lot of damage during that time. So, with great stealth and secrecy, he successfully surprised the Prussians in Charleroi on 15 June 1815.

In Brussels, Charles Lennox, the 4th Duke of Richmond, was in command of reserve forces stationed there to protect the city in case Napoleon attacked it. He and his wife Charlotte decided to host a ball inviting British army officers and European nobility. It was to be held at their house in the rue de la Blanchisserie in a large room on the ground floor to the left of the entrance. Charlotte had requested that an old friend, Captain William Verner, pass out the invitations, telling him:

> 'It might appear extraordinary me giving a ball at such a time, when all the papers as well as all the private communications announced that the French Army had marched to the frontier, and when it was not known the moment our Army might not be ordered out to meet them.'[1]

Luckily for her, Charlotte reported to Verner that the famous 'Iron Duke', Wellington, had already reassured her that she could give the ball with the 'greatest of safety' and 'without interruption'. Attendees included such people as the Prince of Orange, the Duke of Brunswick, Lord and Lady Somerset, Marquis and Marquise D'Assche, Prince Frederic of Orange,

Count and Countess Mercy d'Argenteau, and, of course, Wellington himself, who had arrived rather late and was accompanied by his alleged mistress, Lady Charlotte Greville.

Wellington had never expected Napoleon to attack and had even once thought of launching his own surprise attack against him in Paris. In fact, in May, Wellington had been complacent about the threat that the Emperor posed and sent a dispatch stating, 'I say nothing about our defensive operations because I am inclined to believe that … [we] are so well united and so strong that the enemy cannot do us much mischief'.[2]

Wellington learned at 6pm that Napoleon had made his move and surprised the Prussians. The Duke then ordered some of his men to make haste to Charleroi. However, despite his order, he appeared unconcerned and he and Lady Greville stayed for supper. Some of his men stayed behind too, although they may have regretted that decision the next morning when they were forced to fight wearing their evening attire.

Although Wellington may have seemed calm, most attendees worried about Napoleon's advance. In fact, many participants reported that after the news arrived, it turned into a 'dreadful evening'. One attendee who echoed this sentiment was Katherine Arden, daughter of Baron Alvanley and sister to William Arden, a friend to the Prince Regent who ran in the same circles as the famous dandy 'Beau' Brummell. Katherine wrote to her aunt providing the following sombre details:

> 'On Thursday the 15th of June, we went to the great ball that the Duchess of Richmond gave, at which we expected to see from Generals down to Ensigns, all the military men, who with their regiments had been for some time quartered from 18 to 30 miles from this town, and consequently so much nearer the frontiers; nor were we disappointed, with the exception of 3 generals, every officer high in the army was to be there seen. Though for nearly ten weeks we had been daily expecting the arrival of the French troops on the Frontiers, and had rather been wondering at their delay, yet when on our arrival at the ball, we were told that the troops had orders to march at 3 in the morning, and that every officer must join his regiment by that time, as the French were advancing, you cannot possibly picture to yourself the dismay and consternation that appeared in every face. Those who had brothers and sons to be engaged, openly gave way to their grief, as the last parting of any took

> place as this most terrible ball; others, … who had no near relation, yet felt that amongst the many many friends we all had there, it was impossible that all should escape, and that the next time we might hear of them, they might be numbered with the dead. … We staid at this ball as short a time as we could, but long enough to see express after express arrive to the Duke of Wellington, to hear of Aides de Camp arriving breathless with news, and to see, what was much more extraordinary than all, the Duke's equanimity a *little* discomposed.'[3]

Wellington soon learned that Napoleon had attacked from the east rather than west and that he was making much greater progress than anticipated. Despite displaying a calm demeanour, Wellington supposedly told the Duke of Richmond, 'Napoleon has humbugged me, by God, he has gained 24 hours' march on me'.[4] Wellington also asked the Duke of Richmond for a map and retired with his officers to the study. He realized that his best strategy was to stop Napoleon's progress and it was supposedly while studying the map that he pointed out Waterloo and predicted a major battle would be fought there.

As Wellington rode to join his men, Napoleon left the fiery red-headed Marshal Ney in charge at Quatre Bras and pursued the Prussians. Ney was ordered to keep Wellington's forces occupied and, if possible, defeat him. Unfortunately, Napoleon came to regret that decision because Ney allowed Wellington to escape. Napoleon further become upset at Ney for another reason. General Jean-Baptiste d'Erlon, who was fighting alongside Napoleon at Ligny, was confused as to whose orders to follow after Ney promised to court martial him if he did not return immediately to Quatre Bras. D'Erlon thus ordered his men back to Quatre Bras and, because of all their marching, his troops proved useless to anyone during the fighting.

Another unfortunate event occurred that might have changed the outcome. It was a missed opportunity to capture the Prussian commander, Marshal Blücher. It happened when his grey charger, a gift from the Prince Regent, was shot out from under him and the French Calvary had no idea who he was, which allowed him to safely scramble away on foot although he was badly bruised and half conscious. Still, despite all the problems and failed opportunities, Napoleon essentially won Ligny.

Blücher retreated, and when Wellington learned about his retreat, he retreated too. If Ney had pursued Blücher, he could have severely damaged Wellington's army. Retreating armies are easy prey for pursuing armies partly because they quickly become disorganized, which makes them even more vulnerable to attack. Ney regrettably decided to wait for Napoleon before pursuing Wellington and he thereby allowed the British to escape unscathed.

Although he could not fully capitalize on the surprise attack, Napoleon did have Wellington and Blücher on the run and licking their wounds. On Saturday evening, 17 June, Napoleon's troops reached the small village of Waterloo. Wellington and his men were already settled in, having staked out high ground and obtained the best defensive spots.

The following morning, Napoleon breakfasted off silver plate as Wellington busily supervised and deployed his forces. The battle for supremacy would take place in the open fields of Waterloo, in a battle that Wellington once described as 'a near run thing'. But it would not be a dry or dusty battle. In fact, monumental rains on the 16th and 17th delayed Napoleon from starting the fight. He even waited on the 18th for the fields to dry, but they never did, and the battle turned into a muddy quagmire.

Napoleon was determined to destroy Wellington. He thought he could make an example of him that would discourage other coalition forces and at the same time raise and strengthen the reputation of France as a powerful country. In the French camp where he rallied troops, morale was high and accentuated by the frequent cries of 'Vive l'Empereur'. In fact, Napoleon was so confident of his abilities he said to one man who praised Wellington's skills:

> 'Because you have been beaten by Wellington, you consider him a great general. And now I tell you that Wellington is a bad general, and that the English are bad troops, … we'll settle this matter by lunchtime.'[5]

Wellington may not have had Napoleon's stellar reputation as warrior, but he did have sixteen undefeated battles behind him. He also respected Napoleon, did not underestimate him and never once said anything disrespectful about him. Wellington knew that Napoleon's presence could make a difference and despite being outnumbered by Napoleon's forces, he wisely chose a defensive position and posted his troops skilfully. So, when he looked out over the battlefield, he did not insult his opponent but concentrated on the best way to beat Napoleon.

The morning of the battle must have been a wonderous sight to see. Each side possessed thousands of soldiers probably anxiously anticipating the fight that was about to commence. Nineteenth-century writer George Hooper sets the scene.

> 'Napoleon prepared for the combat with deliberation, and displayed before his intended victim the formidable engines of his power. … The orders of Napoleon put the whole French army in movement. … The drums beat, the bands played, the trumpets sounded. … Light wreaths of smoke curled upwards into the misty air, and through this thin veil the dense dark columns of the French infantry and the gay and gleaming squadrons of French horse were seen moving into the positions assigned them by him who knew so well how to set "his battle in array." Before them was the open valley, yet green with heavy crops; behind them dark fringes of wood, and a thick curtain of dreary cloud. … At ten o'clock they were all in position … a mighty mass of fighting power, revealed as if by magic, in all the majesty of strength and the beauty of order, and trembling with eagerness to rush upon the enemy.'[6]

Napoleon's tactics and strategy at Waterloo were based on his overweening arrogance and lack of respect for his enemy. Of the meeting of these two great forces, Wellington later wrote to his old comrade in arms by the name of Lord Beresford stating:

> 'Never did I see such a pounding match. Both were what the boxers called gluttons. Napoleon did not manoeuvre at all. He just moved forward in the old style in columns, and was driven off in the old style. The only difference was, that he mixed cavalry with his infantry, and supported both with an enormous quantity of artillery. I had the infantry for some time in squares, and we had the French cavalry walking about as if they had been our own. I never saw the British infantry behave so well.'[7]

Waterloo was not necessarily Wellington's finest battle and as Harvey put it, 'The battle had been lost by Napoleon, not won by Wellington'.[8] The Duke made mistakes and was overly cautious, but he had played defensively, brilliantly chosen the right terrain and maintained a cool confidence throughout. Moreover, he perfectly executed the coup de grace when needed and so, in the end, it would not be a glorious victory for Napoleon, despite coming close to victory twice.

One event often retold about Waterloo is when Napoleon decided to send his Imperial Guards into the muddy fray. Initially, he appeared to be leading the charge and morale couldn't have been higher or the French more joyous at the sight of their leader at their head. They knew victory was theirs until Napoleon suddenly veered away, sought shelter and Marshal Ney was forced to take command.

Ney was in the thick of things when his horse was shot out from under him. However, he continued to rally the troops on foot. It was around that time that Wellington struck and caused the previously impervious Imperial Guards to waver. They then retreated, plodding through thick mud. Panic rippled through the French infantry as they saw the guards in retreat. Eventually, they retreated too. The Prussians appeared. Wellington's army rushed forward, throwing themselves with delight upon the French until they were bloodied and unable to withstand the onslaught and folded.

Napoleon's blunders helped Wellington win a victory that did not showcase either man's strategic abilities. To Wellington, his victory may not have seemed like one at all when afterwards he rode through the killing fields, a 'sickening spectacle' of death accompanied by the horrific moaning and groaning of wounded. As usual, the winning side was busy gathering the spoils of war, stripping the dead and looting their bodies. In fact, there were so many dead bodies, five days later the battlefield still had not been cleared of corpses and local peasants resorted to burning them in huge heaps as the intensely hot weather created a critical health hazard.

After the battle, when Wellington reached the village of Waterloo, he immediately requested information on his friends and close acquaintances. Many were dead and just as many were mangled or wounded. Filled with grief, he penned a sorrowful letter:

> 'My heart is broken by the terrible loss I have sustained in my old friends and companions and my poor soldiers. Believe me, nothing except a battle lost can be so melancholy as a battle won. The bravery of my troops has hitherto saved me from the greater evil; but win such a battle as this of Waterloo, at the expense of so many gallant friends, could only be termed a heavy misfortune but for the result to the republic.'[9]

Battle-weary and completely exhausted, he soon fell asleep on the floor of his room. The following day, on 19 June 1815, carriages of tourists appeared at Waterloo to investigate and examine the bloodied battlefield. Wellington in the meantime began sending dispatches. In one, addressed to the Earl of Bathurst, he praised Blücher and the Prussian forces, giving them deserved credit for ensuring his victory:

> 'I should not do justice to my own feelings, or to Marshal Blücher and the Prussian army, if I did not attribute the successful result of this arduous day to the cordial and timely assistance I received from them … and even if I had not found myself in a situation to make the attack which produced the final result, it would have forced the enemy to retire if his attacks should have failed, and would have prevented him from taking advantage of them if they should unfortunately have succeeded.'[10]

Back in England, people waited breathlessly as to the outcome. Mrs. Harriet Ward, the daughter of one of the colonels who commanded the 14th Foot at Waterloo, related how the news reached her family, writing:

> 'My mother anxiously awaited news from the Continent. It came at last, — and in this way; … My brother and I, standing at the front gate of the cottage garden, were one morning attracted by the sound of music, and the gaudy appearances of the coaches coming down the road, streaming with gilded flags that bore the words — WELLINGTON! WELLINGTON! WELLLINGTON! … We repeated them with the passing crowd and … rushed … to my mother "There has been a battle," we said; "they have been fighting the French and *we* have beaten them!"'[11]

As for Napoleon, he fought alongside his men until a portion of the Imperial Guard came to his aid and provided protection for him. He then escaped on horseback, hoping to secure political support back in Paris so that he could remain in power. Two Coalition armies pursued him and he was forced to take a circuitous route home to avoid being captured. He arrived in the capital on 21 June.

Napoleon and his brother Lucien believed that if Napoleon dissolved the chambers and declared himself dictator, he could save France. However, Napoleon soon discovered such an idea was a dream. The ever-wily Fouché was leading parliamentary opposition against him and he could not overcome it. He was forced to abdicate on 22 June and did so in favour of his 4-year-old son, a mere formality as his son was living in Austria and would never assume his father's place.

After Napoleon's abdication, France's provisional government was formed and appointed Fouché as acting president. He then invited Napoleon to leave Paris, which he did by retiring to Josephine's former home, Malmaison, where Marie, accompanied by their son, came one last time to visit.

Napoleon had been crushed in battle by Wellington and he lost his leadership of France. An examination of Napoleon's actions at Waterloo by Harvey concludes:

> 'The key factor at Waterloo was Napoleon's own incompetence. It was not just that he made mistakes: it was that he failed in virtually every respect to exercise the courage or the competence of even a mediocre military commander. … he showed himself to be cowardly, indecisive, poor at man-management, remote haughty, unyielding, unwilling to listen, inept, and, as Wellington had observed, extraordinarily lacking in his old flexibility and ingenuity in tactics. Being so far from the front line and delegating to Ney, he inevitably failed to make the right decisions. By leading his men into battle and then shying away at the last moment, he came across as woefully lacking in his old courage. By being so inert, unapproachable and lacking in energy, he behaved like a conventional general well past his prime, not the extraordinary man-machine of manic energy that had prostrated a whole continent before him. … The only explanation is that his overthrow the year before – which had driven him to attempt suicide – and his months of exile at Elba had changed him as a man.'[12]

Napoleon, of course, never admitted his own mistakes and never thought the defeat at Waterloo was his fault. Instead, he blamed others for his loss, including his incompetent chief of staff Soult, and Emmanuel de Grouchy, whom Napoleon had ordered to intercept Prussian forces. Unfortunately, Grouchy never reached the Prussians and despite hearing booming cannons from Waterloo, he did not return to help Napoleon. Great heaps of blame were also placed upon Ney's head because he had made several mistakes even if he had fought fearlessly.

Chapter 18

Buonaparte

I will never voluntarily accede to the outrage which is done me.
Napoleon on learning he was to be exiled to St Helena

After the Battle of Waterloo, Constant, who was by now no longer bewitched by Juliette, moved to Paris with his wife, Charlotte von Hardenberg, whom he had married in 1808. He then sat in the Chamber of Deputies, the lower legislative house of the Restoration-era government and became one of its most eloquent and respected orators.

Around the same time, Germaine and her husband Rocca travelled to Italy. They were both ill. Germaine had been suffering ever since the birth of her second child and Rocca was stricken with tuberculosis. They thought the mild Italian weather might aid their conditions, but seeing little improvement, the following year, in June, they returned to Coppet. There, the poet George, Lord Byron visited her frequently but was ambivalent when he talked of her. For instance, on one hand he referred to her as a brilliant writer and stated, 'She is … the first female writer of this, perhaps of any age'.[1] Then in the next breath he remarked, 'I do not love Madame de Staël … I admire her abilities, but really her society is overwhelming – an avalanche that buries one in glittering nonsense – all show and sophistry'.[2]

As for Wellington, he was considered a conquering hero in Europe. He was lauded and praised for his illustrious and heroic service and in fact became a beloved national hero back in Britain. He was also well-received in Paris and because of his popularity there he called upon Juliette, but she was not pleased to see him and noted her displeasure in her journal:

> 'I see him again after the battle of Waterloo. He calls upon me the day after his return. I did not expect it. Annoyance this visit occasions me. He returns in the evening, and is denied admission. I again refuse to see him the next day. He writes to Madame de Staël to complain of my treatment of him.'[3]

Wellington believed that Juliette would be delighted by the beating he had given her nemesis Napoleon and in fact, he had rejoiced in the Emperor's defeat by boasting to her, *Je l'ai bien battu*! Instead of pleasure, Juliette was incensed at Wellington's bravado, and, according to her adopted daughter Amélie, because her patriotism was so wounded, she forever 'closed her door upon him'.[4]

Wellington was not the only one thinking of Juliette. Prince Augustus had continued to correspond with her and he saw her once again after he was appointed chief commander of the German forces. In that position, he was tasked with reducing the number of French fortresses. Aided by the Prussian II Corps and the British Battering Train he was successful.

One of the first fortresses he successfully besieged was Maubeuge. From its trenches he declared to Juliette on 8 July: 'The desire of seeing you again will be a very powerful motive with me for pushing on the siege'.[5] Yet, despite his ongoing love for her, nothing would come of their relationship. She would in fact never leave Jacques-Rose.

Napoleon, in the meantime, was busy overcoming his monumental defeat. Waterloo ended his military career forever and it would become a word that today represents insurmountable difficulties and irreversible defeat. His loss left him few options. He thus decided to seek asylum in the United States and was told that two frigates were patiently waiting off shore to take him there. So, on 29 June, he assumed the disguise of a secretary and fled to Rochefort only to discover that the British were already guarding France's shores and that escape was impossible.

He then decided it was best to beg the British for leniency and wrote to the Prince Regent requesting that he be allowed to retire to England. His request included the following memorable lines:

> 'Exposed to the factions which divide my country, and to the hostility of the greatest power of Europe, I have closed my political career. I come, like Themistocles, to seek the hospitality of the British nation. I place myself under the protection of their laws, which I claim from your Royal Highness, as the most powerful, the most constant, and the most generous of my enemies.'[6]

On 15 July 1815, Napoleon surrendered to Captain Frederick Maitland and boarded the HMS *Bellerophon*, which set sail for Plymouth. Maitland offered him no guarantees or promises of any kind. Napoleon's pleasing personality and ability to charm soon resulted in those aboard calling him 'Sire' or 'Your Majesty' and everyone took off their hat when they greeted him on deck.

When the ship anchored at Plymouth on 24 July, curiosity seekers almost immediately filled the docks. Hundreds of boats also occupied the bay with those aboard hoping to catch a glimpse of their notorious arch enemy. Always the showman, Napoleon enjoyed the attention and satisfied their curiosity by frequently walking back and forth on the deck.

During the time that the *Bellerophon* sat in the bay, Madame Tussaud obtained permission to make a wax likeness of him. When this likeness was added to her exhibit, Englishmen could not wait to see their mortal French enemy. In fact, Napoleon would become a centrepiece of her exhibition and, because she had modelled him from real life, her exhibition obtained instant cachet that other wax exhibitors were never fortunate enough to possess.

While in Plymouth, Napoleon was the topic on everyone lips. Newspapers reported daily about him and gave details as to what was happening on the ship. In addition, soon after he arrived in England, the *Kentish Weekly Post* or *Canterbury Journal* stated:

> 'On board the Bellerophon, Bonaparte still play[s] the Emperor. Captain Maitland shewed him his own cabin, and said he should have the whole of it, except one corner, which the Captain said he would close in for his own bed. Bonaparte said he must have the whole to himself, which the Captain politely yielded. … Nothing escapes his [Napoleon's] notice; his eyes are in every place, and on every object, from the greatest to the most minute. He immediately asked an explanation of the ropes, blocks, masts, and yard, and all the machinery of the ship. He sent for the Boatswain, to question; that Officer always fitting out the French ships. He requested the Marines to pass review before him, examined the arms, evolutions, dress, &c and expressed himself highly pleased. He inquired into the situations of the Seamen, their pay, prize money, clothes, food, tobacco, &c.; and when told of their being supplied by a Purser or Commissary, asked if he was not a rogue.'

As Napoleon waited to learn his fate, the British decided he should no longer be called Emperor. Instead, they settled on General and then insulted him again when they reverted to the Italian Buonaparte spelling, hoping to further undermine his legitimacy as the French ruler. Serious consideration was also undertaken as what to do with him. Some people thought he should be allowed to immigrate to Britain, but others opposed such a plan, wary that he might became involved in European politics. Ultimately, the decision was made to exile him to St. Helena and, when he learned about it through a ministerial dispatch, he was furious and angrily stated:

> 'I am the guest of England … and not her prisoner; I came of my own accord to place myself under the protection of her laws; the most sacred rights of hospitality are violated in my person; I will never voluntarily accede to the outrage which is done me; violence alone shall compel me to do so.'[7]

On 4 August, the *Bellerophon* left Plymouth and sailed up the channel with her prisoner. While at sea, Napoleon wrote a formal protest reiterating what he had previously said:

> 'I hereby solemnly protest in the face of heaven and mankind, against the violence that is done me; and the violation of my most sacred rights, in forcibly disposing of my person and liberty. … If this act be consummated it will be in vain for the English henceforth to talk of their sincerity, their laws, and liberties. British will have been lost in the hospitality of the *Bellerophon*.
>
> 'I appeal to history: it will say that an enemy who made war for twenty years against the English people came spontaneously, in the hour of misfortune, to seek an asylum under their laws. What more striking proof could he give of his esteem and confidence? But how did England reply to such an act of magnanimity? It pretended to hold out a hospitable hand to this enemy; and, on giving himself up with confidence, he was immolated!'[8]

Napoleon was right. Britain would long be remembered for refusing to grant to him what was typically granted to other heads of government.

On 7 August, Napoleon boarded a 74-gun third-rate ship of the Royal Navy called the HMS *Northumberland*. It had been repaired ten days prior, but painting and parts of the interior remained unfinished. When the ship sailed, there were 1,080 persons on board. C.B.H. Ross captained the ship and Rear Admiral Sir George Cockburn was appointed to convey Napoleon to St. Helena. Among those on board were General Henri-Gatien Bertrand who had served Napoleon on many campaigns and while he was in Elba, Count Charles Tristan Montholon and his wife and youngest son, Napoleon's valets Louis-Joseph Marchand and Louis Etienne St. Denis, an Irishman serving as a naval surgeon named Barry Edward O'Meara, 32-year-old General Baron Gaspar Gourgaud, and the Marquis Emmanuel-August-Dieudonné, de Las Cases.

Space had been designated for Napoleon between decks, with a bedroom situated near the saloon and dining room. A special mechanical bed was made to offset the ship's rolling motion so that Napoleon would not feel it, but he did not want to use the bed, instead preferring his ordinary camp bed of iron that had two mattresses. In fact, that was the only bed he slept on, something he continued to do even after he reached Saint Helena.

Every day on the ship, Napoleon breakfasted in his own room, never appearing among the English until about four in the afternoon. He then amused himself with chess or the card game piquet until he was escorted to dinner. Supper was always something he finished quickly, eating every dish, always using his fingers instead of a fork and preferring rich dishes over plain ones or vegetables.

During his evening meals, he drank claret from a tumbler and poured from the bottle himself. He also primarily conversed with Cockburn. After eating, he always had coffee and then enjoyed a glass of brandy that was flavoured by fruit kernels, called noyau. An evening stroll was always in order and he walked on deck, usually with Cockburn and sometimes during these walks questioned the sailors about their actions and then astonished them with his knowledge.

Napoleon's uneventful 67-day trip ended on 15 October 1815 at half past ten when the *Northumberland* anchored at St. Helena. The only advantage to the island was that it was so remote, it greatly reduced the risk that Napoleon might escape. The island was also where its first explorers supposedly found nothing but goats and pheasants. However, they must have missed the rats, because it was loaded with them, something the Count of Montholon mentioned during his stay:

> 'Their number was so great at Longwood … that they frequently came running under our table whilst we were at dinner, and walked about in rooms without appearing at all

> disturbed by our presence. We were never able to destroy them entirely, though we waged a deadly war with them during more than five years.'[9]

Bertrand disembarked first, went in search of temporary lodgings and obtained them. That night, Napoleon slept aboard the ship. By the next morning, word had spread that Napoleon had arrived, which caused him to refuse to disembark until around seven in the evening, as noted by Cockburn's secretary John R. Glover:

> 'Bonaparte, at his own particular request, delayed disembarking until it was dark, to avoid the gaze of the inhabitants, who were crowded on the wharf to see a person who had heretofore kept nations in a state of warfare and dread for nearly twenty years.'[10]

On the morning of the 17th, Napoleon and Cockburn travelled about 6km to Longwood House, the home of the lieutenant-governor designated as Napoleon's future residence. Napoleon seemed satisfied but because Longwood House needed to be repaired, refurbished and enlarged, he stayed temporarily at the Briars homestead that was housing William Balcombe and his family.

Balcombe was an English merchant who became a purveyor to Napoleon and who established a brewery on the homestead. The homestead also had the Briars house where the Balcombes lived, and a single-room pavilion with a tent attached to it where Napoleon resided. The Briars was also situated in a secluded glen, with an avenue of banyan trees leading to the front door and surrounded by a garden complete with an aloe and prickly pear hedge.

Balcombe had a precocious 13-year-old daughter nicknamed Betsy. She was initially afraid when she learned that Napoleon was to live there. Newspapers had described him as a demon and thus her imagination took over. She was greatly relieved when she saw he was an ordinary looking man. However, she did recollect that she felt dread mingled with admiration.

Because she was the only one in the Balcombe family who spoke French, she became the family's translator. She later published her memories describing her time with him and claimed she once threatened him with a sword. After she was disarmed, she reported that he violently pinched her ear and then tweaked her nose causing it to remain red all day. However, the two became great friends. After he moved to Longwood, Betsy continued to visit him and, years later, she remarked on his sweet smile, amiability and kindness to her.

In direct opposition to Betsy, the island's governor, Sir Hudson Lowe, never got along with Napoleon. Part of the reason was that he became suspicious of the relationship between Napoleon and the Balcombe family. He saw plots everywhere and believed the Balcombes might be smuggling out secret messages for Napoleon. Betsy once related how the exiled Emperor viewed his relationship with Lowe:

> 'Napoleon, wishing to learn English, procured some English books; amongst them "Aesop's Fables," were sent him. In one of the fables the sick lion, after submitting with fortitude to the insults of the many animals who came to exult over his fallen greatness, at last received a kick in the face from the ass. "I could have borne everything but this," the lion said. Napoleon showed the wood-cut, and added, "It is me and your governor."'[11]

Chapter 19

Death

I begged Heaven to age this angel to reduce her divinity a little.
Chateaubriand about Juliette

Napoleon moved into Longwood House in December 1815. The location was windswept with no trees and the poorly done repairs to the house made it damp and unhealthy. There, Napoleon's health would decline and cause many people to blame the British for purposely trying to hasten his death. Perhaps it was so, because although Longwood was deemed inadequate, unsuitable and temporary, the construction of the new Longwood House did not happen until he had been on the island about three years.

Life on the island was far from ideal for Napoleon. English papers reported that he was usually in 'bad humour' and that he insisted upon being treated as an Emperor, something the British refused to do. He also hated his poor living conditions, tired of guards constantly watching him and resented the restrictions Cockburn applied to him. Still, he tried to make the best of a bad situation. He took long walks, received guests, reminisced and dictated his memoirs, even mentioning Germaine on 21 October of 1816 as he was dressing:

> 'Her house … had become quite an arsenal against me. People went there to be armed knights. She endeavoured to raise enemies against me, and fought against me herself. She was at once Armida and Clorinda. It can not be denied that Madame de Staël is a very distinguished woman, endowed with great talents, and possessing a considerable share of wit. She will go down in posterity. It was more than once hinted to me in order to soften me in her favour, that she was an adversary to be feared, and might become a useful ally. It might, no doubt, have proved advantageous to me if she had spoken in my praise instead of reviling me as she did, for her positions and abilities

> gave her absolute sway over the saloons, and their influence in Paris is well known.
>
> 'Notwithstanding all that she has said against me, and all she will say yet, I am certainly far from saying or thinking she had a bad heart. The fact is, that she and I have waged a little war against each other, and that is all.'[1]

Napoleon and his physician O'Meara were getting along well on the island. O'Meara encouraged Napoleon to maintain his health through physical exercise and Napoleon followed his suggestion. That was until shortly after Lowe arrived on the island in April of 1816. Lowe was constantly suspicious about what Napoleon was doing, lacked tact when dealing with him and created petty rules for Napoleon to follow. Lowe also had a slew of restrictions for Napoleon, chief among them was that he was required to have an escort wherever he went. So, Napoleon's long walks eventually stopped, as did his horse riding, which then resulted in his mental and physical health declining.

While Napoleon dealt with the irascible Lowe, Germaine returned to Paris in the winter of 1816-17. When Juliette saw her, she was deeply concerned for her friend's health. However, Juliette was not the only one who thought Germaine looked terrible. Her appearance had drastically changed, and she was suffering terrible physical pain. In fact, she was so uncomfortable at night she could barely sleep and developed insomnia. The doctors finally diagnosed her with 'gradual paralysis', but that created a new problem as their prescription was opiates, which often causes patients to develop a tolerance to the medication and thereby creates a requirement for increasingly larger amounts to gain the same sense of relief.

Despite being ill, Germaine resumed holding her salon. It quickly filled with a variety of literary people, politicians and distinguished foreigners. Lafayette was there, as was Canova and Wellington. In fact, Wellington and Germaine had forged a rather warm friendship over the years and that friendship allowed her to influence him so that he significantly reduced the size of the army occupying Paris.

Another visitor to Germaine's salon was Chateaubriand. Although he was a descendant of an old and renowned aristocratic family from Brittany, he was also a man who was completely enamoured by himself and critical of others. For instance, he once compared Napoleon to Nero and then, when Napoleon fell in 1814, Chateaubriand rallied to the Bourbons' side and wrote a scathing indictment against him.

Chateaubriand was also critical of others and so vocal about his opinions, he sometimes was his own worst enemy. This was demonstrated after he gained a position with Louis XVIII, where soon after he disgraced himself by criticizing the king and lost his job. Chateaubriand then switched sides and joined the opposition, siding with an ultra-royalist group that supported the future Charles X.

In 1792, Chateaubriand was under pressure from his family to marry a woman he did not know and had never met. She was a 17-year-old heiress and aristocratic woman from his home town of Saint-Malo, Céleste Buisson de la Vigne. She was not a particularly pretty woman and was scarred from smallpox. After their marriage, he took her to Paris but was unhappy, left her, and joined the Royalist Army until he was wounded and discharged. He then travelled to England, where he began an affair with his landlord's daughter and then followed that relationship up with a long string of other lovers.

When Juliette met Chateaubriand for a second time in 1816, he was forty-eight and, by many accounts, still a handsome and magnetic individual. Nineteenth-century historian Mathurin François Adolphe de Lescure wrote a biography of him in 1892 and described his physical appearance at age thirty-two, stating:

> 'His manhood was in full bloom. His height was average, and he was a little high-shouldered. All his masculine vitality was centred in his head, which was superb and full of fascination. He had a broad forehead, black curly hair, and eyes with a profound expression, like the colour of the sea, and when he wanted to please, he had a smile both captivating and irresistible.'[2]

Chateaubriand had also become a close friend to Germaine over the years. Unfortunately, day-by-day her condition worsened until she was forced to stay in bed. The only time Germaine left her bed was when weather permitted her to be carried to the garden to enjoy the fresh air, but that did little to help or stop the inevitable progress of her illness. Luckily, Germaine remained sharp intellectually and, every morning after waking, her maid brought her writing materials and she wrote until noon. She then received her most intimate friends and, besides Chateaubriand, Wellington dropped by regularly, as did Juliette who called on her dear friend daily.

As Germaine's health continued to decline, Wellington, Chateaubriand, and Juliette helplessly watched. Finally, she suffered a paralyzing seizure on 5 January 1817, but the attack did not kill her. She lingered for months, apparently too stubborn to die. The night before her death, Juliette and Chateaubriand visited her and then sat down together for dinner. Chateaubriand recorded the event:

> 'Madame de Staël was not in the drawing-room and was even unable to come into dinner; but she did not know that the fatal hour was so nigh. We sat down … [and] I found myself sitting by Madame Récamier. It was twelve years since I had met her, and then I had seen her for but a moment. I did not look at her, she did not look at me; we did not exchange a word. When towards the end of the dinner, she timidly addressed a few words to me on Madame de Staël's illness, I turned my head a little and raised my eyes.'[3]

Germaine died the following morning at 5am on 14 July 1817 of a cerebral haemorrhage. A few days later, the French moralist and essayist Joseph Joubert, who was a stranger to Germaine, penned a letter to his friend Madame de Vintimille. In the letter, he claimed that few people mourned Germaine:

> 'Happily … my heart is still living, but it lives entirely for you alone; perhaps, too for Madame de Staël, whom I have never seen, whom I avoided a thousand times, who seemed to me a fatal and pernicious being, whose death, though I hold it a good, yet saddens me when I see the coldness with which the friends of that woman, so long worshipped, and still so living, have seen her go down to the grave! Everywhere I have sought for regrets – not one true one has been expressed … The day of praise has been displaced for her; she received it during life – beyond life there was none. … I have been truly grieved at this calamity of so great a fame; and when I saw that no one would think of the poor woman, I set to thinking of her alone, and to regret, with inconsolable bitterness, the bad use she has made of so much mind, of so much strength and goodness.'[4]

Joubert's assessment was not particularly accurate. Juliette and Chateaubriand experienced great sadness at her death, Mathieu also mourned her and so did her emaciated husband who was completely grief-stricken. After her funeral, he travelled to the French Riviera and died six months later at the city's oldest resort, Hyères, on 31 January 1818. Moreover, in tribute to Germaine, one British newspaper wrote a lengthy paragraph after her death, noting that she was admired for her elegance, vivacity and wit.

Constant was never the same after Germaine's death. He lost a part of himself the day she died, and he buried it with her. In honour of their special relationship, he also wrote a biographical article for the *Moniteur Universalle* that was published on 27 July 1817. It began:

> 'At the time that death took Mme de Staël, many of her friends felt the need of paying a last act of homage to the memory of a woman whose mind, superior as it was, formed the least part of her merit. I hope that others may succeed in the accomplishment of this duty; the more I try to perform the sad task, the more I feel that it is beyond my strength.'[5]

Back on St. Helena, Napoleon's health was going downhill just like Germaine's. He was losing strength and continually got worse because he was not exercising. His health suffered even more after August of 1818 when his doctor O'Meara was court-martialled and banished from the island.

O'Meara's replacement was another Irish doctor, James Verling. Napoleon might have agreed to see Verling if he did not tell Lowe everything about his health, but because he did, Napoleon refused to see him. Moreover, Napoleon had once told a doctor he had little faith in the medical profession and further stated 'that his own remedies were starvation and the warm bath'.[6]

While Napoleon was being stubborn and refusing to see Verling, 41-year-old Juliette was thinking about love. She had completely forgotten about Augustus and although she was still married to Jacques-Rose, she was focused on a budding relationship she had begun with the notorious and unfaithfully married 50-year-old Chateaubriand.

She had met him for the first time, years earlier in 1800, while she and her husband were living in their elegant mansion on the rue du Mont-Blanc. Chateaubriand was an unknown writer at the time and did not impress her. However, he found their meeting memorable and her unforgettable, noting:

> 'One morning, about a month later, I was at Madame de Staël's … suddenly Madame Récamier entered wearing a white dress;

> she sat down in the centre of a blue silk sofa; Madame de Staël remained standing and continued her conversation, in a very lively manner and speaking quite eloquently: I scarcely replied, my eyes fixed on Madame Récamier. I asked myself whether I was viewing a picture of ingenuousness or voluptuousness. … I think I begged Heaven to age this angel to reduce her divinity a little, to set less distance between us. When I dreamed of my Sylph, I endowed myself with all the perfections to please her, when I thought of Madame Récamier I lessened her charms to bring her closer to me: it was clear I loved the reality more than the dream.'[7]

When Juliette suddenly became interested in Chateaubriand, her male friends were unhappy. Moreover, they were probably perplexed as to why she liked him. Besides being a womanizer, Chateaubriand was described by his contemporaries as being a tedious, self-centred windbag. So, it was somewhat surprising that a woman described as being sweet, generous in character, gentle, charming and exquisitely tactful, was so enamoured of him.

Ballanche certainly felt uneasy about Juliette's relationship with Chateaubriand. It didn't matter that Ballanche and Juliette were meeting and dining regularly, he probably worried that his time with her might stop because of Chateaubriand. Mathieu also did not want to be relegated to second place. He continued to hope that he might somehow capture Juliette's heart. Thus, when Mathieu noticed a chill and honed in on Juliette's interest in Chateaubriand, he remonstrated bitterly and expressed his jealousy in a note:

> 'I opened with great emotion, the note; which is better than such incredible silence, such sudden coldness, which I could not qualify or explain. But why should I tell you all I have felt about it? It seems to me, that it was not an unworthy feeling that made me afraid to provoke an explanation, and be the first to complain. … It may be, that this pure, unchangeable affection is worth far more than all those passing illusions that fascinate you at present.'[8]

Despite the best efforts of Ballanche and Mathieu to deter Juliette from having a relationship with Chateaubriand, her relationship with him grew day by day. Before long, her interest in him was so strong that his schedule became hers and her thoughts constantly centred on him. Ultimately,

Ballanche and Mathieu realized they could not stop the affair and reluctantly resigned themselves to the inevitable.

Lowe had also resigned himself to the fact that Napoleon was stubborn and not going to see Verling under any circumstances, even if he fainted, which is exactly what happened in January of 1819. Napoleon's family became so worried about his health that they sent their own doctor to attend him, Francesco Antommarchi, who was born in Corsica but studied medicine in Italy.

He arrived on 19 September, but Napoleon quickly discovered that the doctor was grossly incompetent, although he did see him a few times. Antommachi encouraged the out-of-shape and overweight man to garden, which he did. So, for a short time the fresh air and activity improved Napoleon's physical health and mental outlook. Feeling better, he reminisced about his life and once mentioned Juliette and her relationship with Augustus that resulted in the following story:

> 'The emperor again alluded to Mme. de Staël, of whom, however, he said nothing new, except mentioning some letters seen by the police, which related to Mme. Récamier and a Prussian prince. The prince, in spite of his rank, had conceived the idea of espousing the friend of Mme. de Staël, and confided it to the latter, whose poetical imagination readily seized upon a plan that would give to Coppet so romantic a reputation. Though the young prince was recalled to Berlin, absence made no change in his feelings, and he still ardently prosecuted his suit. But, whether through her Catholic prejudices against divorce, or through her natural generosity, Mme Récamier constantly declined this unlooked-for elevation.'[9]

Although Napoleon's health had temporarily improved after Antommarchi's arrival, it did not last. For the next year and half, it seemed as if Napoleon always had some complaint. He would also never occupy the new residence that was being built to house him because in February of 1821, his health rapidly deteriorated to the point that he suffered constant pain and could not keep food down. He died at 5:49pm on 5 May 1821 from stomach cancer.

After his death, rumours swirled that he had been poisoned. The belief was that European leaders had made it happen because they feared he might escape and retake France. Stories emerged that his food was poisoned with arsenic and although arsenic was present in his body at higher levels than in most people today, later studies by researchers have ultimately shown that he was not poisoned and that he most likely died of cancer.

Despite, his death, the fascination people held for Napoleon would continue. This was demonstrated in 1842 when Madame Tussaud opened two rooms known as the Napoleon Rooms. The 'Shrine of Napoleon' or the 'Golden Chamber' was filled with his relics that she had been purchasing for years. The room contained such items as the camp bed on which he died and a wax figure of him dressed in clothes that he wore while living in exile. There was also another wax figure of him standing next to his wax son, who was lying in his original cradle. Other interesting objects in the room included Napoleon's blue cloak from Marengo, a painting of him by artist Robert Lefévre, and a portrait of Marie Louise by Gérard. The second room contained similar priceless items. There was the 'Table of the Marshals', Sèvres porcelain china presented to Napoleon from the city of Paris and his coach captured at Waterloo.

The Duke of Wellington made his first visit to Madame Tussaud's establishment in July of 1835, which was the same year that he allowed her to model him. When the Napoleon rooms opened in 1842, he was quick to visit and thereafter became a fascinated and regular patron. He was often seen walking through the Napoleon rooms and reportedly spent a great deal of time staring at the figure of Napoleon. In fact, his visits became so well-known that Sir George Hayter produced a painting that shows Wellington with his back to the viewer looking at Napoleon's wax figure lying on his camp-bed with his imperial crown sitting atop a table behind them. Hayter titled it 'Wellington Visiting the Effigy of Napoleon'.

In his will, Napoleon asked to be buried on the banks of the Seine River, but wary that his body might become a shrine, Lowe buried him on Saint Helena under a willow tree in Geranium Valley, a spot of solitude that Napoleon sometimes visited and belonged to a Jamestown shopkeeper named Mr. Torbet. A discussion also ensued about what Napoleon's tombstone should read. The French wanted 'Napoleon' or 'Emperor Napoleon', but it had to be 'Napoleon Buonaparte' or nothing, so he was buried in an unmarked grave.

On 9 May, Lowe provided a grand funeral for Napoleon. His body passed a line of 2,000 troops with four musical bands playing on the side of the road. The coffin was placed on a hearse drawn by four carriage horses and his pall consisted of a blue cloak, embroidered with silver, that he wore at the battle of Marengo and placed atop it was his mantle and sword worn at the battle of Waterloo. He was carried to the grave by 24 grenadiers where he received a priest's blessing and his coffin was then deposited by pulleys under three discharges of eleven artillery pieces. It was topped with an enormous stone slab and covered with bricks, clay, and stones.

The coffin builder also later provided his version of the events, writing:

> 'After his decease he was dressed in full uniform, with cocked hat, boots and spurs, and laid out in state.
>
> 'The same morning I received orders for the coffins for the illustrious deceased, which were of course executed with all possible dispatch. The shell was made of one-inch mahogany, lined with tin and covered with lead outside. The tin was afterwards covered with white satin; pillow and mattress of the same. The outside coffin was made of Spanish mahogany, the top and sides fine solid curls; and I dove-tailed it together and polished it with my own hands in the highest manner that my poor abilities would allow … There was no inscription on the coffin.
>
> 'On Wednesday morning I rode up to Longwood and enclosed the body in the coffins, with silver-head screws. Enclosed with him in the coffin were a silver urn containing his heart, and another containing his stomach, and all the coins that were issued during his reign; together with a knife and fork, a spoon, and one plate, all of silver.'[10]

Chapter 20

Continued Fascination

She begs you to come as little beautiful as you can.
Madame de Krüdener about Juliette

Juliette's nemesis was at last dead. She wouldn't immediately hear about his death or ever know that he had mentioned their contentious relationship one dark and stormy night on St. Helena. It happened in February of 1816 when Napoleon and those exiled were sitting around a table after dinner. The topic of conversation landed on finance *agents* who had become rich during the French Revolution and it was then that Napoleon said:

> 'Scarcely had I become First Consul … when I found myself at issue with Madam Recamier. Her father had been placed in the Post-office Department. I had found it necessary to sign in confidence a great number of appointments, but I soon established a very rigid inspection in every department. A correspondence was discovered with the Chouans, going on under the connivance of M. Bernard, the father of Madame Recamier. He was immediately dismissed, and narrowly escaped trial and condemnation to death. His daughter hastened to me, and upon her solicitations I exempted M. Bernard from taking his trial, but was resolute respecting his dismissal. Madame Recamier, accustomed to obtain[ing] everything, would be satisfied with nothing less than the reinstatement of her father. Such were the morals of the times. My severity excited loud animadversions. It was a thing quite unusual. Madame Recamier and her party, which was very numerous, never forgave me.'[1]

Juliette might not have forgiven Napoleon, but she would find that she would have to forgive her husband. In 1818, she had unwisely put her fortune in his hands and, due to faulty speculation on his part, he lost 100,000 francs.

Still they were able to purchase a new home in the rue d'Anjou for themselves, which was to also accommodate Juliette's father, her father's friend Simonard, Amélie and Amélie's husband.

Unfortunately, no one resided there long because Jacques-Rose soon became involved in another risky speculation scheme and lost more of Juliette's money. This second loss caused Juliette to permanently separate herself and her finances from her husband. Nevertheless, she continued to aid him financially even though they remained separated from this point forward.

When she moved out from her husband, possibly to avoid guilt, she decided to settle in a religious community known as Abbaye-aux-Bois (Abbey of the Woods), a Bernardine convent in Paris that was founded in the thirteenth century. Her new home held certain advantages. Living at Abbaye-aux-Bois made it look as if she had never had a disagreement with her husband because men were not allowed to reside in or near the Abbey. The Abbey was also situated in the rue de Sèvres, surrounded by an iron fence and located in the same immediate area where her husband, her father and her father's friend lived, which made visiting them easy.

Although she visited her husband, Juliette was passionately in love with Chateaubriand, and he was the man with whom it was rumoured she finally consummated her love. In addition, because her life revolved around him, she saw him daily, precisely at three o'clock when he came with 'his cane in his hand, his head in the air, and his fingers buried in his waistcoat'.[2] Moreover, at these three o'clock visits, Juliette never admitted anyone without Chateaubriand's prior consent.

Despite his capricious temperament, Chateaubriand was at heart a man who loved routine and Juliette's contemporaries noted that no one seemed to understand him like she did. He wrote to her daily and she in turn, 'cheered him, not, perhaps, entering so much into his feelings, as flattering imperceptibly his vanity, which was naturally soothed by a beautiful woman, who had been such a star in the world of society.'[3]

As Juliette was busy with Chateaubriand, in mid-January of 1826, Mathieu was named tutor to the 6-year-old Duke of Bordeaux, heir to the throne. The public had nothing but good wishes for Mathieu in his new position and he was thrilled at the vote of confidence. He appeared to be the picture of good health as he began to perform his duties with exacting zeal, and if there was any sign that something was wrong, it was that he was 'slightly indisposed' around the beginning of Holy Week. However, by Good Friday, on 24 March, he was feeling better and attended services at the Church of St. Thomas d'Aquin in the fashionable and historic district known as Faubourg Saint-Germain. No one could have guessed what would happen next.

> 'While he was prostrate at the foot of the tomb of his Divine Saviour, his noble head was suddenly bent lower, as though in an excess of fervour. Those about him feared at first to disturb his pious meditations; but it was soon perceived that he had ceased to live.'[4]

Juliette was heartbroken over Mathieu's death, but time was marching on and others were feeling their age. Jacques-Rose was one. In early March of 1830, he began to suffer from breathing problems. He requested that he be taken to Juliette's home because he thought the air there might help him breath more freely. His wish was granted and it was there he died at the age of seventy-nine on 29 March 1830 surrounded by his wife, family and friends.

Constant's death was next and happened the same year. He had suffered a severe fall several years earlier as he descended the Tribune and he was thereafter forced to rely on crutches to get around. However, in the early months of 1830, his legs became swollen making it even more difficult to walk and by October, he acknowledged in a letter to his cousin that paralysis was slowly taking over his body, affecting his feet, tongue and other body parts. Things were worse by December as he could not climb the stairs. His secretary visited him on Wednesday, 8 December and left this account:

> 'The day of his death I brought him early in the morning the last printed page of his book. "I'm glad," he said, "I was afraid of dying before I had finished it." … At the end of the day, when he was dying, he called me to him. He asked me for his folder, it was next to him on his bed. I gave it him, he put it under his pillow. A quarter of hour later he passed away.'[5]

Constant's death created a sensation in Paris. No one had expected him to die so quickly and so his funeral turned into a lavish event attended by thousands of people honouring him as a defender of constitutional principles and for his perpetual struggle against aristocracy and oppressive powers. Services were held on Sunday at the Protestant church in the rue Saint Antoine. His funeral was attended by the entire Chamber of

Deputies, the Prime Minister and even Lafayette, the papers reporting that a 'warm' and 'affecting' eulogy was given. He was interred at the Père Lachaise cemetery.

A few years passed before another of Juliette's friends died. This time it was her one-time love Prince Augustus. He had continued to think of her and had seen her in Aix-la-Chapelle and once again in 1818 in Paris, the same year that he commissioned Gérard to paint a posthumous portrait of Germaine as her character Corrine. Augustus then presented the painting to Juliette as a souvenir of his passion and in honour of her deep and abiding friendship with Germaine.

Now, on 19 July 1843, Augustus was dead. He had never married and had no legitimate heirs, so his substantial estate reverted to the crown. However, the painting by Gérard that Juliette had sent to him in 1808 and that he hung in his palace upon its arrival, was, according to his wishes, returned to her in 1845.

Ballanche was the next to die. Over the years, he and Juliette had developed a deep and abiding friendship, so when the writer and French counter-revolutionary perished, Juliette took his death extremely hard. He had been living upon a diet of 'milk and vegetables' for some time, and although the diet was enough to sustain him, he was feeble and barely surviving when he died from an inflammation of the lungs on 12 June 1847.

'Good Ballanche' was buried in Cimetiere de Montmartre in Paris. In honour of their close friendship, Juliette made room for him close to her burial spot and, as the days passed, Juliette's grief for him supposedly increased and became more profound. Yet, she was not the only one mourning him. Chateaubriand also mourned him and immortalized him in his *Mémoires d'outre-tombe*.

The deaths of her husband and close friends caused Juliette to age. However, contemporaries noted that she remained beautiful and there were numerous reports that she continued to eclipse all women in beauty, even into her late sixties. She was slightly bent in her later years and although the bloom of youth had faded, Amélie claimed she never experienced the infirmities of old age like many others, because she always accepted the effects of her aging graciously.

Old age never appeared to affect Juliette until Chateaubriand died. It happened on 4 July 1848 after an illness had confined him to his bed. His death left an unmistakable void in her life. There was no obvious signs of grief other than a sad smile that pulled at the edges of her lips. Perhaps, she knew that she would soon be reunited with him in death.

His life was celebrated on 8 July in the church of the Foreign Mission in the rue du Bac. From there, his body was removed to Saint-Malo, where he had requested to be buried. Obtaining this burial spot had been a hard-fought battle as he had applied in 1828 to be buried there, but the municipal council refused his request, citing a litany of obstacles. Subsequently, a friend intervened on Chateaubriand's behalf in 1831 and this time the municipal council agreed. A note from the mayor granting Chateaubriand's request arrived on his doorstep on 27 October 1831 that stated:

> 'The resting-place you wish for on the sea-shore, within a few steps of the spot where you were born, will be prepared by the piety of the inhabitants of St. Malo. But a sad thought intrudes itself amidst the performance of this duty. May the monument continue long unoccupied; though honor and glory survive that which is transient on the earth!'[6]

The tomb was placed on the tidal island of Grand Bé, located at the mouth of the Rance River, near the walls of Saint-Malo and is located on the island's western tip. It faces the sea and can only be accessed when the tide is out. Chateaubriand had requested that there be no inscription on his tomb. There is none, but on a wall behind the grave has a plaque that reads: 'the Great French writer wanted to find peace, to hear the sea'.

As for Juliette, life marched on. She read, joined in conversations and thanked her friends for their attention, but the real reason for her life seemed to have been lost when Chateaubriand died. Nevertheless, his death did not stop guests from visiting her, but now instead of the snowy whiteness that had so long marked her wardrobe, she appeared every day clad in morbid black.

Much like Napoleon, she also continued to fascinate people despite her age, infirmities and subtleties of talent. Her ability to fascinate has been well-documented and can easily be demonstrated by a short story that involves the Baroness Barbara Juliane von Krüdener, a German mystic born in 1764, who from an early age learned French and German, read Voltaire and the Encyclopaedists and accessed French culture.

Once when Juliette attended Madame de Krüdener's popular salon that she held during the Empire and Bourbon Restoration periods, her entrance caused so much commotion and distraction that Madame de Krüdener later wrote to Constant and entreated him to ask Juliette to make herself less charming. He complied with Madame Krüdener's request by sending Juliette the following lines:

> 'I acquit myself with a little embarrassment of a commission which Mme de Krüdener has just given me. She begs you to come as little beautiful as you can. She says that you dazzle all the world, and that consequently every soul is troubled and attention is impossible. You cannot lay aside your charms, but do not add to them.'[7]

Another mention of her ability to fascinate was made by the famous German dramatist, August Friedrich Ferdinand von Kotzebue. He travelled from Berlin through Switzerland to Paris in the year 1804 and soon thereafter met Juliette. He noted that before meeting her he had become 'prepossessed' against her because he had heard so frequently that she was irresistible and charming. However, he quickly changed his mind upon meeting her.

> 'I thought I should find her a vain coquet, enveloped in clouds of incense, hardened by wealth, seeing and loving no other in the world but herself, receiving homage as a duty with chilling pride; and to make a distinguished figure, throwing aside every thing decorous and becoming. Indeed, I don't know how many unfavourable things I was induced to conceive of her, owning to the calumnies contained in the public papers; I was therefore curious to see, without wishing to become acquainted with her. It was at the opera that my curiosity was first gratified. "There sits Madame Recamier," said a neighbor, and I very naturally turned my head suddenly towards her box, which he pointed out. My eyes sought her in the front row, more brilliant in diamonds than in beauty; but there she was not to be found. Withdrawing from the public gaze, like a violet in the grass, this lovely female sat with her hair unadorned, in the plainest white dress, and the graces of modesty clung to her as to their sister. She seemed to blush at being so beauteous. The first appearance made a very favourable impression on me, and I was now glad to be introduced at her house.'[8]

One English visitor to France in 1835 was the novelist Frances Trollope. She also attested to Juliette's appeal and remarked that she was the perfect specimen of a Frenchwoman. Years earlier, when Juliette had visited London, someone had pointed out Juliette to Trollope and then pronounced Juliette the most beautiful woman in Europe. Trollope had agreed, declaring her to be the model of grace.

Years later when Trollope visited France and saw Juliette, she still thought everything about her was spectacular – her voice, dress, person, manner, and movement – were 'quite perfect.' She also marvelled at Juliette's charisma and noted that although she had passed the age when her beauty was at its height, admiration still surrounded her.

> 'She is followed, sought, looked at, listened to, and moreover, beloved and esteemed, by a very large circle of the first society in Paris, among whom are numbered some of the most illustrious literary names in France.'[9]

In 1849, cholera hit Paris. This outbreak was as devastating as the outbreak that had arrived seventeen years earlier. Parisians were concerned about cholera and because they feared it, they wanted to know what they could do to avoid it. The *Journal des Debats* obliged and provided the following tips:

> 'The medical journals of Paris recommend particular attention to the slightest disorder of the bowels or derangement of the digestive organs; and, above all, the avoidance of excessive fatigue, by which the nervous system is exhausted and a predisposition to cholera at once excited. Strict attention to diet and regime, abstinence from ices, refrigerating drinks, unripe fruit, shell-fish, and crude vegetables – and the avoidance of impure air on the one hand, and cold draughts on the other, are indispensable measures of prevention, the neglect of which is literally suicidal.'

Juliette had long feared cholera and no doubt she followed the newspaper's advice. Furthermore, because the immediate area surrounding Abbaye-aux-Bois was infected, she decided to pack up and leave. She suffered no health problems upon her departure, despite being feeble and now almost blind. Moreover, there was no reason for anyone to suspect anything amiss with her. She returned home on a brief errand on 9 May 1849 and later that same day, before dinner, she received visitors.

The first indication that something was wrong occurred the following day. She felt slightly unwell, but later she was chipper enough to enjoy her great-niece reading to her. Then, around 4pm, as Juliette was dressing for dinner, she suddenly felt strange and immediately called for Amélie. By the time she reached her, Juliette could barely speak. The doctor was immediately summoned and prescribed a warm bed and some other remedies. A letter written to Juliette's nephew in Lyon provides more details about the suddenness of her illness:

> 'On Thursday I had been with her [Juliette] from ten in the morning till half-past three, and when I went out for a little fresh air I left her perfectly well. At four o'clock when I returned I found her in bed and very unwell.'[10]

When Juliette awoke, Amélie was filled with terror upon seeing how much her countenance changed. Another doctor was immediately summoned and this time his diagnosis left no hope. Juliette had been stricken with cholera. A distressed Amélie wrote of her adopted mother's next few hours:

> 'For twelve hours, this angelic woman was … prey to the most agonizing suffering: still her courage, sweetness, and celestial tenderness never abandoned her for one instant. She asked for her confessor, and received extreme unction. She also wished to receive the holy viaticum, but her state did not permit the gratification of this pious desire.'[11]

Complete tranquillity followed, and she was conscious to the end, dying the following day, 11 May. Juliette asked to be buried near her mother in the Montemartre Cemetery in the Récamier family tomb. Next to her was also her beloved Ballanche so that he reposed in death by the woman that he loved most in life. Juliette's funeral took place on 13 May at the church of Notre Dame des Victories.

Juliette had written her will on four small pages of blue paper and signed it on 15 September 1842. Amélie was appointed her residuary legatee. In that regard, Juliette's picture of Corrine was presented to the Lyon Museum in her name and that of Ballanche. There was also a bas-relief – the martyrdom of Eudorus and Cymodocea – that Juliette had commissioned from the Italian sculptor Pietro Tenerani in honour of Chateaubriand's *Les Martyrs*. It was bequeathed to the Saint-Malo Museum.

The rapidity of Juliette's disease had astounded everyone, and they were surprised to learn that although cholera tends to leave 'frightful traces,' those present at her death found Juliette spared any signs of cholera. Her beauty that had won her admirers and lovers remained perfectly intact as if she was a statue of grace and sweetness. This was echoed by the French poet and novelist Marceline Desbordes-Valmore, who on 22 June 1849 stated in a letter to a friend:

> 'Adieu to Mme. Recamier … to her grace and her gentle hands, which were so courageous too, in drawing to herself and sustaining those who were suffering the most. The loss of M. de Chateaubriand uprooted her from the earth. Her beautiful eyes had become blind, and this creature, judged as frivolous because she smiled through her tears, wanted to die. She told me so … Adieu!'[12]

Notes

Chapter 1

1. A. Decaux, *Napoleon's Mother*, translated by Len Ortzen (London: Crescent Press, 1962), p68
2. W.H. Ireland and G. Cruikshank, *The Life of Napoleon Bonaparte* v. 4 (London: J. Cumberland, 1828), p137
3. L.J. Abrantès, *Memoirs of Napoleon, His Court and Family* v. 1 (R. Bentley, 1836), p12
4. *The Court and Camp of Bonaparte* (New York: J. & J. Harper, 1833), p23
5. H.C. Hopkins, *Dixie: A Monthly Magazine* v. 2-3 (Dixie Publishing Company, 1899), p344
6. H.N. Williams, *The Women Bonapartes: The Mother and Sisters of Napoléon I* v. 1 (London: Methuen, 1908), p20
7. D. Archer, 'Does Napoleon's Birthplace Still Exist?' *The Sphere*, November 1, 1924, p30
8. M. Broers, *Napoleon: Soldier of Destiny* (New York: Pegasus Books LLC, 2014), p39
9. A. Fournier, *Napoleon the First: A Biography* (New York: Henry Holt and Company, 1903), p6
10. L.A.F. de Bourrienne, *Memoirs of Napoleon Bonaparte*, 3 vols. v. 1 (New York: Charles Scribner's Sons, 1891), p15

Chapter 2

1. The *Western Chronicle*, 'Bits From Books', May 24, 1907, p6
2. A. Lenormant and I.M. Luyster, *Memoirs and Correspondence of Madame Récamier*, 4th ed. (Boston: Roberts Brothers, 1867), p2
3. Ibid. p3
4. J. Turquan, *A Great Coquette: Madame Recamier and Her Salon* (New York: Brentano's, 1913), p34
5. A. Lenormant, and I. M. Luyster, p6

Chapter 3

1. R. Harvey, *The War of Wars: The Epic Struggle Between Britain and France: 1789-1815* (Little, Brown Book Group, 2009), p67
2. M. Broers, p70
3. Ibid., p71
4. E. Herriot, *Madame Récamier from the French of Édouard Herriot*, 2 vols. v. 1 (New York: G.P. Putnam's Sons, 1906), p11
5. *London Times*, 'France', September 10, 1792, p1
6. E. Herriot, p13
7. M. Broers, p79-80
8. Ibid., p81
9. E. de Pressensé and J. P. Lacroix, *Religion and the Reign of Terror: Or, The Church During the French Revolution* (New York: Carlton & Lanahan, 1869), p211

Chapter 4

1. A. Stuart, *Josephine: The Rose of Martinique* (London: Pan Macmillan, 2011), p36
2. A. Cunningham, *Anecdotes of Napoleon Bonaparte and His Times* (Philadelphia: J.B. Perry, 1855), p39
3. L. Mühlbach, *The Empress Josephine* (New York: P.F. Collier, 1902), p272
4. M.E.C. Mohl, *Madame Récamier: With a Sketch of the History of Society in France* (London: Chapman and Hall, 1862), p11
5. A. Lenormant, and I. M. Luyster, p8
6. H.N. Williams, *Madame Récamier and Her Friends* (London: Harper & Brothers, 1906), p1
7. A.T. Thomson and P. Wharton, *The Queens of Society* v. 2 (London: Porter & Coates, 1890), p5
8. I.M. Luyster, *Memoirs and Correspondence of Madame Récamier*, 6th ed. (Boston: Roberts Brothers, 1868), p12

Chapter 5

1. C. Hill, *Maria Edgeworth and Her Circle in the Days of Buonaparte and Bourbon* (New York: John Lane, 1910), p19
2. A. Lenormant, and I. M. Luyster, p13
3. *Putnam's Monthly and the Critic* v. 1 (G.P. Putnam's Sons, 1907), p324-5
4. J.M. Thompson, ed., *Letters of Napoleon* (Read Books Ltd, 2013), p21
5. L.J. Abrantès, p144

6. A. Lenormant, and I. M. Luyster, p14
7. A. Lenormant, and I. M. Luyster, p17
8. A.G. Mason, *The Women of the French Salons* (New York: The Century Co., 1891), p132-3
9. Dena Goodman, *Enlightenment Salons: The Convergence of Female and Philosophic Ambitions*, 3rd ed. 22 (John Hopkins University Press, Spring, 1989); Eighteenth-Century Studies, p331
10. D. Austrian, *Juliette Recamier* (Chicago: R.F. Seymour, 1922), p19
11. Ibid, p144
12. *Mémoires d'une femme de qualité sur le Consulat et L'Empire* (Paris: Mercure de France, 1987), p80
13. F. Gendron and J. Cookson, *Gilded Youth of Thermidor* (Montreal: McGill-Queen's University Press, 1993), p34
14. *The Athenaeum*, 1600 vols. no. 1584 (London: British Periodicals Limited, 1858), p302
15. H.N. Williams, p34

Chapter 6

1. T.E. Evans, *History of the Political Institutions, of the Nations of Europe and America: With the constitutions, charters, and fundamental laws, by which they have been, and are now governed. From the French* v. 1 (London: Black, Young, and Young, 1824), p229
2. A. Lenormant, and I. M. Luyster, p18
3. I.M. Luyster, p19
4. M.E. Braddon, *Belgravia* v. 38 (London: Willmer & Rogers, 1879), p445
5. L. Bonaparte, *Memoirs of the Private and Political Life of Lucien Bonaparte: Prince of Canino,* 2 vols. v. 1 (London: Henry Colburn, 1818), p153
6. J. Turquan, p94
7. Ibid.

Chapter 7

1. J. Turquan, p107
2. Countess C. Granville, ed., *Lord Granville Leveson Gower (first Earl Granville): Private Correspondence, 1781 to 1821*, 2 vols. v. 1 (New York: E.P. Dutton and Company, 1916), p376–77
3. A. Lenormant, and I.M. Luyster, p45
4. Ibid., p207
5. J.M. Thompson, ed., p159

6. D. Barry, 'Monumental Meaning at Marengo 1800', Napoleon.org, https://www.napoleon.org/en/history-of-the-two-empires/articles/monumental-meaning-at-marengo-1800/
7. R. Harvey, p349
8. *The Spirit of the English Magazines* v. 10 (Boston: Monroe and Francis, 1822), p457
9. W.H. Ireland, *The Napoleon Anecdotes: Illustrating the Mental Energies of the Late Emperor of France; and the Characters and Actions of His Contemporary Statesmen and Warriors* v. 1 (London: C. S. Arnold, 1822), p16
10. I.M. Luyster, p39
11. *The Spirit of the English Magazines* v. 10 p458
12. *Bruce Herald*, 'Napoleon and Madame de Staël,' October 16, 1905, 81, p3

Chapter 8

1. J.C. Herold, *Mistress to an Age: A Life of Madame de Staël* (New York: Grove Press, 2002), p95
2. *Otago Daily Times*, 'Napoleon's Green-Room', January 14, 1905, p8
3. Ibid.
4. Ibid.
5. J.M. Price, *Dame Fashion: Paris - London (1786 - 1912)* (London: Editorial Maxtor Libreria, 2015), p31
6. H.N. Williams, p48
7. J. M. Price, p31
8. S. Englund, *Napoleon: A Political Life* (New York: Scribner, 2010), p224
9. H.N. Williams, p58
10. Ibid., p60
11. L.A.F. de Bourrienne, *Memoirs of Napoleon Bonaparte*, 3 vols. v. 2 (London: R. Bentley and Son, 1885), p144
12. *The International Review* v. 8 (New York: A.S. Barnes, 1880), p638
13. S. Englund, p226
14. M. Broers, p276

Chapter 9

1. L. J. Abrantès, *The Autobiography and Recollections of Laura, Duchess of Abrantès (widow of General Junot): With Reminiscences of Her Life in Corsica, Paris, and in Spain and Portugal* v. 3 (New York: C. Scribner, 1893), p51

2. Frédéric Masson, *Napoleon and His Coronation* (Philadelphia: J.B. Lippincott Company, 1907), p228–29
3. Ibid, p232
4. Ibid., p234-55
5. J. L. David, *Account of the Celebrated Picture of the Coronation of Napoleon* (London: G. Schulze, 1822), p4
6. E.L. Whipple and J.E. McLean, eds., *The Metaphysical Magazine* v. 1 (New York: Metaphysical Publishing Company, 1895), p511
7. W. Scott, *Life of Napoleon Buonaparte: With a Preliminary View of the French Revolution* (Edinburgh: Robert Cadell, 1842), p138
8. *Staffordshire Advertiser*, 'The Revolutionary Plutarch', September 8, 1804, p3
9. *St. James' Magazine and United Empire Review* v. 10, no. 1 (London: W. Kent, 1864), p349
10. A. Lenormant, and I.M. Luyster, p53
11. A.L.I. de Saint-Amand and I. de Saint-Amand, *The Wife of the First Consul* (New York: Charles Scribner's Sons), p24
12. A. Lenormant, and I. M. Luyster, p55
13. *The Illustrated American* v. 8, no. 85 (1891), p311
14. A. Lenormant, and I.M. Luyster, p56
15. *The Illustrated American* v. 8, no. 85 (1891), p311

Chapter 10

1. A. Lenormant, and I.M. Luyster, p58
2. G. Ducrest and S.C. Durand, *Memoirs of the Empress Josephine, with Anecdotes of the Courts of Navarre and Malmaison*, 2nd ed. (London: H. Colburn, 1829), p54
3. E. Sampson, G. Chittenden and H. Croswell, *The Balance and Columbian Repository* v. 5 (New York: Sampson, Chittenden & Croswell, 1806), p192
4. I. M. Luyster, p63
5. J.C. Herold, *The Age of Napoleon* (Mariner Books, 2002), p187
6. J.M. Thompson, ed., p394
7. J.H. Agnew, ed., *The Eclectic Museum of Foreign Literature, Science and Art* v. 3 (New York: E. Littell, 1843), p337
8. R. Harvey, p535
9. A.T. Mahan, *The Influence of Sea Power Upon the French Revolution and Empire, 1793-1812* v. 2 (Little, Brown, 1897), p329
10. Ibid., p328

Chapter 11

1. J.M. Thompson, ed., p343
2. Ibid., p129–30
3. *The Edinburgh Review* v. 179 (London: A. and C. Black, 1894), p388
4. J. Turquan, p125
5. Ibid, p125
6. E. Herriot, p157
7. Ibid, p159–60
8. Ibid, p163
9. J. Turquan, p133
10. A. Lenormant, and I. M. Luyster, p64–65

Chapter 12

1. R. Winegarten, *Germaine de Staël and Benjamin Constant* (New Haven: Yale University Press, 2008), p14
2. E. d. Nolde and C. Harwood, eds., *Madame de Staël and Benjamin Constant* (New York: G.P. Putnam's Sons, 1907), p80
3. A.J.M.R. Savary, *Memoirs of the Duke of Rovigo* (London: H. Colburn, 1828), p18
4. *The National and English Review* v. 8 (London: National Review Limited, 1887), p103
5. E. Herriot, p225
6. L.A.F. d. Bourrienne, p446
7. E. Herriot, p233

Chapter 13

1. H.N. Williams, p84
2. A. Lenormant, and I.M. Luyster, p67
3. Ibid., p78
4. G. Long, *France and Its Revolutions: A pictorial history 1789-1848* (London: Charles Knight, 1850), p306
5. I.M. Luyster, p78
6. *The London Literary Gazette and Journal of Belles Lettres, Arts, Sciences, Etc* no. 1482 (London: Henry Colburn, 1845), p373
7. I.M. Luyster, p85
8. Ibid.
9. A. Lenormant, and I.M. Luyster, p5
10. M.E.C. Mohl, p51
11. H.N. Williams, p107
12. I.M. Luyster, p93

Chapter 14

1. P.P. de Ségur, *History of the Expedition to Russia: Undertaken by the Emperor Napoleon in the Year 1812* v. 1 (New York: Harper & Brothers, 1872), p105
2. Ibid., p108–9
3. Ibid. p125
4. P.P. de Ségur, *History of the Expedition to Russia: Undertaken by the Emperor Napoleon in the Year 1812* v. 2 (London: A. Sherman, 1826), p302
5. Ibid., p261
6. *The Nation* v. 63 (New York: J.H. Richards, 1896), p46
7. I. de Saint-Amand and Perry. T.S., *Marie Louise and the Decadence of the Empire* (New York: Charles Scribner's Sons, 1902), p71
8. R. Harvey, p810
9. P.P. de Ségur, p286
10. Ibid., p286–88

Chapter 15

1. A. Lenormant, and I. M. Luyster, p97
2. E.D. Mansfield, ed., Monthly *Chronicle of Interesting and Useful Knowledge: Embracing Education, Internal Improvements, and the Arts. With Notices of General Literature and Passing Events* v. 1 (Cincinnati: A. Pugh, 1839), p416
3. J.M. Thompson, ed., p275
4. L.E. Saint-Denis and F. H. Potter, *Napoleon from the Tuileries to St. Helena* (New York: Harper & Brothers, 1922), p67–69
5. A.J.F.B. Fain, *The Manuscript of 1814. A history of events which led to the abdication of Napoleon, etc. Translated from the French* (London: Henry Colburn, 1834), p267–68
6. Ibid., p268
7. M. Glover, *The Napoleonic Wars: and Illustrated History 1792-1815* (London: B.T. Batsford, Ltd., 1979), p206
8. J.M. Thompson, ed., p283
9. H.N. Williams, p128
10. Ibid., p131
11. *Kentish Gazette*, 'Too Late', August 14, 1849, p4

Chapter 16

1. L. Mühlbach, p524
2. T.P. O'Connor and H. Jackson, 'Napoleon in the Fox Skin', *T. P.'s Weekly* v. 8, no. 204 (1906): p426

3. L. de l'Ardeche, *History of Napoleon: From the French of M. Laurent de L'Ardeche* v. 2 (London: W. Strange, 1841), p287
4. A.M. Elliott, ed., *Modern Language Notes* v. 20 (Baltimore: Johns Hopkins Press, 1905), p96
5. Antony Brett-James, *The Hundred Days* (New York: St. Martin's Press, 1964), p3
6. L. de l'Ardeche, p289
7. A. Brett-James, p7
8. M. Glover, p208
9. H.N. Williams, p149
10. A. Lenormant, and I. M. Luyster, p111-2
11. F. vicomte de Chateaubriand and A. T. de Mattos, *The Memoirs of François René, Vicomte de Chateaubriand, Sometime Ambassador to England: Being a Translation by Alexander Teixeira de Mattos of the Mémoires D'outre-tombe, with Illustrations from Contemporary Sources*, 6 vols. v. 4 (London: Freemantle and Company, 1902), p198
12. L. de l'Ardeche, p301-2
13. J.E. Hall, ed., The Port Folio X (Philadelphia: Harrison Hall, 1820), p346

Chapter 17

1. A. Brett-James, p39
2. A.W.D. Wellington and J. Gurwood, *Selections from the Dispatches and General Orders of Field Marshall the Duke of Wellington* (London: J. Murray, 1842), p842
3. *The Eclectic Magazine of Foreign Literature, Science, and Art* v. 67 (New York: Leavitt, Trow, & Company, 1898), p350
4. *The Nineteenth Century* v. 33 (London: Henry S. King & Company, 1893), p419
5. A. Roberts, *Napoleon and Wellington: The Battle of Waterloo and the Great Commanders who Fought it* (New York: Simon & Schuster, 2001), p1
6. G. Hooper, *Waterloo, the Downfall of the First Napoleon* (London: Smith, Elder and Co., 1862), p184–86
7. J.H. Settle, *Anecdotes of Soldiers in Peace and War* (London: Methuen & Company, 1905), p192
8. R. Harvey, p899
9. T. Dwight and J. Hawthorne, *The World's Great Classics: Decisive battles of the world, by E.S. Creasy* (New York: Colonial Press, 1899), p396

10. A.W.D. Wellington, and J. Gurwood, p860
11. A. Brett-James, p193–94
12. R. Harvey, p901

Chapter 18

1. A. Stevens, *Madame de Staël: A Study of Her Life and Times, the First Revolution and the First Empire* v. 2 (New York: Harper & Brothers, 1881), p195
2. Ibid., p196-97
3. H.N. Williams, p136
4. I.M. Luyster, p106
5. A. Lenormant, and I.M. Luyster, p67
6. L. de l'Ardeche, p334
7. Ibid, p337
8. Ibid., p339
9. C.J.T. marquis of Montholon, *History of the Captivity of Napoleon at St. Helena* (New York: E. Ferrett & Company, 1846), p60
10. J.R. Glover, *Taking Napoleon to St. Helena: From a Manuscript Diary of the Trip* (1893), p90
11. L.E.B. Abell, *Recollections of the Emperor Napoleon: During the First Three Years of His Captivity on the Island of St. Helena: Including the Time of His Residence at Her Father's House, 'The Briars,'* (London: John Murray, 1844), p242–43

Chapter 19

1. J.S.C. Abbott, *Napoleon at St. Helena: Or, Interesting Anecdotes and Remarkable Conversations of the Emperor During the Five and a Half Years of His Captivity* (New York: Harper, 1871), p426
2. M. Lescure, *Chateaubriand. Paris 1892* (Paris: Hachette, 1892), p64
3. F. v. d. Chateaubriand, and A. T. d. Mattos, p206
4. J. Kavanagh, *French Women of Letters: Biographical Sketches* (London: Hurst and Blackett, 1862), p267–68
5. E. d. Nolde and C. Harwood, eds., p289
6. L.E.B. Abell, p59
7. F. vicomte de Chateaubriand and A.S. Kline, *Mémoires d'Outre-Tombe* (Poetry in Translation, 2005)
8. I.M. Luyster, p124
9. A. Lenormant, and I. M. Luyster, p68
10. *Oxford Journal*, 'Napoleon Bonaparte', August 4, 1821, p2

Chapter 20

1. J.S.C. Abbott, p94
2. F.H. Gribble, *Chateaubriand and His Court of Women* (New York: Charles Scribner's Sons, 1909), p242
3. H.N. Williams, p180
4. A. Lenormant, and I. M. Luyster, p247
5. Dennis Wood, *Benjamin Constant: A Biography* (London: Routledge, 1993), p261
6. F. vicomte de Chateaubriand, *Memoirs of Chateaubriand: From His Birth in 1768, Till His Return to France in 1800* (London: Henry Colburn, 1849), p37–38
7. A.G. Mason, p280
8. A.F.F. von Kotzebue, *Travels from Berlin, through Switzerland, to Paris in ... 1804*, v. 3 v. 1 (London: T. Gillet, 1804), p205-6
9. Henry M. Trollope, *The Salon of Madame Necker*, 2 vols. v. 1 (London: Chapman and Hall, Limited, 1882), p270-1
10. E. Herriot, *Madame Recamier from the French of Édouard Herriot*, 2 vols. v. 2 (London: W. Heinemann, 1906), p361
11. A. Lenormant, and I. M. Luyster, p407
12. E. Herriot, p364

Bibliography

Abbott, J.S.C. *Napoleon at St. Helena: Or, Interesting Anecdotes and Remarkable Conversations of the Emperor During the Five and a Half Years of His Captivity*. New York: Harper, 1871.

Abell, L.E.B. *Recollections of the Emperor Napoleon: During the First Three Years of His Captivity on the Island of St. Helena: Including the Time of His Residence at Her Father's House, "The Briars"*. London: John Murray, 1844.

Abrantès, L. J. *Memoirs of Napoleon, His Court and Family* v. 1. R. Bentley, 1836.

Abrantès, L. J. *The Autobiography and Recollections of Laura, Duchess of Abrantès (widow of General Junot): With Reminiscences of Her Life in Corsica, Paris, and in Spain and Portugal* v. 3. New York: C. Scribner, 1893.

Agnew, J.H. ed. *The Eclectic Museum of Foreign Literature, Science and Art* v. 3. New York: E. Littell, 1843.

Austrian, D. *Juliette Récamier*. Chicago: R.F. Seymour, 1922.

Bonaparte, L. *Memoirs of the Private and Political Life of Lucien Bonaparte: Prince of Canino.* 2 vols. v. 1. London: Henry Colburn, 1818.

Bourrienne, L. A. F. d. *Memoirs of Napoleon Bonaparte.* 3 vols. London: R. Bentley and Son, 1885.

Braddon, M. E. *Belgravia* v. 38. London: Willmer & Rogers, 1879.

Brett-James, Antony. *The Hundred Days*. New York: St. Martin's Press, 1964.

Broers, M. *Napoleon: Soldier of Destiny*. New York: Pegasus Books LLC, 2014.

Browning, O. *The Despatches of Earl Gower, English Ambassador at Paris from June 1790 to August 1792*. Cambridge: University Press, 1885.

Chateaubriand, F. v. d. *Memoirs of Chateaubriand: From His Birth in 1768, Till His Return to France in 1800*. London: Henry Colburn, 1849.

Chateaubraind, F.v.d., and Kline, A.S. *Mémoires d'Outre-Tombe*. Poetry in Translation, 2005.

Chateaubriand, F. v. d., and **Matto, A. T. d.** *The Memoirs of François René, Vicomte de Chateaubriand, Sometime Ambassador to England: Being a*

Translation by Alexander Teixeira de Mattos of the Mémoires D'outre-tombe, with Illustrations from Contemporary Sources. 6 vols. v. 4. London: Freemantle and Company, 1902.

Cunningham, A. *Anecdotes of Napoleon Bonaparte and His Times.* Philadelphia: J.B. Perry, 1855.

David, J. L. *Account of the Celebrated Picture of the Coronation of Napoleon.* London: G. Schulze, 1822.

Decaux, A. *Napoleon's Mother, translated by Len Ortzen.* London: Cressent Press, 1962.

Ducrest, G., and **Durand, S.C.** *Memoirs of the Empress Josephine, with Anecdotes of the Courts of Navarre and Malmaison.* 2nd ed. London: H. Colburn, 1829.

Dwight, T., and **Hawthorne, J.** *The World's Great Classics: Decisive battles of the world, by E.S. Creasy.* New York: Colonial Press, 1899.

Elliott, A.M.ed. *Modern Language Notes* v. 20. Baltimore: Johns Hopkins Press, 1905.

Englund, S. *Napoleon: A Political Life.* New York: Scribner, 2010.

Evans, T. E. *History of the Political Institutions, of the Nations of Europe and America: With the constitutions, charters, and fundamental laws, by which they have been, and are now governed. From the French* v. 1. London: Black, Young, and Young, 1824.

Fain, A.J.F.B. *The Manuscript of 1814. A history of events which led to the abdication of Napoleon, etc. Translated from the French.* London: Henry Colburn, 1834.

Fournier, A. *Napoleon the First: A Biography.* New York: Henry Holt and Company, 1903.

London Times. "France." September 10, 1792.

Gendron, F., and Cookson, J., *Gilded Youth of Thermidor.* Montreal: McGill-Queen's University Press, 1993.

Glover, J. R. *Taking Napoleon to St. Helena: From a Manuscript Diary of the Trip.* 1893.

Glover, M. *The Napoleonic Wars: and Illustrated History 1792-1815.* London: B.T. Batsford, Ltd., 1979.

Goodman, D., *Enlightenment Salons: The Convergence of Female and Philosophic Ambitions.* 3rd ed. 22. John Hopkins University Press, Spring, 1989; Eighteenth-Century Studies.

Granville, C.C., ed. *Lord Granville Leveson Gower (first Earl Granville): Private Correspondence, 1781 to 1821.* 2 vols. v. 1. New York: E.P. Dutton and Company, 1916.

Gribble, F. H. *Chateaubriand and His Court of Women*. New York: Charles Scribner's Sons, 1909.

Hall, J.E, ed. *The Port Folio* X. Philadelphia: Harrison Hall, 1820.

Harvey, R. *The War of Wars: The Epic Struggle Between Britain and France: 1789-1815*. Little, Brown Book Group, 2009.

Herold, J. C. *Mistress to an Age: A Life of Madame de Staël*. New York: Grove Press, 2002.

Herold, J. C. *The Age of Napoleon*. Mariner Books, 2002.

Herriot, E. *Madame Récamier from the French of Édouard Herriot*. 2 vols. v. 2. London: W. Heinemann, 1906.

Herriot, E. *Madame Récamier from the French of Édouard Herriot*. 2 vols. v. 1. New York: G.P. Putnam's Sons, 1906.

Hill, C. *Maria Edgeworth and Her Circle in the Days of Buonaparte and Bourbon*. New York: John Lane, 1910.

Hooper, G. *Waterloo, the Downfall of the First Napoleon*. London: Smith, Elder and Co., 1862.

Hopkins, H. C. *Dixie: A Monthly Magazine* v. 2-3. Dixie Publishing Company, 1899.

Ireland, W. H. *The Napoleon Anecdotes: Illustrating the Mental Energies of the Late Emperor of France; and the Characters and Actions of His Contemporary Statesmen and Warriors* v. 1. London: C. S. Arnold, 1822.

Ireland, W. H., and **Cruikshank, G.** *The Life of Napoleon Bonaparte* v. 4. London: J. Cumberland, 1828.

Kavanagh, J. *French Women of Letters: Biographical Sketches*. London: Hurst and Blackett, 1862.

Kotzebue, A. F. F. v. *Travels from Berlin, through Switzerland, to Paris in … 1804*. v. 3 v. 1. London: T. Gillet, 1804.

l'Ardeche, L. de. *History of Napoleon: From the French of M. Laurent de L'Ardeche* v. 2. London: W. Strange, 1841.

Lenormant, A., and Luyster, I.M., *Memoirs and Correspondence of Madame Récamier*. 4th ed. Boston: Roberts Brothers, 1867.

Lescure, M. *Chateaubriand. Paris 1892*. Paris: Hachette, 1892.

Long, G. *France and Its Revolutions: A pictorial history 1789-1848*. London: Charles Knight, 1850.

Luyster, I. M. *Memoirs and Correspondence of Madame Récamier*. 6th ed. Boston: Roberts Brothers, 1868.

Mahan, A. T. *The Influence of Sea Power Upon the French Revolution and Empire, 1793-1812* v. 2. Little, Brown, 1897.

Mansfield, E.D. ed. *Monthly Chronicle of Interesting and Useful Knowledge: Embracing Education, Internal Improvements, and the Arts. With Notices of General Literature and Passing Events* v. 1. Cincinnati: A. Pugh, 1839.

Mason, A. G. *The Women of the French Salons*. New York: The Century Co., 1891.

Masson, Frédéric. *Napoleon and His Coronation*. Philadelphia: J.B. Lippincott Company, 1907.

Mémoires d'une femme de qualité sur le Consulat et L'Empire. Paris: Mercure de France, 1987.

Mohl, M. E. C. *Madame Récamier: With a Sketch of the History of Society in France*. London: Chapman and Hall, 1862.

Montholon, C.J. T. marquis of. *History of the Captivity of Napoleon at St. Helena*. New York: E. Ferrett & Company, 1846.

Mühlbach, L. *The Empress Josephine*. New Yor: P.F. Collier, 1902.

Nolde, E. d and **Harwood, C.**, eds. *Madame de Staël and Benjamin Constant*. New York: G.P. Putnam's Sons, 1907.

Pressensé, E. de, and **Lacroix, J.P.** *Religion and the Reign of Terror: Or, The Church During the French Revolution*. New York: Carlton & Lanahan, 1869.

Price, J. M. *Dame Fashion: Paris - London [1786 - 1912]*. London: Editorial Maxtor Libreria, 2015.

Roberts, A. *Napoleon and Wellington: The Battle of Waterloo and the Great Commanders who Fought it*. New York: Simon & Schuster, 2001.

Saint-Amand, A.L.I. de, and **Saint-Amand, I. de.** *The Wife of the First Consul*. New York: Charles Scribner's Sons.

Saint-Amand, I. de, and **Perry. T.S.** *Marie Louise and the Decadence of the Empire*. New York: Charles Scribner's Sons, 1902.

Saint-Denis, L. E., and **Potter, F.H.** *Napoleon from the Tuileries to St. Helena*. New York: Harper & Brothers, 1922.

Sampson, E., Chittenden, G. and **Croswell, H.** *The Balance and Columbian Repository* v. 5. New York: Sampson, Chittenden & Croswell, 1806.

Savary, A. J. M. R. *Memoirs of the Duke of Rovigo*. London: H. Colburn, 1828.

Scott, W. *Life of Napoleon Buonaparte: With a Preliminary View of the French Revolution*. Edinburgh: Robert Cadell, 1842.

Ségur, P. P. de. *History of the Expedition to Russia: Undertaken by the Emperor Napoleon in the Year 1812* v. 2. London: A. Sherman, 1826.

Ségur, P. P. de. *History of the Expedition to Russia: Undertaken by the Emperor Napoleon in the Year 1812* v. 1. New York: Harper & Brothers, 1872.

Settle, J. H. *Anecdotes of Soldiers in Peace and War*. London: Methuen & Company, 1905.

Stevens, A. *Madame de Staël: A Study of Her Life and Times, the First Revolution and the First Empire* v. 2. New York: Harper & Brothers, 1881.

Stuart, A. *Josephine: The Rose of Martinique*. London: Pan Macmillan, 2011.

Thompson, J.M., ed. *Letters of Napoleon*. Read Books Ltd, 2013.

Thomson, A. T., and **Wharton, P.** *The Queens of Society* v. 2. London: Porter & Coates, 1890.

Trollope, Henry M. *The Salon of Madame Necker.* 2 vols. v. 1. London: Chapman and Hall, Limited, 1882.

Turquan, J. *A Great Coquette: Madame Récamier and Her Salon*. New York: Brentano's, 1913.

Wellington, A.W.D. and **Gurwood, J.** *Selections from the Dispatches and General Orders of Field Marshall the Duke of Wellington*. London: J. Murray, 1842.

Whipple, E.L. and McLean, J.E. eds. *The Metaphysical Magazine* v. 1. New York: Metaphysical Publishing Company, 1895.

Williams, H. N. *Madame Récamier and Her Friends*. London: Harper & Brothers, 1906.

Williams, H. N. *The Women Bonapartes: The Mother and Sisters of Napoléon I* v. 1. London: Methuen, 1908.

Winegarten, R. *Germaine de Staël and Benjamin Constant*. New Haven: Yale University Press, 2008.

Wood, Dennis. *Benjamin Constant: A Biography*. London: Routledge, 1993.

Online Sources

Barry, D. 'Monumental Meaning at Marengo 1800' https://www.napoleon.org/en/history-of-the-two-empires/articles/monumental-meaning-at-marengo-1800/.

Newspapers and Periodicals

Eclectic Magazine of Foreign Literature, Science, and Art
Edinburgh Review
Illustrated American

International Review
Kentish Gazette.
London Literary Gazette and Journal of Belles Lettres, Arts, Sciences, Etc
National and English Review
Putnam's Magazine: An Illustrated Monthly of Literature, Art and Life
Putnam's Monthly and the Critic
St. James' Magazine and United Empire Review
Spirit of the English Magazines
Staffordshire Advertiser.
The Athenaeum.
The Nineteenth Century
The Principality.
T.P's Weekly

Index

Balcombe, Betsy, 84, 153-154
Balcombe family, 84, 153-154
Ballanche, Pierre-Simon, 104, 108, 126, 160, 161, 171
  burial, 167
  philosophy, 109
Barras, Paul, 22, 25, 26, 31, 32
Battle of Eylau, 81-82
Bourrienne, Louis Antoine Fauvelet de, 7, 78, 85, 90
Beauharnais, Josephine de, 25, 30, 31, 40, 50-52, 58, 61, 68, 82, 83, 84, 86-88, 147
  coronation, 69-71
  divorce, 99
  death, 129
  marriage to Alexandre de Beauharnais, 24
  marriage to Napoleon Bonaparte, 26-27
  relationship with Hippolyte Charles, 87
Berlin Decree, 81, 84
Bernard, Jean, 9, 10, 13, 75, 164
Bernard, Madame, 9, 12, 13, 56, 75, 79-80
Berthier, Louis-Alexandre, 139-140
Blücher, Gebhard Leberecht von 93, 122, 142-143, 146
Bonaparte, Carlo, 1, 3-6
Bonaparte, Caroline, *see* Murat, Madame Caroline
Bonaparte, Joseph, 3, 8, 44, 51, 53, 60, 69, 95, 121-122
Bonaparte, Letizia, 1-6, 17, 58, 61, 69
Bonaparte, Lucien, 2, 17, 34, 36, 39, 42-47, 69, 78, 132, 146
  love letters to Juliette, 37, 45-46
  wife, Christine Boyer, 37, 45
Bonaparte, Louis, 53, 79
Bonaparte, Marie Louis, 99-100, 108, 122-123, 128-129, 162
Bonaparte, Napoleon,
  abdication, 122, 123, 125, 147
  Battle of Bailén, 95-96
  Battle of Eylau, 81-82
  birth, 1-3
  bulletins, 52, 115-116, 118, 131, 134
  coup d'état of 18 Brumaire, 42-44
  Continental System, 81-82, 84-85, 95
  death, 161
  Flight of the Eagle, 132
  funeral, 162-163
  health, 130, 139, 159, 161
  leaves Elba, 131
  Ligny, 142
  Luxembourg fete, 29-30
  Maison Bonaparte, 6

Marengo, 51-52
nicknames, 83, 134
on Germaine, 53, 155
One Hundred Days, 131-147
opinion of the Duke of Wellington, 143
pamphlet Le souper de Beaucaire (Supper at Beaucaire), 21
relationship with Marie Walewska, 86-87
Russian Campaign, 111-118
Siege of Toulon, 21-23
Six Days Campaign, 121-122
suicide attempt, 123-124
Treaties of Tilsit, 82-83
wedding to Josephine, 26-27
wedding fete to Marie Louis, 100
Buonaparte, Carlo, *see* Bonaparte, Carlo
Buonaparte, Letizia, *see* Bonaparte, Letizia
Buonaparte, Napoleone di, *see* Bonaparte, Napoleon

Cabarrus, Thérésa Cabarrus, *see* Tallien, Madame
Cadoudal Affair, 63
Campbell, Sir Neil, 128, 130-131
Canova, Antonio, 108-110, 125-126
Cavendish, Georgiana, Duchess of Devonshire, 61-62
Charles, Hippolyte, 87
Chateaubriand, François-René, Vicomte de, 66, 155-160, 165, 167-168, 171-172
Chevreuse, Madame, 105-106, 108
cholera, 170-172
Congress of Vienna, 129, 132, 134-135
Constant, Henri-Benjamin, 96-98, 101-102, 132, 135, 137-138, 148, 159, 166, 168
Continental System, 81-82, 84-85, 95
Coppet, 32-33, 80, 88-93, 96, 98, 102, 132, 148, 161
Coquille, Jacques François Coquille, *see* Dugommier
Corsica, 1-2, 4-8, 16-18, 20, 123, 136, 161
coup d'état of 18 Brumaire, 42-44
Cyvoct, Amélie, 103, 107-108, 110, 149, 165, 167, 171

David, Jacques-Louis, 40-41, 72, 83, 93
Directory, 3, 22, 25, 27, 29, 31, 40, 42-43
Ducos, Roger, 42-44
Dugommier, 21-23

Elba, 123, 125, 128-132, 147, 152

Federalists, 21
Fesch, Joseph, 4, 66, 68
Fontenay, Jean Jacques Devin, 28
Fouché, Joseph, 42, 60, 64, 72-77, 105, 120, 146-147
Frederick William III, 50, 80, 82

Gérard, François, 40-41, 93, 162, 167
guerrilla strategy, 95
Grand Duke of Mecklenburg-Strelitz, George, 50

Hôtel Jacques-Rose, 34-35, 48

incroyables, 27

La Pagerie, Josèphe Rose Tascher de, *see* Beauharnais, Josephine de
les merveilleuses, 27-28
Louis XVIII, 11, 52, 59, 64, 126, 130, 132, 134, 136, 139, 157
Luynes, Duchess of 106, 108
Lyon, 9-10, 14, 73-74, 105-109, 111, 126, 134, 171

Madame de Staël, *see* Staël-Holstein, Anne Louise Germaine de
Madame Tussaud, 11, 61, 83, 150, 162
Marie-Antoinette, 10, 13, 33, 99
masked balls, 48-51
Matton, Marie-Julie, *see* Bernard, Madame
Mohl, Mary Elizabeth (Clarke), 19, 109
Montmorency-Laval, Mathieu of, 39, 57-58, 80, 102, 108, 158, 160-161, 165
Moreau, Jean-Victor-Marie, 39, 56, 58-59, 63-66, 72, 75
Murat, Madame Caroline, 2, 17, 69, 76, 119-121, 136
Murat, Joachim, 76, 81, 95, 120-121, 135-136

Narbonne-Lara, Comte de, Louis Marie Jacques Amalric, 39, 49, 57-58, 96-98, 115, 132
National Convention, 2, 14, 20, 25, 28, 31, 105
Necker, Jacques, 31-32, 51
Neipperg, Count Adam Adalbert von, 128-129
Ney, Michel, 134, 142-143

Pichegru Conspiracy, 63, 74,
Paoli, Pasquale, 5, 16-17
Prince Augustus of Prussia, 86, 88-94, 149, 159, 161, 167, 169

Ramolino, Letizia, *see* Bonaparte, Letizia
Récamier, Jacques-Rose, 14, 16, 18-20, 24, 28, 31, 34, 36, 39, 44, 48, 78-80, 90-91, 96, 165-166
Récamier, Juliette
- adopted daughter, *see* Cyvoct, Amélie
- bedroom, 34-35
- beauty 13, 18, 28, 30, 40, 62-63, 89, 125, 167, 169-170, 172
- childhood, 10, 12, 14
- Clichy, 35-37, 75, 77
- death, 171
- exile at Châlons-sur-Marne, 102-105, 107, 110
- father, *see* Bernard, Jean
- François Gérard painting, 40-41, 93
- Gabriel-Julien Ouvrard's party, 46
- marriage, 18
- meeting Lucien Bonaparte, 36-37
- meeting Prince Augustus of Prussia, 89
- mother, *see* Bernard, Madame
- opinion of Canova's sculpture of her, 125-126

relationship at Coppet with Prince Augustus of Prussia, 90-92
rue du Mont Blanc house, 31, 79, 159
shawl dance, 107
trip to England, 62-63
visit to Albano, 109-110
wedding reception, 19
Richmond Ball, 140-142
Rocca, Albert Jean Michel de, 108, 148
Russian Campaign, 111-118
Battle of Borodino, 113
Berezina River, 116-118
desertion of soldiers, 114
lice, 114
Moscow, 113-114
suicide, 114
starvation, 114-115

September Massacres, 2, 19, 20, 32
Siege of Toulon, 21-23
Sieyès, Abbé Emmanuel Joseph, 42-44
Simonard, 13, 96, 105, 165
St. Helena, 84, 130, 151-152, 159, 164
Staël-Holstein, Anne Louise Germaine de, 31-33, 39, 48, 51, 53-58, 72, 75, 80, 88-90, 92-93, 96-99, 101-105, 108, 115, 132, 135, 137-138, 148, 155-159, 167
banishment, 54
Corrine, or Italy, 90
death, 158
De l'Allemagne, 96, 99, 101
dislike for Napoleon, 53-54
Delphine, 53
feelings about love, 98
letters to Juliette, 92, 101-102, 105, 126
son Auguste de Staël, 102-103, 105, 107

Talleyrand-Périgord, Charles Maurice de, 30-32, 40, 42, 58, 86, 120-123, 129-130
Tallien, Madame, 28, 40, 46
Talma, François Joseph, 76-77
Treaty of Amiens, 61
Treaties of Tilsit, 82-83
Tsar Alexander, 67, 82, 111, 122-123, 129
Tussaud, Madame, *see* Madame Tussaud
Tuileries Palace, 2, 12, 51, 59-60, 70, 100, 136-137

Vicomte de Barras, Paul François Jean Nicolas, *see* Barras, Paul

Walewska, Marie, 86-87, 128, 139
Waterloo, 141-149, 162
Wellesley, Arthur, *see* Wellington, Arthur Wellesley, Duke of
Wellington, Arthur Wellesley, Duke of, 29, 96, 121, 126-127, 139-149, 156-158, 162